Theater in a Post-Truth World

Methuen Drama Agitations: Text, Politics and Performances

Theater has always offered immediate responses to political, social, economic and cultural crisis events that are local, national, and global in dimension, establishing itself as a prime medium of engagement. Methuen Drama Agitations interrogates these manifold intersections between theater and the contemporary: What is the relationship between theater and reality? Which functions does the theater perform in public life? Where does the radical potential of the theater reside and how is it untapped?

Methuen Drama Agitations addresses issues from across a number of spectrums, including contemporary politics, environmental concerns, issues of gender and race, and the challenges of globalization. The series focuses on text as much as performance, on theory as much as practice. It investigates the lively dialogues between theater and contemporary lived experience.

Series Editors
William C. Boles (Rollins College, USA)
Anja Hartl (University of Konstanz, Germany)

Advisory Board
Lynnette Goddard (Royal Holloway, University of London, UK)
Anton Krueger (Rhodes University, South Africa)
Marcus Tan (Nanyang Technological University, Singapore)
Sarah J. Townsend (Penn State University, USA)
Denise Varney (University of Melbourne, Australia)

*Theater of Lockdown: Digital and Distanced
Performance in a Time of Pandemic*
Barbara Fuchs

Forthcoming Titles

*Performing Statecraft: The Postdiplomatic Theatre of
Sovereigns, Citizens, and States*
Edited by James R. Ball III

*Contemporary Black Theatre and Performance:
Acts of Rebellion, Activism, and Solidarity*
Edited by Martine Kei Green-Rogers, Khalid Y. Long, and
DeRon S. Williams

Performing the Queer Past: Bodies Possessed
Fintan Walsh

Theater in a Post-Truth World

Text, Politics, and Performance

Edited by
William C. Boles

methuen | drama

METHUEN DRAMA
Bloomsbury Publishing Plc
50 Bedford Square, London, WC1B 3DP, UK
1385 Broadway, New York, NY 10018, USA
29 Earlsfort Terrace, Dublin 2, Ireland

BLOOMSBURY, METHUEN DRAMA and the Methuen Drama logo
are trademarks of Bloomsbury Publishing Plc

First published in Great Britain 2022
This paperback edition published 2024

Copyright © William C. Boles and contributors, 2022, 2024

William C. Boles has asserted his right under the Copyright, Designs and
Patents Act, 1988, to be identified as Editor of this work.

For legal purposes the Acknowledgments on pp. ix–x constitute
an extension of this copyright page.

Series design by Ben Anslow
Cover image: Topshot US Vote Trump (© MANDEL NGAN/AFP/Getty Images)

All rights reserved. No part of this publication may be reproduced or transmitted in any
form or by any means, electronic or mechanical, including photocopying,
recording, or any information storage or retrieval system, without prior
permission in writing from the publishers.

Bloomsbury Publishing Plc does not have any control over, or responsibility for, any
third-party websites referred to or in this book. All internet addresses given in this
book were correct at the time of going to press. The author and publisher regret any
inconvenience caused if addresses have changed or sites have ceased to exist, but
can accept no responsibility for any such changes.

A catalogue record for this book is available from the British Library.

Library of Congress Cataloging-in-Publication Data
Names: Boles, William C., 1966– editor.
Title: Theater in a post-truth world : texts, politics, and performance /
edited by William C. Boles.
Description: London ; New York : Methuen Drama 2022. |
Series: Methuen Drama agitations: text, politics and performances |
Includes bibliographical references and index. |
Identifiers: LCCN 2021058079 (print) | LCCN 2021058080 (ebook) |
ISBN 9781350215856 (hardback) | ISBN 9781350215894 (paperback) |
ISBN 9781350215863 (epub) | ISBN 9781350215870 (ebook)
Subjects: LCSH: Theater–Moral and ethical aspects. | Theater and society. |
Truthfulness and falsehood in literature. | American drama–21st century–History
and criticism. | English drama–21st century–History and criticism. |
Theater–United States–History–21st century. |
Theater–Great Britain–History–21st century. | Truthfulness and falsehood.
Classification: LCC PN2049 .T4375 2022 (print) | LCC PN2049 (ebook) |
DDC 792–dc23/eng/20220309
LC record available at https://lccn.loc.gov/2021058079
LC ebook record available at https://lccn.loc.gov/2021058080

ISBN: HB: 978-1-3502-1585-6
PB: 978-1-3502-1589-4
ePDF: 978-1-3502-1587-0
eBook: 978-1-3502-1586-3

Series: Methuen Drama Agitations: Text, Politics and Performances

Typeset by Newgen KnowledgeWorks Pvt. Ltd., Chennai, India

To find out more about our authors and books visit www.bloomsbury.com
and sign up for our newsletters.

For family in Colorado: Carrington, Will, and Maddi and good friends in Florida: Greg and Julie

Contents

Acknowledgments — ix

Post-Truth: A Brief Introduction — 1
William C. Boles

Part 1 Text

1 Post-Truth but Not Post-Race: The Repeating Realities of Anna Deavere Smith's *Twilight: Los Angeles, 1992* — 39
   Heidi E. Bollinger
2 Knowing Not What It "Seems": Re-Viewing Caryl Churchill's Post-Truth World in *Glass, Kill, Bluebeard's Friends,* and *Imp* — 58
   Mamata Sengupta

Part 2 Politics

3 The Alternative Realities of David Henry Hwang's *Soft Power* and Anne Washburn's *Shipwreck* — 77
   William C. Boles
4 Negotiating the Fifth Wall — 96
   Lynn Deboeck
5 When the Play Is Not the Thing: The Mueller Report and the Limits of Documentary Drama — 114
   Victoria Scrimer

Part 3 Performance

6 Australian Biographical Theater on the Post-Truth Stage — 135
   Stephen Carleton and Chris Hay

7	Performing Reality: Tina Satter's Verbatim Staging of an FBI Transcript in *Is This A Room* *Helen Georgas*	155
8	Seductive Frames: Digital Aesthetics in Kip Williams's Staging of Bertolt Brecht's *The Resistible Rise of Arturo Ui* (2018) *Susanne Thurow*	176
9	Satanic Panic: Performance in the New Culture War *Lewis Church*	196

Notes on Contributors	217
Index	221

Acknowledgments

This volume is the second in the Methuen Drama Agitations series, which I co-edit with the inestimable Anja Hartl. Its genesis occurred on a glorious spring afternoon in Florida when I spoke with Bloomsbury publisher, Mark Dudgeon, about a potential book project on various crises points in British theater. However, I expressed concerns about the idea because of the numerous paths I wanted to explore, including the Great Recession, climate change, the housing crisis, race relations, terrorism, the influence of Brexit and Trump, and other sociopolitical pressure points. A covering of all these issues would cause the volume to be more of a survey, and an in-depth look at one or two items would ignore the rest. Mark asked: Why limit the question to one volume? Why not start a series? And so, Methuen Drama Agitations was born. So, my first thanks needs to go to Mark, Anja, and Anna Brewer, who has been my longtime contact at Bloomsbury and who put me in touch with Mark when I shared my idea with her.

Second, I want to thank the contributors to this volume, who, in the midst of a pandemic, have managed to navigate online teaching; local, state, and national lockdowns; the political football of Covid vaccines and masks; personal struggles with family illnesses (Covid-related and not); and the omnipresent dread of what might come next. In the midst of all the chaos, they have kept on point, crafting compelling chapters that examine the intersections between theater and our post-truth world. It has been a difficult year for all of us, and I thank them for their time, energy, focus, and good-natured bonhomie.

I also must thank Rollins College and the Hugh F. and Jeannette G. McKean Endowed Chair for their continuing financial support of my research.

Finally, my thanks and love go out to my wife, Leslie Tate Boles, and daughter, Emma, who have traveled with me to London, New York,

Chicago, and Los Angeles to see plays that, well, were not exactly their first choice for a night out at the theater. They have graciously, with only a little bit of eye-rolling, journeyed with me into the darkness of the theater, even though they never exactly knew what they were about to see.

Post-Truth: A Brief Introduction

William C. Boles

The Smokiness of Post-Truth: Science, Profit, and Cigarettes

The birth of our post-truth world can be traced to a meeting that occurred on December 15, 1953, in the iconic Plaza Hotel, situated on the southeast corner of Central Park.[1] Gathered together in the hotel conference room was a rare sight—almost all of the heads of the major cigarette corporations, including Philip Morris, R. J. Reynolds, Brown and Williamson, American Tobacco, U.S. Tobacco, and Benson and Hedges. What had drawn them all together a mere ten days before Christmas? All had concerns about the future profitability and viability of their product. Not only had the stock prices of their respective companies been dropping but also for the first time the annual consumption of cigarettes had decreased. Even more concerning was the cause of this financial reversal. In 1952, *Reader's Digest*, one of the most respected magazines in the United States, had published "Cancer by the Carton," which linked cigarettes with cancer. By the time of the December meeting, 40 percent of polled US citizens believed that lung cancer was caused by smoking cigarettes (Hilts 1996: 3). Adding to the corporate bigwigs' woes, a 1953 article in the scientific journal *Cancer Research* indicated a direct link between cigarettes and cancer, based on an experiment where cigarette tar brushed on mice caused the growth of cancerous tumors.

The CEOs of the companies needed to combat the scientific and media offensive against their product. Luckily for them, also in attendance was John Hill of Hill and Knowlton, a public relations firm. Public relations had become an "aggressive new industry which sought to shape feelings rather than facts" (Hilts 1996: 5). This focus on "feelings" rather than "facts" would later become the core attribute of post-truth when it came to the forefront in 2016. Hill's suggestion to the assembled leaders was that rather than acquiesce to the science and, in turn, find themselves regulated by the government, they "should sponsor a public relations campaign which is positive in nature and entirely 'pro-cigarettes'" (Hilts 1996: 6). Hill recommended they create their own committee dedicated to finding out if there was any truth to the emerging science. Entirely funded by the cigarette manufacturers, they created the Tobacco Industry Research Committee (TIRC). It would have multiple functions: push back against the recent studies linking cigarettes with cancer; stress to the media that they had an obligation to provide a balanced coverage of the topic; and lobby government officials so they would not interfere with the sales of cigarettes (Rabin-Havt 2016: 26–7). In addition, TIRC would hire and fund its own scientists, whose unstated goals would be to refute the research that was prejudicial against the industry. Hill's recommendations were unanimously approved. Philip Hilts summed up the significance of this decision:

> Thus began the conspiracy. Money was at its center, and public relations forestalled any serious look at the issue or any conscience-searching at the time. The plan was to spend large amounts of money every year indefinitely into the future to prevent, not sworn adversaries, but *scientists and public health officers*, from warning people of a potential hazard in the normal manner. (1996: 6–7)

The decision by the CEOs was an act of self-survival to maintain the money flowing into the company's coffers and stockholders' pockets.

Dollars trumped the facts being reported about the fatal effects of their product. An essential part of the campaign involved the production of public relations material that convinced smokers that the cigarette manufacturers were looking out for their best interests, despite the growing evidence about the cancer-causing aspects of the product. The chairman of the British American Tobacco company best summed up the difficult position they now found themselves in:

> It was very difficult when you were asked, as Chairman of a Tobacco Company, to discuss the health question on television. You had not only your own business to consider but the employees throughout the industry, retailers, consumers, farmers growing the leaf, and so on, and you were in a much too responsible position to get up and say: "I accept that the product which we and all our competitors are putting on the market gives you lung cancer," whatever you might think privately. (Hilts 1996: 28)

Under the auspices of TIRC, Ligget and Myers duplicated in 1955 the same lab experiment done in the *Cancer Research* article. Their hope was to prove that while other cigarette companies' products might cause cancer, theirs did not. The scientists not only duplicated the same result but also discovered it caused cancerous tumors in rabbits. It is worth noting at this point that during that seminal meeting in 1953 all agreed that if their own research proved that cigarettes did cause serious health issues, then they would cease their public relations campaign. They espoused that "public health is paramount to all else" (Hilts 1996: 6). However, instead of publicly sharing discoveries like the Ligget and Myers study, the results were kept secret, and they continued their assault on scientists.

In addition to duplicating research being done by legitimate labs, the TIRC self-produced a pamphlet called *Tobacco and Health*, which was sent to over 170,000 doctors and 15,000 media outlets. The material praised the health benefits of cigarettes in an aim to stem the tide of the negative publicity from the previous two years. The campaign proved a success, helping to staunch the fiscal bloodletting. Thirty-five years after the pamphlet was disseminated, Judge H. Lee Sarokin examined industrial documents that had been kept secret, like the failed experiment by Ligget and Myers. Citing *Tobacco and Health*, he noted that the pamphlet "was a blatant and biased account of the smoking 'controversy'" (Hilts 1996: 21). Based on paperwork that was revealed in later litigation, there were thirty tests run over a twenty-year period that continued to replicate the research already established in 1953 linking cigarettes with cancer. Hilts noted that "it is clearly a testament to brazenness of company executives that they could step up before Congress, swear an oath, and say, as they did in 1994, it has not been proven" (1996: 37). While the tobacco industry in the 1950s wrapped themselves in the argument that the evidence linking their product explicitly to cancer had not yet been categorically proven because of other factors that also could contribute to the cause of medical ailments (including where one worked, what one's economic position was, and where one lived), forty years later it was apparent that what had begun as a campaign to push back against science had now turned into a cottage industry of blatant lying, best documented in an interview by *The Wall Street Journal* with Ross Johnson, who had been CEO of R. J. Reynolds. He had always denied the dangers and addictive properties of cigarettes. After retiring, he was asked if nicotine was addictive. "Of course it's addictive. That's why you smoke the stuff" (qtd. in Hilts 1996: 64).

As listed above in the three points that came from the 1953 meeting, the media was another tack used by the tobacco companies to push back against the science linking their product with cancer. Aiding this push was the passing of the Fairness Doctrine in 1949, which stated that broadcast television was required to present a balanced look at controversial issues that may impact the viewing public. TIRC vigilantly took advantage of this doctrine, encouraging the media to present both sides of the issue and convincing newspaper and magazine editors to change their more damning stories and television shows to be more balanced. Perhaps their greatest success was convincing Edward R. Murrow, who was one of the most respected journalists of the United States, to represent the side of the scientists employed by the cigarette companies. After a meeting in 1956, Murrow and his producer Fred Friendly agreed to explore the issue surrounding cigarettes "with special effort toward a balanced perspective and concrete steps to show that the facts still are not established and must be sought by scientific means such as the research activities the Tobacco Industry Research Committee will support" (qtd. in Oreskes and Conway 2010: 19). This successful technique by TIRC and John Hill of advocating for an evenhanded presentation of "facts" from both sides led to future tenuous political, medical, and scientific positions to gain traction precisely because the media allowed so-called experts, not scientists but individual spokespersons, to assert opinion against the facts cited by bona fide experts. Nowhere was this more prominent than in the recent brouhaha about the connection between childhood vaccines and autism, where

> some argued that vaccines cause autism, and they were given an equal amount of airtime as the experts who stressed the importance of vaccines for public health and who rejected the fraudulent claim of a causal relationship between autism and vaccines. Through this policy, the media asserted the importance of various values other than truth, in particular a certain conception of equality—everyone is entitled to his or her opinion as much as anyone else. (Dumouchel 2010: 10)

Jenny McCarthy, an actress, television personality, game show judge, and former *Playboy* Playmate of the Year, became not only the face of the anti-vaccine movement but also a perfect representation of what Hill's plan of attack for the cigarette companies wrought. After her son was diagnosed with autism, she appeared on various television programs, and her platform was given credence on *The Oprah Winfrey Show*, where she proudly announced that "the University of Google is where I got my degree from," when questioned about her expertise on the subject (Vanden Heuvel 2013). She also appeared on *Frontline*, *Good Morning America*, and *The Larry King Show*, where she debated with a doctor over the efficacy of vaccines. This movement toward allowing nonspecialists to have equal airtime as experts on the subject has contributed to the rise of the muddying of facts and expert testimony, so key to the post-truth era in which we find ourselves.

> While this may have been a reasonable or even laudable goal when it came to opinion-based topics, it proved to be a disaster for science coverage. By allowing "equal time," the media only succeeded in creating "false equivalence" between two sides of an issue even when there were not really two credible sides. (McIntyre 2018: 77)

However, it has not just been the Jenny McCarthys of the world who have benefited and been given voice due to that meeting back in 1953. Other industries with economic and political connections to controversial policies and products followed the playbook created by Hill. Similar tactics can be traced to successful campaigns challenging guns and gun safety, climate change, issues surrounding health care, immigration reform, Voter ID laws, abortion, gay marriage, and many other political and professional hot topics. Matthew d'Ancona makes the case why these groups have embraced this method of pushing back against the experts:

> Their purpose is invariably to sow doubt rather than to triumph outright in the court of public opinion … As the institutions that traditionally act as social arbiters—referees on the pitch, as it were—have been progressively discredited, so well-funded pressure groups have encouraged the public to question the existence of conclusively reliable truth. (2017: 46)

In addition, the rise of twenty-four-hour news channels in the 1990s that desperately needed content to fill out its schedule provided the perfect opportunity for institutions aiming to push back against fact and science. Their opportunities were becoming more numerous and the audience for their alternative perspective was larger, since the cable news programs, feeling like they were obligated to provide two different sides to every story, would fill their airtime pitting experts against nonexperts, who were only there to confuse the issue in the five-minute slot dedicated to the topic. Ultimately, this method of countering truth through sound bites and misdirection led to the success of Brexit and

Trump's election win, both of which were seen as the reasons why the term post-truth became the ubiquitous word of 2016.

What Is Post-Truth? A Political Perspective

The first documented use of the term "post-truth" occurred in 1992 in *The Nation*, where Steve Tesich in a short essay titled "A Government of Lies" suggested that "in a very fundamental way we, as a free people, have freely decided that we want to live in some post-truth world" (1992: 13). How is it that we decided to live in such a world? Tesich traces this desire to two instances from the previous decades. First, he connected the rise of post-truth to the politics of the late 1960s and early 1970s, name-dropping President Richard Nixon and the Vietnam War as two of the main instigators for our current, tenuous relationship with the truth and facts.

> Either because the Watergate revelations were so wrenching and followed on the heels of the war in Vietnam ... or because Nixon was so quickly pardoned, we began to shy away from the truth. We came to equate truth with bad news and we didn't want bad news anymore, no matter how true or vital to our health as a nation. We looked to our government to protect us from the truth. (Tesich 1992: 12)

Second, he posited that President Ronald Reagan keenly understood American citizens' desire to avoid hearing the truth. His demeanor, advanced age, Hollywood background, and folksiness assuaged the public's reliance on a truthful government. Tesich suggested that "President Reagan perceived correctly that the public really didn't want to know the truth. So he lied to us, but he didn't have to work hard at it. He sensed that we would gladly accept his loss of memory as an alibi" (1992: 12). According to George Schultz, who was Reagan's secretary of state, the president "could rearrange facts to make a good story better ... Sometimes President Reagan simply did not seem to care that much about facts and details" (qtd. in Keyes 2004: 126).

Nothing better summed up this mindset of Reagan than the Iran Contra scandal, where his reliance on storytelling and disregard for facts were finally caught out by John Tower's commission investigating the scandal. In a national address to the country from the White House, Reagan finally admitted to the disconnect between the facts and his own public pronouncements: "A few months ago I told the American people that I did not trade arms for hostages. My heart and my best intentions still tell me that is true, but the facts and evidence tell me it is not" (Cannon 1987). Tesich, writing twenty-four years before the rise of Trump, was prescient in what was barreling to the United States in the ensuing decades. One of his arguments about embracing this post-truth world was that "we are rapidly becoming prototypes of a people that totalitarian monsters could only drool about in their dreams" because of our complete disconnect from pursuing truth from our leaders (1992: 13). President Donald J. Trump, like Reagan before him, is a performer and understands audience and what generates "ratings" among the voting public. His own political pronouncements, based on his gut feelings—not his heart, like Reagan—and not facts, are direct descendants from Reagan's own pronouncements in the 1980s. It is understandable then that the electorate, having been honed over the years to divorce themselves from a truthful government by Vietnam, Nixon, Reagan, President William Clinton's prevarications about his extramarital relationships, and President George W. Bush administration's claim of weapons of mass destruction in Iraq, was of a mindset in 2016 to no longer believe in the presence or importance of truth when it came to politics and government.

However, at this point it is important to note the difference between the omnipresence of political lies and the larger concept behind post-truth. Post-truth rhetoric and political lying are not one and the same thing. Colin Wight notes the distinction between the two: "Post-truth resides not in the realm of production, but in the realm of reception. If lies, dissembling, spinning, propaganda and the production of bullshit have always been part and parcel of politics, then what has changed is how publics respond to them" (2018: 22). This shift can clearly be seen in the public's response to Trump's rhetoric leading not only to his election but also to a more bifurcated, angry, and at times violent state of the country with protests appearing on both sides of the political spectrum. The strident language and attitude were apparent from the "Lock her up" demands for Hillary Clinton to go to jail by his supporters to the increase in violent attacks against non-white ethnic groups and protestors at his rallies. The rhetoric and the public's strident reaction of support no longer relied on his citing of facts, but instead on how they felt in reaction to his statements. If they believed what he said was true, then it was true. Tesich's post-truth world had now gone mainstream. And not surprisingly, with the phrase having such a predominant presence in the media due to Trump and Brexit's successes, Oxford Dictionaries selected it as the word of the year in 2016, beating out "alt-right" and "Brexiteer."[2] The post-Tesich definition of the term by the *Oxford Dictionary* states that post-truth is where "objective facts are less influential in shaping public opinion than emotional appeals" ("'Post-Truth' Declared" 2016). Lee McIntyre clarifies how the term works when it is used in a political context, since "post-truth is not so much a claim that truth *does not exist* as that *facts are subordinate to our political point of view*" (2018: 11; emphasis in the original). Wight offers another glossing of the term and its real-world applications, arguing that "if levels of trust in public institutions have declined to the extent that it is now assumed everyone is lying … then accepting the narrative that fits best with one's worldview makes perfect sense" (2018: 27). Of course, the most extreme example of the public's acceptance of Trump's rhetoric occurred on January 6, 2021, which we will examine later in this introduction.

Trump's campaign in 2015–16 as well as the Brexit campaign in the UK demonstrated Wight's distinction. Trump emulated the rhetorical device of lies used by politicians but, as many have documented, lying was nothing new to Trump, as he had always relied on lies to grow the stature of his public and business persona. He honed the skill of what he termed "hyperbole" through his books, his posing as his own press agent, and the successful television show *The Apprentice* and its spin-off

The Celebrity Apprentice. Writing in the early 1990s, F. G. Bailey precisely defined the method upon which Trump based his electoral campaign as well as his own reputation: "When politicians assert that something is true, they mostly have an eye not on anything in the objective world but more on rhetoric and persuasion. 'Will it fly?' takes precedence over 'Is it true?'" (1991: 125). Trump, especially, was one interested in clicks, ratings, and press mentions as signposts of his importance. The idea of "will it fly" was, in a sense, his mantra. Will it get him headlines, will it get retweets, will he appear on the news is what drove his professional and social life and then, later, his political career. Sissela Bok's seminal text on lying explains the pre-post-truth effect of lying:

> How is the liar affected by his own lies? The very fact that he *knows* he has lied, first of all, affects him. He may regard the lie as an inroad on his integrity; he certainly looks at those he has lied to with a new caution. And if they find out that he has lied, he knows that his credibility and the respect for his word have been damaged. (1978: 24; emphasis in the original)

In a post-truth world none of the answers to the question of what happens to a liar hold true anymore. Lies do not affect the liars, witnessed by the success of Trump, Boris Johnson, Leave campaigners, countless other politicians, cigarette manufacturers, and nonexpert talking heads. But even more importantly, the reaction to the liar has changed dramatically. Respect and credibility have not been damaged. In fact, a fervor exists in the followers, who make the lies a mantra and, in turn, through the repetition (either through exposure through media outlets or the follower's own statement to others) it becomes truth. The 2020 election was stolen.[3] Hillary should go to jail. Covid is a hoax. Democratic pedophiles are using a DC pizza parlor as its base of operation. With the public now digesting and spouting the lies instead of acknowledging them exactly as such, the dramatic shift to the new post-truth normal was complete and, with it, Trump won the presidency.

For his reelection campaign in 2020 he doubled down on the same rhetoric, sometimes replaying the same talking points as in 2015–16, but he added a new caveat about the upcoming election, suggesting that there was no way he could lose to a candidate like "Sleepy Joe" Biden and, if he did lose, it would only be because the election was rigged. This talking point was one he constantly repeated, ingraining in his followers the idea that the only way he could lose was if the system worked against him, disenfranchising their votes, while hundreds of thousands of fake urban votes were snuck in to ensure a Democratic victory. Even though there were no facts to support such electoral corruption on local, state, and national scales, Trump stated the accusation from podiums carrying the presidential seal, indoctrinating his followers to believe his highly dubious claims. Shortly after the election, on November 5, 2020, Trump addressed members of the media as well as the nation from the Press Room of the White House, where what had previously been a hypothetical claim of possible fraud now became a stated "fact" that the election had been stolen.

> We think there's going to be a lot of litigation because we have so much evidence, so much proof. And it's going to end up, perhaps, at the highest court in the land ... because we can't have an election stolen by—like this ... I have been talking about this for many months with all of you. And I've said very strongly that mail-in ballots are going to end up being a disaster. Small elections were a disaster. Small, very easy-to-handle elections were disastrous.
> This is a large-scale version, and it's getting worse and worse every day. We're hearing stories that are horror stories—absolute horror stories. And we can't let that happen to the United States of America. ("Remarks" 2020)

Broadcasters immediately pulled out of the White House feed, interrupting Trump's screed as offended national anchors insisted that they were not going to be party to the president of the United States lying to the American public about the veracity of the nation's electoral system. And yet, it is worth a short digression here to note the hypocrisy of the networks' decision to stop covering Trump at this moment, since the previous five years they had had no issues broadcasting his lies throughout both election campaigns and his presidency. Trump, after all, had been a boon to the bottom line of news outlets. He helped bolster profits, drawing massive ratings for both the more liberal-leaning news stations as well as the conservative ones. "If there is one true thing that Donald Trump said in his book *The Art of the Deal* it is that the media loves controversy more than truth" (McIntyre 2018: 82). Jane Suiter cited another factor that underlined the media's love/hate relationship to Trump—the emotional response of their audiences:

> We know that using emotional cues helps to get audiences' attention and to prolong engagement ... Talk radio and Fox News understand this logic well, tapping into a market for anger and unabashed partisanship that is amplified by social media. Being fair and balanced does not drive ratings. This is the bedrock of the post-truth environment where truth is simply a matter of assertion. (2016: 27)

The ubiquitous appearance of Trump on national television screens created a desensitization to all of his mistruths, hence also contributing to our current easy dismissal of facts and truth. *The Washington Post* Fact Checker team, which cataloged Trump's lies, stated that by the end of his presidency he had amassed more than thirty thousand misstatements, meaning, on average, he lied twenty-one times a day (Kessler, Rizzo, and Kelly 2021). Writing almost forty years before Trump's presidency, Bok noted the ramifications of such a massive amount of dishonesty in the political arena: "Political lies ... cannot be trivial when they affect so many people and when they are so peculiarly likely to be imitated, used to retaliate, and spread from a few to many" (1978: 15). Indubitably, the media's Trump obsession shared the same bottom line that drove the campaign by cigarette companies from the 1950s onward: profits, which drove both to be significant contributors to our post-truth world.

There are repercussions, though, for the preponderance of lies that the public embraces. The fabric of our nation is threaded tightly together by a reliance on not only the normalcy of truth telling, but also on the recognition and rejection of falsehoods. When this structure begins to collapse, as we have seen with the rise of post-truth rhetoric and politics, the fabric of social interactions and political behavior unwinds. Ralph Keyes noted the danger of when such a tipping point is reached. "Our social contract cannot survive lying so routine that citizens consider it normal," and, as a result, "post-truthful behavior by specific individuals picks away at our social contract as a whole" (Keyes 2004: 228). Keyes's words would prove to be prophetic come the lunchtime hours of January 6, 2021, the day the 2020 election results were to be ratified by Congress. After hearing Trump and other Trump allies decry the stolen election and the need to reclaim their country, a mob of pro-Trump protestors marched to the Capitol and soon thereafter stormed the government building, wreaking havoc inside and out for several hours before being dispersed by Capitol police and members of the National Guard. The takeover of the building resulted in five deaths and over seven hundred arrests. What had been a months-long, post-truth rhetorical exhortation by Trump to rally his followers had morphed into a social-contract defying, violent, bloodshedding event. As Keyes predicted, the social contract, which had been stretched dangerously thin throughout Trump's tenure by events like the Charlottesville protest and the clearing out of protesters in front of the White House, so he could stand in front of a St. John's Episcopal Church holding a Bible, finally snapped on that unforgettable afternoon of January 6. The post-truth age, which had spates of violence tied to its rhetoric, had exploded into a full-fledged, riotous insurgency against lawmakers, the Constitution, and the concept of what the United States stands for.

Despite the horrific images of the event and the immediate across-the-aisle condemnation of the mob by politicians, who hid under desks and in bathrooms, post-truth posturing has (as I write this introduction), of course, begun to redefine what happened on that day. At a May 12, 2021, hearing by the US House of Representatives looking at the attack a few Republicans described a picture of what occurred that was different from what was depicted by the news media. Andrew Clyde of Georgia stated:

> Watching the TV footage of those who entered the Capitol and walked through Statuary Hall showed people in an orderly fashion staying between the stanchions and ropes, taking videos, pictures. You know, if you didn't know the TV footage was a video from January the 6th, you would actually think it was a normal tourist visit. (Itkowitz 2021)

Others wondered whether the invaders were Trump supporters at all. With future hearings scheduled in a pursuit of what happened on that day, no doubt the refusal to acknowledge the truth of that day will continue by politicians, and their supporters will embrace their statements, believing their words and their feelings that Trump's second term was stolen rather than the facts of Biden's election.

The rise of Trump was mirrored in the UK by the surprise result of the Brexit vote in 2016, which also relied on the same post-truth rhetoric that had catapulted Trump to the Republican nomination in the summer of 2016. Just as Trump played fast and loose with the truth, members of the Leave campaign were equally less concerned with sharing truthful statements in their campaign. "The promoters of Brexit openly admitted that they had pushed ideas that they fully knew were not 'true,' but they did so 'because there really are no facts,' and what really counts is 'that we truly believe this' … what I *want* to be true *is* true in a post-truth culture" (Wilbur 2017: 25; emphasis in the original). Making this strategy possible was the changing mindset of the voting British public, which had begun to rely less on experts and more on social media for information. The distrust of experts arose because of "the Iraq War, the 2008 financial crisis, and the 2009 MPs' expenses scandal. These events caused the public to mistrust academics (and other 'experts'), politicians, journalists, and, indeed, the 'system' as a whole" (Marshall and Drieschova 2018: 98). This lack of trust was a key component of the Leave campaign's success, and they publicly acknowledged their reliance on the voting public's disbelief in specialists. "Faced with a challenge to name the economists backing Leave, after many prominent economists had publicly supported

Remain, [Michael] Gove [member of parliament] simply dismissed the question: 'People in this country have had enough of experts'" (Ball 2017: 58). The result of such a mindset and sociopolitical condition is that, according to Matthew d'Ancona, one no longer has "to make an intellectual case" (2017: 127). Brexit demonstrated how intellectual argument and facts lost out to the public's reliance on their own feelings. Arron Banks, a co-founder of the Leave.EU campaign, explained that the Remain campaign lost because it "featured fact, fact, fact, fact … You've got to connect with people emotionally" (qtd. in d'Ancona 2017: 17). How they did that was through three key points that stressed: (1) the amount of money dedicated to the European Union (350 million pounds a week being sent to the continent); (2) the increasing migration numbers of European Union members to the UK; (3) and the future threat of other countries, like Turkey, joining the EU. As a result, "the narrative of the Vote Leave campaign had traction with the public in a way the Vote Remain campaign did not … [However], it is worth noting that the three key messages the public remembered are, at best, misleading, and at worst, outright false" (Marshall and Drieschova 2018: 94). D'Ancona views the Brexit campaign as the quintessential definition of how post-truth rhetoric works. It was "the triumph of the visceral over the rational, the deceptively simple over the honestly complex" (2017: 20). Marshall and Drieschova see Brexit's victory as far more dangerous, arguing that "the Brexit referendum suggests that post-truth politics represents a serious threat to democracy as it is commonly understood" (2018: 100), which, as we have seen, turned out to be true in the United States in the early days of 2021.

Other Post-Truth Originations

While Tesich placed the word into play in the 1990s and Trump and Brexit made it a household term in 2016, the roots of post-truth did not actually begin to form in 1953. Scholars have traced it back over the millennia. Steve Fuller suggests that Socrates and Plato embodied a post-truth mentality because they were "concerned more with the mix of chance and skill in the construction of truth than with the truth as such" (qtd. in Myres 2018: 392). D'Ancona notes that *The Prince* by Machiavelli also features a harbinger of post-truth dictums. The Italian argued that a ruler should "be a great pretender and dissembler; and men are so simple, and so subject to present necessities, that he who seeks to deceive will always find someone who will allow himself to be deceived" ([1532] 1998). According to Yve-Alain Bois, Heinrich von Kleist in "Primer of French Journalism" (1821), which was composed in response to Napoleon's propaganda machine, exposed "the process by which fake news is manufactured and disseminated in the media" by Napoleon and his advisors (2017: 127). Of course, the most noted example of post-truth before Tesich coined the term can be found in the writing of George Orwell. While d'Ancona suggests that *Looking Back on the Spanish War* is "an early premonition of the Post-Truth era" (2017: 5), Orwell's novel *1984* is the most cited example of post-truth ideas, as the government of Oceania constantly discounts factual instances in its effort to promote its latest governmental narrative, erasing previously praised individuals entirely from its historical records, and instantaneously changing the status of an ally to an enemy and an enemy to an ally in its ongoing battle with the two other superstates. Through the eyes of Winston Smith, who works at the Ministry of Truth in the Records Department, we learn how the government under the auspices of Big Brother erases facts, people, and the past to reflect the current mindset of the government. In turn, the citizens believe every utterance, despite the clear inconsistencies of statements made day-to-day and sometimes, moment to moment.

One of the strongest influences for the rise of our post-truth world can be traced to colleges and universities, where faculty members challenged their students through their postmodernist publications and pedagogy. D'Ancona forthrightly declares that "post-modernist texts paved the way for Post-Truth" (2017: 96), while McIntyre agrees, suggesting that "the godfather of post-truth" is postmodernism (2018: 150). The element of postmodernism that ties directly into the rise of our post-truth era was that of challenging the concept of truth through the valuing of multiple readings of a text. When there is never a wrong interpretation, pressure then arises on what is truth. Postmodernism argued that there was no truth, only social constructs, which allowed each individual to decide their own truth.

> Indeed the notion of truth itself was now under scrutiny, for one had to recognize that in the act of deconstruction, the critic was bringing his or her own values, history, and assumptions to the interpretation as well. This meant that there could be *many* answers, rather than just one, for any deconstruction. (McIntyre 2018: 125)

The result of such a situation, obviously, takes us back to the example of Jenny McCarthy and her anti-vaccine campaign. If, as postmodernism says, everyone constructs their own truth, and, in turn, truth itself is relative, then the position Jenny McCarthy holds and stridently argues is completely viable. The same would hold true for anti-Covid vaxxers, who believe that Bill Gates is using the serum to insert a tracker into everyone's body, or climate change deniers, or those believing Trump should still be president. All would stem, then, from a position of validity and, therefore, should be considered as equally valid as other more factual positions, meaning that one could make the case that a Holocaust denier's truth is equal to the truth of a Holocaust survivor. This problematic result from postmodernism creates a position of "ethical absurdity" (Keyes 2004: 140). In addition, the denying of facts as truth has led to the confusion and uncertainty surrounding scientific findings, as we saw with the cigarette and anti-vaccine campaign, when no confusion should exist at all. "The standard postmodern claim became, very quickly, that there was 'no difference between science and poetry,' … If science itself was not discovering anything like truth, then clearly truth itself simply did not exist" (Wilbur 2017: 94).

In the classroom professors pushed their students to give voice to their ideas and argue alternative interpretations of texts. Colin Wight highlighted this pedagogical aspect as contributing to our current atmosphere of reliance on alternative realities, according to the facts we consume:

> The facts, as we constantly remind our students, don't directly speak for themselves. Which facts matter, and what to make of them, is always a matter of interpretation. Thus, post-truth finds intellectual legitimation in the necessary and critical approach to the construction of knowledge that is an essential element of academia. Academics necessarily, and rightly, take a sceptical attitude to all truth claims. (2018: 23).

While Wight places the rise of post-truth as a pedagogical decision, Ken Wilbur is more critical of the role academics and the institution have played as contributors to the emergence of our post-truth era. He writes that the current challenge to truth, which has become dominant in not only politics but also in internet search engines and social media, could not happen "without virtually every university in the world spewing out postmodern poststructuralist nostrums centering on the idea that 'truth' itself is the single greatest oppressive force in the history of humankind?" (2017: 36). McIntyre shares the same level of discomfort with the role academia has played in contributing to the post-truth era, acknowledging that "it is … embarrassing to admit that one of the saddest roots of the post-truth phenomenon seems to have come directly out of colleges and universities" (2018: 123). Keyes, when he was a university student, experienced the omnipresence of the postmodern mindset and witnessed how the openness of interpretation led students to see how far they could push their analysis. He saw that "on campus it became fashionable for obscurity, duplicity, and outright fabrication to be considered acceptable. In this intellectual climate, dissembling was not just condoned but virtually celebrated" (Keyes 2004: 142). As the number of students attending college and universities have increased over the decades, so too has the dissemination of postmodern ideas. Wight argues that over the last thirty years students who have enrolled in humanities and social sciences classes "have not escaped exposure to these ideas" and they are "now deeply ingrained in western societies"

(2018: 25). Precisely because of this increased exposure, the institution now finds itself in a bit of a conundrum. "If academics make a difference and publics no longer seem to care about facts, truth and reason, then we cannot be absolved of all responsibility for this situation. Indeed, if we do deny our responsibility, we as good as admit that we have little impact on society" (Wight 2018: 26).

Within the academic setting "postmodernists see themselves as intellectual pranksters. Deception, they argue, can be a creative, playful act" (Keyes 2004: 143). However, that playfulness has now been smartly appropriated, as seen through the rhetoric of Donald Trump. His cries of fake news, hoaxes, and witch hunts parrot the same wording ("obscurity, duplicity, and outright fabrication") noted by Keyes about his classmates joyfully challenging the facts as presented. The postmodern concept of no truth has escaped "the walls of the academy and become a key source of our eroding commitment to truth telling" (Keyes 2004: 146), and the serious repercussions of this jailbreak can be seen, most specifically, in the realm of Trumpian politics, where now the rejection of truth is no longer about philosophical considerations or classroom pedagogical choices but instead about the quest for power and dominance over others. Wilbur accuses collegiate institutions of hypocrisy as they now see bombastic figures like Donald Trump and Boris Johnson relying upon the postmodern questioning of truth, text, and narrative at every press conference.

> Teaching that "no truth" idea in an ivory tower, divorced from any practical reality to unsuspecting college students is one thing; seeing it in real action is quite another. And around the world, coming out of essentially every university in existence, there has arisen a thunderous silence … After hearing somebody like Trump constantly claiming that there is no truth and that all news agencies who disagree with him are fake news, no self-respecting scholar can even repeat those words. The notion itself has become a massive embarrassment. (Wilbur 2017: 122–3)

Instead, a hypocritical sea change has taken place, and Wilbur argues truth has now become the totem of academicians, even though "that sentiment is utterly inconceivable coming out of post-modern academia anytime during the past half century—until just about three weeks after Trump's inauguration, and now it is the banner headline under which all good men and women everywhere are meant to march" (Wilbur 2017: 139). McIntyre chides scholars that "they must acknowledge some responsibility for undermining the idea that facts matter in the assessment of reality, and not foreseeing the damage this could cause" (2018: 127). Finally, Daniel Dennett provides perhaps the harshest reprimand for the postmodernist's role in the rise of post-truth rhetoric and its poster child Donald Trump, rebukingly writing, "what postmodernists did was truly evil" (qtd. in Perrin 2017).[4]

Enter the Theater: Post-Truth, Climate Change, and the Stage

The previous sections have provided a brief history of the term post-truth over the last seventy years, especially in the world of business and politics. Where does the stage and our post-truth era overlap? While the theater has always been a site where playwrights have pushed back against perceived misstatements and misleading government policies and actions, in the 1990s and into the 2000s, some writers embraced documentary, also known as verbatim drama, to challenge important political and social issues. This format, which positions itself as only relying upon truth and facts, professes to offer a more in-depth, focused, and honest exploration of an issue or event than journalism, which is limited by word count or spare minutes offered between commercials. Richard Norton-Taylor, perhaps the most successful verbatim dramatist in the UK, argued that the documentary method allows the theater to be "an extension of journalism in the best possible way—that is, by communicating and explaining contemporary issues, scandals and events in a unique, fair, positive and intellectually honest manner" (2008: 122). Relying on government documents, transcripts of public hearings and trials, news accounts, and personal interviews, docudramatists create a detailed examination through the presentation of multiple perspectives. These authors argue that this methodology allows for a purer look at the issues under consideration, as it is unfiltered and unbiased, all with the consequence of a performative piece that is truthful and factual. Two of the most powerful dramas that also effected change in their respective countries over the last twenty-five years were docudramas. In England, Norton-Taylor's *The Colour of Justice*, about the murder of Stephen Lawrence, was an influential instrument in revealing racism in the London Metropolitan Police Department, while Moisés Kaufman and his Tectonic Theater production of *The Laramie Project*, which chronicled the murder of Matthew Shepard, who was killed for being gay, and its aftermath on the Wyoming town of Laramie, was one of the most produced plays in the United States, educating audiences about the brutality behind homophobia and the grace of forgiveness. Both plays' reliance on truth and accuracy was endemic to their success and, in turn, aided an explosion of docudramas in the UK and United States.

However, the claim of verbatim theater being the "truth" and presenting what really happened is not a universal belief. Doubters exist about the veracity of the form because of the author's own bias, which becomes clear through "the creative editing of materials, textual manipulations, artistic license in converting the texts to a theatrical form, and the excision of material that does not support the chosen representation of an individual character or overall theme of the piece" (Boles 2017: 219). Clouding the fact-based nature of the genre is the emerging presence of mockumentary plays, which follow the same narrative format as docudramas, purporting to be true, but are actually partly or completely false. Dennis Kelly's *Taking Care of Baby* included harrowing interviews with mothers whose infants had died in their cribs. And yet, those interviews were all fictional. As Clare Finburgh Delijani noted, Kelly's play was a perfect post-truth signifier, as he crafted "a dizzying piece of theatre which ... blurs the boundaries between reality and fiction" (2021: 3). The same confusion between fact and fiction occurred with David Henry Hwang's *Yellow Face*, which appears to be a documentary-style, autobiographical play about Hwang's life after winning the Tony for *M. Butterfly* and his father's involvement in illegal political contributions by Chinese citizens to Bill Clinton's presidential campaign but is actually a mix of truth and fiction, confusing the audience and critics about what was truth and what was not. In numerous interviews Hwang was pressed to clear up the confusion but, unlike Kelly, Hwang would not confess to the fictional components of the play, admitting that "part of the fun of the play, I believe, is not knowing what is true and what is invented, so I'm going to duck that question" (Maher 2013). The overlap between documentary theater and post-truth rhetoric is rich with material and since three of the chapters in this volume (Chapters 1, 5, and 7) specifically analyze the overlap between the format and post-truth rhetoric by three American playwrights, I will focus the rest of this section on a group of British playwrights, whose plays pushed back against the claims being espoused in the media by climate change deniers.

The playbook created in the 1950s to push back against the cancer-causing agents of cigarettes had been retooled, rewritten, and perfected by the time climate change became an eco-political talking point. Energy companies successfully challenged the increasing scientific studies of rising carbon dioxide readings, ozone loss, and melting ice caps, leading experts to suggest that "global warming is perhaps the most egregious case of modern science denial" (McIntyre 2018: 27). While there was the fleeting sense of inroads being made in the 1990s against climate change with the Kyoto Protocol being signed by the United States and 140 other countries, they were promptly scuttled by well-prepared foes of the agreement who convinced George W. Bush to drop out upon becoming president in 2001. The post-truth battle over climate change came to the forefront with the success of Al Gore's documentary *An Inconvenient Truth* (2006) and his sharing of the 2007 Nobel Peace Prize with the Intergovernmental Panel on Climate Change (IPCC). The IPCC had released their fourth climate statement in 2007, convincingly arguing about humanity's role in the earth's changing climate and rising temperatures. Polls indicated the public was invested in moving forward to address climate change, and governments were open to creating eco-friendly policies. However, in 2009 this new awareness about the delicate nature of the earth's environment was overwhelmed by an international scandal that anti-climate change advocates used to great advantage. In mid-November a hacker broke into the servers of the Climactic Research Unit (CRU) of the University of East Anglia, accessing over 4,500 emails and documents tied to the IPCC report of 2007. By November 20, parts of the emails appeared in *The New York Times* and *The Wall Street Journal*. The emails, taken out of context, seemed to indicate that scientists, including Michael Mann, who was one of the creators of the famous hockey-stick graph that was used to such dramatic effect in Gore's documentary, had manipulated their research to strengthen the case for climate change, refused to release requested information to inquisitors wielding the Freedom of Information Act, and followed unethical procedures while doing their research. As a result, the scandal was termed Climategate. (Later, it was discovered, via an independent committee, that the charges of reckless scientific behavior were unfounded, although a separate review did find fault with the handling of the Freedom of Information Act request as well as sloppiness in how they handled their emails and their reactions to the press.) The anti-climate change rhetoric in response to the released information was immediate and brutal, as numerous skeptics attacked the report, the scientists, and the IPCC. James Sensenbrenner, a member of the House of Representatives, argued that the emails were evidence of "scientific fascism," and Competitive Enterprise Institute Director Myron Ebell accused scientists of "unethical conniving" (Lee 2011: 36). Even those who believed in the science found the behavior of the scientists as problematic. "Climategate has tarnished the image of climate research, but hasn't undermined its substance. At the risk of invoking the silver-lining cliché, maybe climategate will spur scientists to change how they conduct their research and engage with critics" (Begley 2009).[5] Even the scientists realized that the public relations of Climategate hurt their standing. Before the hearing in Parliament of the

Science and Technology Committee, Phil Jones, the head of the CRU at the University of East Anglia acknowledged: "Yes, I have obviously written some very awful emails" (Darwall 2013: 195).

Climategate halted the growing calls for governmental climate policies. The difference in two polls conducted by *The Guardian*, one just after the news began to break about the hacked emails and the second taken a couple of months later, showed how dramatic an impact the scandal had on the public perception of science and the issue of climate change. The first poll taken in December

> suggests that scientists continue to be held in retain [*sic*] relatively high esteem: 83% of the electorate trust scientists "to tell the truth about climate change," as against just 14% who do not trust them at all. But the email row may have reduced the extent of the trust. Just 36% trust the scientists "a lot" as against 47% who trust them only a little. (Clark 2009)

A follow-up poll from February of 2010 highlighted that the distrust that had begun to bubble up in December had increased as well as a change in perspective about the seriousness of climate change. "The proportion of adults who believe climate change is 'definitely' a reality dropped by 30% over the last year, from 44% to 31%, in the latest survey by Ipsos Mori" (Jowit 2010).[6] A BBC poll from the same month indicated that in February 2010, 34 percent now believed that climate change was connected to human behavior, whereas, in November of 2009, 50 percent of the population believed the same thing (Corbyn 2010: 10).[7] The poll numbers were no different in the United States. "In 2008, 71% of Americans said 'yes,' global warming is happening. By 2010, however, this number had dropped to 57%. Meanwhile the proportion that said 'no,' global warming is not happening doubled from 10% to 20%, whereas those who said 'don't know' increased from 19% to 23% of the public" (Leiserowitz et al. 2012: 824).

With the media breathlessly covering the scandal, the British theater community took notice. While there had been a few plays prior to Climategate that took on the rapidly warming planet, including

Crown Prince (2007) by John Godber, which was about the effect of flooding on the country, it was *The Contingency Plan* (2009) by Steve Waters that hit a nerve, critically and commercially. There had always been questions about how to stage the climate crisis. Waters solved it through an insightful, fact-based, and emotional play that presented the effect a major, climate change–caused flood has on a personal as well as political level. He had turned what had previously been subject matter for bad disaster movies into a powerful theatrical examination of the threat climate change posed for the British Isles. The viability of the topic had been proven by Waters, and the resultant poll numbers about Climategate showed that almost everyone had an opinion. It is not surprising then that the number of plays dedicated to climate change suddenly grew in number, leading to a two-week stretch in 2011 where three climate change plays all had premieres at major London venues.

Playwrights in the aughts and teens of the twenty-first century turned their theatrical eye to the post-truth arguments surrounding climate change and offered their own representations of the scientific perspective on stage as well as a new venue for documenting truths and facts when it came to the fate of the planet. Following *The Contingency Plan*, Mike Bartlett's *Earthquakes in London* (2010) was another critical and financial success, as his play, innovatively directed by Rupert Goold, mixes climate change science with the family drama between three distinctly different sisters. Other plays from this time period also seen as being climate change plays include Simon Stephens's *Wastwater* (2011), Duncan Macmillan's *Lungs* (2011), and Tonya Ronder's *Fuck the Polar Bears* (2015). It is also worth noting that Richard Bean's *The Heretic* (2011) provides a comedic look from the other side of the climate change controversy by focusing on a university scientist who, based on her research, does not agree with her colleagues about the warming planet, finding herself the object of threatening letters. Perhaps a perfect representation of science and the theater partnering together could be seen at the National Theatre with *Greenland* (2011), a play written by Moira Buffini, Matt Charman, Penelope Skinner, and Jack Thorne. The play stitches together numerous narratives, including scientists in the Arctic, a disgruntled young woman viewing the crumbling fate of the earth, future, and the failed 2009 Copenhagen international summit on climate change. Unlike *The Contingency Plan*, the play was not a success, and was panned ruthlessly in the press (except there was great praise for a polar bear that appears on stage at one point), but what differentiated it from other climate change productions was the inclusion of educational material in the lobby throughout the play's run and the opportunity for the audience to interact with scientists. The seriousness of climate change, then, was not just limited to the running time of the play but was enlarged to create an educational experience for not only ticket holders but also anyone who might be in the National Theatre lobby during the play's run. The space, then, became a post-truth free zone, allowing the facts to stand on their own, and for audiences and visitors to make up their own minds without anyone muddying the issue.

However, the most significant response by the theater to the post-truth slamming of scientists and their climate change research was Katie Mitchell's directorial decision to bring the science directly to the stage via two productions at the Royal Court: *Ten Billion* (2012) and *2071* (2014). Rather than having actors play scientists as occurred in the plays previously discussed, in each production Mitchell put one scientist alone on the stage, providing him with the platform, time, and visual support (through digital projections) to make their case about the state of the world to the audience. In doing so, Mitchell upended John Hill's public relations strategy to disparage scientists and their research. The expert, whose reputation over the years had become trampled and disrespected, whose science was attacked, whose profession grew less and less believed, was now given the stage for ninety minutes, without interruption, and allowed to speak and explain without the eye-rolling, loud-voiced hijinks of alternative truth speakers so endemic to the rise of post-truth. In *Ten Billion* Stephen Emmott, head of Computational Science for Microsoft as well as a visiting professor at Oxford and University College London, methodically works his way through the environmental and economic repercussions of the earth's population hitting ten billion, including the rising threat of earth's temperature. His thorough journey through the dramatic challenge the world faces eventually leads him to surmise that "technologizing our way out of this does not look likely" (2013: 184). Instead, he turns to the opportunity for everyone and every government to change their behavior in handling such a crisis point, but he has little hope in our ability to change, believing we still stick with the status quo. As the piece draws to a close, he refers back to his profession as a scientist to support his position: "As a scientist what do I think about our current situation? Science is essentially organized skepticism. I spend my life trying to prove my work wrong or look for alternative explanations for my results. I *hope* I'm wrong. But the science points to my not being wrong" (2013: 214). A few years later *2071* featured Chris Rapley, a climate scientist, who was not quite as dour about our fate. Like Emmott before him, he too focused on the scientific studies about the rising temperatures on earth, but his summation suggested a faith in science, as he tells his audience nightly, "My hope lies with the engineers" (2015: 190), who can "create the conditions for a massive effort of innovation and roll-out of energy technologies that will make existing fossil fuels redundant" (2015: 191). However, he too ends with an acknowledgment of the limit of science, which "cannot answer moral questions, value questions" (2015: 201). Ultimately, he ends the play with a call to consider the future generations, like his eldest granddaughter who will be Rapley's current age in 2071, asking us about what kind of future we are creating through our current actions. Both plays are perfect examples of how the theater used its format and physical space to offer an opportunity for science to reclaim its position of authority when it came to climate change.

No doubt, my brief examination of the theater's response to Climategate and the climate change debate only begins to dip into the material, but the examples perfectly capture some of the many times that the theater has involved itself with the issues that have arisen in the post-truth era. And what follows in the ensuing pages of this book highlights not only the interwoven complexity of theater's engagement with our post-truth world but also the theatrical and performative world that is so intrinsic to politicians, who have benefited from their own post-truth manipulations.

Theater in a Post-Truth World: Texts, Politics, and Performance

Amanda Stuart Fisher has posited that "the role of theatre as a mode of truth telling becomes ever more critical" in these post-truth times (2020: 180). My brief discussion of British theater's response to the controversy surrounding climate change is one of many examples of the way the theater has turned to truth telling to respond to post-truth rhetoric. As of the writing of this introduction, this volume is the first book to examine the intersections between theater and the rise of post-truth.[8] This work examines three different paths where we can see the intersection of post-truth and theater: texts, politics, and performance. The text section features close readings of plays to examine how post-truth elements have been addressed by playwrights. The politics section, while occasionally relying on close readings, considers how the realm of post-truth politics are rendered through plays, while also considering the theatrical component of being a politician. Finally, the last section looks at specific productions and how the artists have incorporated or responded to the rise of post-truth rhetoric and its challenge to truths and facts.

The text section of the book focuses on Anna Deavere Smith and Caryl Churchill, two important contemporary theatrical voices in the United States and Great Britain, respectively. Heidi E. Bollinger in her examination of *Twilight: Los Angeles, 1992* (Chapter 1) argues that Smith's work "anticipates the public's susceptibility to the rampant conspiracy theories and fake news of our post-truth era" through her dramatic positioning of alternative testimonies about the riots against one another, echoing the device used by the media to have two talking heads face off with one another. Bollinger also notes that "questions of truth and facts are intimately bound up with questions of crime, justice, and racial bias," ultimately suggesting that audience members' response to the paired monologues will be influenced by their own feelings about race rather than the facts presented. Meanwhile, in Chapter 2, through a close reading of Caryl Churchill's set of four short plays, *Glass*, *Kill*, *Bluebeard's Friends*, and *Imp*, performed at the Royal Court in 2019, Mamata Sengupta explores how the playwright "grapples with the divergent pulls of a world where misrepresented realities, politicized data, and misappropriated reportage loom large." Churchill's plays demonstrate how individuals consciously avoid facts and realities (*Glass*), how fictions usurp reality (*Kill*), how money influences our ignoring of reality (*Bluebeard's Friends*), and how difficult it is to control one's life in a post-truth world (*Imp*). Ultimately, Sengupta argues that the plays stress "the indomitable human will to survive every crisis."

The next section of the volume addresses the role of post-truth politics when it comes to not only the stage but also the theatrical world that politicians create around themselves. In Chapter 3, William C. Boles notes the overlap between Kellyanne Conway's "alternative fact" defense of Sean Spicer and Donald Trump's assertion of a massive inauguration crowd and David Henry Hwang's *Soft Power* and Anne Washburn's *Shipwreck*. Both playwrights turn the tables on the administration's use of alternative facts by staging alternative Trumpian realities. Hwang's musical play posits a world where the US's descent into chaos after Trump's election allows China to become not only the world's sole superpower but also the victor who dictates an alternative history of America, while Washburn's *Shipwreck* brings to life Trump's alternative fact that he was the only one to protest the Iraq War. Both playwrights use these alternative realities to provoke their audiences to challenge the lies that surround us. In Chapter 4, "Negotiating the Fifth Wall," Lynn Deboeck works from the premise that politicians "actively push away truth and/or those seeking it." Building upon the concept of the fourth wall, Deboeck argues that politicians in press conferences and other televised events have constructed a fifth wall, which acts like a moveable and flexible shield, as they "deflect, ricochet, and mirror challenging (or outright accusatory) questions and statements away from themselves and onto other targets." While acknowledging that this has long been a political device, she applies the concept to the four years of Trump's tenure, using examples from Trump, Nancy Pelosi, Lindsey Graham, and Sean Spicer. Chapter 5, the last chapter in the section, is by Victoria Scrimer, who focuses on the multiple performative elements surrounding the Mueller Report, which reported on the influence of Russia on the 2016 presidential election. She splits her chapter into two parts, first analyzing the performance of Mueller himself during his testimony before Congress and his failure, as seen by the Democrats, to bring his text to life before the committee. She then turns to another attempt to bring the report to life by examining Robert Schenkkan's theatrical adaptation. Through her analysis Scrimer determines his production to be a failure on many levels because of its political hobbyism, whereby it "cheapens its important subject matter in predictable ways" and tries "to transform a document, rather than trying to transform the audience."

The final section of the volume considers how theatrical performances explore the complexities of performing truth in our contemporary world. In Chapter 6, Stephen Carleton and Chris Hay focus on two plays by Tommy Murphy. Using a close reading of *Mark Colvin's Kidney* and *Packer & Sons*, they "argue that the post-truth age has altered the form of biographical theater on the Australian stage," as emotion now trumps fact in the theatrical authentication of "biographical truth." What has resulted is "a new kind of post-truth biographical Australian playwriting genre." Tina Satter's *Is This A Room*, which stages the transcription of the FBI's interrogation of Reality Winner, who leaked classified information, is the subject of Chapter 7. Helen Georgas takes "us on a post-truth exploration of r(R)eality," where she not only analyzes the "truth" of the onstage Reality but also the "truth" of the production through its use of music, costumes, set design, and other elements of mise-en-scène. Through close study of the performance she argues that the play "serves as both a troubling of reality and a word-for-word recreation of a troubled 'reality.'" In

Chapter 8, Susanne Thurow discusses Kip Williams's 2018 production of Bertolt Brecht's *The Resistible Rise of Arturo Ui*, which integrates a digital component that projects the live stage performance onto a screen behind the actors. In so doing, Williams forces the audience to decide which performance to watch, the live actor or the manipulated images on the screen. She argues that his production is a "sophisticated and timely example of artistically thinking through contemporary image making practices that site the classical text firmly within our age of post-truth and sensory voracity" and as a result it demonstrates how power and influence are consolidated through the manipulation of media. Chapter 9, the final chapter, details the accusations made by the documentary *Out of Shadows* that the performance artist Marina Abramović is part of a satanic group that eats and abuses children. Lewis Church ties the accusations to the rise of alt-right groups over the last two decades and compares the charges against Abramović to the attacks against performance artists in the late 1980s and early 1990s. His chapter documents the rise of post-truth cultural contexts, in which works like Abramović's can become ensnared, and finally argues that through "systematically debunking" such accusations and "by insisting on a recontextualization" they can be undone.

After viewing the Royal Court production of *Ten Billion*, Michael Billington surmised that theater "gains immeasurably from engaging with momentous political, social or scientific issues" (2012). The hope is that this volume will do precisely the same thing by documenting how the theater has taken up the challenges posed by our post-truth era and provided audience members with the opportunity to look anew at the rhetoric surrounding us. Finding a way to navigate through the misinformation, alternative facts, fake news, and other examples of counterknowledge is key to regaining the stability lost over the last five years. The chapters here provide examples of how playwrights, directors, and theater companies have joined the fray against forces that have attacked the position of experts and the solidity of facts. Time will only tell whether truth, fact, and expertise will eventually win in this new era we have entered.

Notes

1 Ironically, Donald J. Trump, who many see as the poster child for the post-truth era, would own the same hotel a few decades later.
2 The use of the term "post-truth" increased over 2000 percent from its 2015 use ("'Post-Truth' Declared" 2016).
3 A poll in June of 2021 found that 32 percent of Americans continued to believe that the election was stolen from Trump (Cillizza 2021).
4 While a majority of writers have drawn a connection between postmodernism and the rise of post-truth positions, not all critics are convinced. A. J. Perrin pushed back, arguing:

> Writers on the left and the right who blame postmodernism for the horrors of post-truth politics are effectively fleeing toward concreteness, pining for a space safe from power and contention. But such a base is a mirage ... Instead, we have to come to terms with the reality that radical complexity and ideological pluralism are at the core of contemporary life. Far from undermining democracy, postmodernist-influenced thought provides valuable resources for understanding and supporting democracy. Its insistence on interrogating the origins and implications of claims and ideas would be welcome additions to a flailing public sphere. (Perrin 2017)

5 The doubt about the science being done by the CRU was not limited to just the researchers on that project. Due to Climategate, the research by other East Anglia professors also became tainted. See Corbyn (2010).
6 Pollsters acknowledged other factors could have also contributed to the changing numbers, including the failure of the United Nations Climate Change Summit in Copenhagen in December 2009 as well as a colder winter than normal. Others, though, were more certain of the effect of Climategate on the polls. One study argued the scandal "deepened and perhaps solidified the observed declines in public beliefs that global warming is happening, human-caused, and of serious concern. It also helps to explain the erosion of public trust in scientists as sources of information on global warming" (Leiserowitz et al. 2012: 828).
7 Some surmised that the numbers were skewed too high since the persons polled were aged between sixteen and sixty-four years old and it was

believed that the older population would be more likely to be skeptical about climate change than a younger population.

8 While this may be the first book connecting theater and the post-truth era, I must note that in the summer of 2018 *Canadian Theatre Review*, edited by Barry Freeman and Matt Jones, published an issue that focused entirely on theater and post-truth.

References

Bailey, F. G. (1991), *The Prevalence of Deceit*, Ithaca, NY: Cornell University Press.

Ball, J. (2017), *Post-Truth: How Bullshit Conquered the World*, London: Biteback.

Begley, S. (2009), "The Truth about 'Climategate': Hacked E-Mails Have Compromised Scientists—but Not the Science Itself," *Newsweek*, 154 (24), December 14. *Proquest* (accessed July 12, 2021).

Billington, M. (2012), "*Ten Billion*—Review," *Guardian*, July 19. Available online: https://www.theguardian.com/stage/2012/jul/19/ten-billion-review-royal-court (accessed September 3, 2021).

Bois, Y. (2017), "Fake News and Alternative Facts: Three Antidotes from History," *October Magazine*, 160 (Spring): 127–30.

Bok, S. (1978), *Lying: Moral Choice in Public and Private Life*, New York: Pantheon Books.

Boles, W. C. (2017), "Inspiration from the 'Really Real': David Henry Hwang's *Yellow Face* and Documentary Theatre," *Comparative Drama*, 51 (2): 216–33.

Cannon, L. (1987), "Reagan Acknowledges Arm-for-Hostages Swap," *Washington Post*, March 5. Available online: https://www.washingtonpost.com/archive/politics/1987/03/05/reagan-acknowledges-arms-for-hostages-swap/7a5cd7cc-a112-4283-94bd-7f730ad81901/ (accessed July 25, 2021).

Cillizza, C. (2021), "1 in 3 Americans Believe the 'Big Lie,'" *CNN.com*, June 21. Available online: https://www.cnn.com/2021/06/21/politics/biden-voter-fraud-big-lie-monmouth-poll/index.html (accessed July 25, 2021).

Clark, T. (2009), "Three in Four UK Voters Believe Climate Change Is Important Problem," *Guardian*, December 15. Available online:

https://www.theguardian.com/environment/2009/dec/15/ guardian-icm-poll-climate-change-problem (accessed July 5, 2021).

Corbyn, Z. (2010), "Climategate: The Cold Comfort Is That It Is Now a Hot Topic," *Times Higher Education*, 8 (April): 10–11.

d'Ancona, M. (2017), *Post-Truth: The New War on Truth and How to Fight Back*, London: Ebury Press.

Darwall, R. (2013), *The Age of Global Warming: A History*, London: Quartet Books.

Delijani, C. F. (2021), "Introduction," in *DNA by Dennis Kelly*, 1–44, London: Methuen.

Dumouchel, P. (2010), "After-Truth," *Contagion: Journal of Violence, Mimesis, and Culture*, 27: 1–13.

Emmott, S. (2013), *Ten Billion*, New York: Vintage Books.

Fisher, A. S. (2020), *Performing the Testimonial: Rethinking Verbatim Dramaturgies*, Manchester: Manchester University Press.

Hilts, P. J. (1996), *Smoke Screen: The Truth behind the Tobacco Industry Cover-Up*, Reading, MA: Addison-Wesley.

Itkowitz, C. (2021), "'Normal Tourist Visit': Republicans Recast Deadly Jan. 6 Attack by Pro-Trump Mob," *Washington Post*, May 12. Available online: https://www.washingtonpost.com/politics/trump-riot-capitol-republicans/2021/05/12/dcc03342-b351-11eb-a980-a60af976ed44_story.html (accessed May 17, 2021).

Jowit, J. (2010), "Sharp Decline in Public's Belief in Climate Threat, British Poll Reveals," *Guardian*, February 23. Available online: https://www.theguardian.com/environment/2010/feb/23/british-public-belief-climate-poll (accessed July 5, 2021).

Kessler, G., S. Rizzo, and M. Kelly (2021), "Trump's False or Misleading Claims Total 30,573 over 4 Years," *Washington Post*, January 24. Available online: https://www.washingtonpost.com/politics/2021/01/24/trumps-false-or-misleading-claims-total-30573-over-four-years (accessed June 25, 2021).

Keyes, R. (2004), *The Post-Truth Era: Dishonesty and Deception in Contemporary Life*, New York: St. Martin's Press.

Lee, J. (2011), "Climategate: Anatomy of a Scandal," *Mother Jones*, 36 (May/June): 36. *Proquest* (accessed July 12, 2021).

Leiserowitz, A. A., E. W. Maibach, C. Roser-Renouf, N. Smith, and E. Dawson (2012), "Climategate, Public Opinion, and the Loss of Trust," *American Behavioral Scientist*, 57 (6): 818–37.

Machiavelli, N. ([1532] 1998), *The Prince*, trans. W. K. Marriott. Available online: https://www.gutenberg.org/files/1232/1232-h/1232-h.htm (accessed July 16, 2021).

Maher, A. (2013), "An Interview with David Henry Hwang," *London Magazine*, May 30. Available online: https://www.thelondonmagazine.org/an-interview-with-david-henry-hwang/ (accessed October 26, 2021).

Marshall, H., and A. Drieschova (2018), "Post-Truth Politics in the UK's Brexit Referendum," *New Perspectives: Interdisciplinary Journal of Central & East European Politics and International Relations*, 26 (3): 89–105.

McIntyre, L. (2018), *Post-Truth*, Cambridge, MA: MIT Press.

Myres, J. D. (2018), "Post-Truth as Symptom: The Emergence of a Masculine Hysteria," *Philosophy Rhetoric*, 51 (4): 392–415.

Norton-Taylor, R. (2008), "Richard Norton-Taylor," in Will Hammond and Dan Steward (eds.), *Verbatim, Verbatim: Contemporary Documentary Theatre*, 103–31, London: Oberon.

Oreskes, N., and E. M. Conway (2010), *Merchants of Doubt: How a Handful of Scientists Obscured the Truth on Issues from Tobacco Smoke to Global Warming*, New York: Bloomsbury.

Perrin, A. J. (2017), "Stop Blaming Postmodernism for Post-Truth Politics," *The Chronicle of Higher Education*, August 4. Available online: https://www.chronicle.com/article/stop-blaming-postmodernism-for-post-truth-politics (accessed August 19, 2021).

"'Post-Truth' Declared Word of the Year by Oxford Dictionaries" (2016), *BBC News*, November 16. Available online: https://www.bbc.com/news/uk-37995600 (accessed January 14, 2021).

Rabin-Havt, A., and Media Matters (2016), *Lies, Incorporated: The World of Post-Truth Politics*, New York: Anchor Books.

Rapley, C., and D. Macmillan (2015), *2071: The World We'll Leave Our Grandchildren*, London: John Murray.

"Remarks by President Trump on the Election" (2020), Trump White House Archives, November 5. Available online: https://trumpwhitehouse.archives.gov/briefings-statements/remarks-president-trump-election/ (accessed July 7, 2021).

Suiter, J. (2016), "Post-Truth Politics," *Political Insight*, December: 25–7.

Tesich, S. (1992), "A Government of Lies," *Nation*, January 6/13: 12–14. *Academic Search Ultimate* (accessed May 25, 2021).

Vanden Heuvel, K. (2013), "Jenny McCarthy's Vaccination Fear-Mongering and the Cult of False Equivalence," *Nation*, July 22.

Available online: https://www.thenation.com/article/archive/jenny-mccarthys-vaccination-fear-mongering-and-cult-false-equivalence/ (accessed August 19, 2021).

Wight, C. (2018), "Post-Truth, Postmodernism and Alternative Facts," *New Perspectives: Interdisciplinary Journal of Central and East European Politics and International Relations*, 26 (3): 17–29.

Wilbur, K. (2017), *Trump and a Post-Truth World*, Boulder, CO: Shambhala.

Part One

Text

1

Post-Truth but Not Post-Race: The Repeating Realities of Anna Deavere Smith's *Twilight: Los Angeles, 1992*

Heidi E. Bollinger

We live in an America that is post-truth but not post-race. This is strikingly clear in the conflicting interpretations of cellphone videos documenting the disfigurement and death of Black Americans at the hands of police. Viewers who do not want to believe that racism is still devastatingly alive search in the video footage for evidence of criminality, recalcitrance, and conspiracy to rationalize police violence perpetrated against unarmed Black citizens. The deeply divided public reaction to these brutal encounters reveals that Americans exist in starkly different racial realities without a shared language of facts or truth. In this post-truth but not post-race America, Anna Deavere Smith's work of documentary theater *Twilight: Los Angeles, 1992* (1994, 2003) remains hauntingly resonant and relevant.

Smith's play offers a medley of perspectives on the police beating of Rodney King in 1991, the legal trial of the officers in the white suburb of Simi Valley, and the violent uprising in South Central Los Angeles that followed their acquittal in April of 1992. These events remain eerily familiar today when protesters continue to chant "No Justice, No Peace!" following another incident in another American city while commenters on social media debate the simple premise that "Black Lives Matter." To compose *Twilight: Los Angeles, 1992*, Smith interviewed approximately two hundred witnesses from the Los Angeles community across dividing lines of race, ethnicity, class, gender, and geography (Smith 1994: xvii). From her collection of witness testimonies, Smith selected approximately twenty-five to perform as a series of loosely connected monologues in her one-woman show. As such, Smith's solo performance gives voice to a cacophonous collection of conflicting truths. *Twilight: Los Angeles, 1992* juxtaposes contradictory and often dubious perspectives without a definitive verification or refutation. The play anticipates the public's susceptibility to the rampant conspiracy theories and fake news of our post-truth era, and it debunks our nostalgia for an earlier time of unanimity. Smith's exploration, as an African American dramatist, of conflicting truths following the Rodney King incident reveals that Americans have never shared a common reality. At the same time, *Twilight: Los Angeles, 1992* reveals the impossibility of a post-race era by voicing past racial grievances that return and repeat without end. Ultimately, Smith's play does not offer a model for helping us to "all get along," in the words of Rodney King, but instead challenges viewers to confront the recurring consequences of living in utterly disparate racial realities.

Background Context

Twilight: Los Angeles, 1992 is part of Smith's ongoing series of performances, *On the Road: A Search for American Character*, which also includes *Fires in the Mirror* (1993), her examination of the 1991 riots in Crown Heights, Brooklyn. Ironically, the first performance of *Fires in the Mirror* was canceled because of "events in Los Angeles and concern that the unrest might spread to New York" in April 1992 (Wright 1992). Because of the acclaim that *Fires in the Mirror* garnered, Smith was commissioned by the Mark Taper Forum in Los Angeles to "create a one-woman performance piece about the civil disturbances in that city" (Smith 1994: xvii). As a discordant chorus of witnesses to the violence, the play resembles a trial in which many testimonies are heard, and no verdict is reached. As theater critic and playwright Damon Wright has observed, "that they [Smith's interviewees] might be in direct contradiction of one another does not mitigate their utter conviction that what they say is truth" (1992). Justice means something different to each witness whose testimony Smith voices, and the beating of Rodney King is only one of the injustices put on trial during the play. The complexity and scope of the injustices far outreach the ability of any legal trial or work of drama to achieve resolution, as witnesses connect the police brutality against Rodney King to a multitude of other race-based and class-based injustices. These other incidents include the 1991 killing of African American teenager Latasha Harlins by Korean American shop owner Soon Ja Du, and the beating of Caucasian truck driver Reginald Denny by African American protesters of the Simi Valley trial verdict, events that were both sensationalized by the news media and widely debated in the public sphere.

Documentary theater, the tradition with which Smith is often associated, blurs the boundary between fact and fiction. Sometimes called found theater, journalistic theater, or living history, documentary theater is composed from historical documents, including newspapers, diaries, interviews with witnesses, government records, and filmed events. In *Theatre of Real People*, Ulrike Garde and Meg Mumford describe what they call the "Authenticity-Effects" of incorporating verbatim interviews or nonprofessional performers into documentary theater. They argue that incorporating these elements creates the impression of "the sincere and genuine and therefore credible, in the sense of honest and free from pretense or counterfeit, or really originating from its reputed maker or source ... and that of unmediated and intimate contact with people who actually exist or have existed" (2016: 70). In this vein, Smith, who has described herself as a "repeater," claims to reproduce the exact words of each witness in her performances and, through her technique of repetition, to invoke the bodily persona of the witness through their characteristic gestures and mannerisms (Pellegrini 1997: 71). As an interviewer and performer, Smith is particularly interested in repetition: in the moments when her subjects repeat themselves and stammer over words as they struggle to articulate their sense of racial grievance. Smith attempts to inhabit her interview subjects through these vocal patterns: "Her interest lies not so much in what is said as how it comes out. She rehearses with earphones on and plays back unedited talk and speaks the words until images and gestures emerge from [speech] rhythms" (Connor 2001: 167). As such, Smith has been cited as the "seminal example" of verbatim theater (Parenteau 2017). As a dramatist, Smith presents herself as a transparent medium or instrument. In terms of authorship, she resembles a mixologist who samples audio tracks, or a sculptor who constructs assemblages from found objects.

The seemingly unedited, raw aesthetic of *Twilight: Los Angeles, 1992* is created in large part by comments that the speakers address to Smith, which continually remind us of the play's genesis from interviews. Television writer Joe Viola interrupts his account to give Smith advice about whom to interview: "This is the one you ought to track down!" (Smith 1994: 92). Real estate agent Elaine Young gives Smith explicit permission to impersonate her: "You can repeat whatever I say / I mean I will tell you *exactly*" (Smith 2003: 36; emphasis in the original). With these self-referential statements, Smith capitalizes on the truth-value associated with witness testimony, and the compelling yet misleading idea that testimony offers direct access to historical events. At the same time, these meta-remarks highlight Smith's role as a dramatic intermediary between the witnesses and her audience. The effect of hearing Smith repeat another person's words and imitate their affect has a kind of uncanny effect, of something being "off"—like watching a film where the audio is slightly out of sync, or the subtitles do not match the dialogue—that subtly undermines their claims. In *Insecurity: Perils and Products of Theatres of the Real*, Jenn Stephenson identifies this paradoxical blend of authenticity and artifice as a possible avenue for interrogating truth: "What theatres of the real are producing instead of reality is insecurity. It is through insecurity that we are impelled to move past simply noting the proliferation of free-floating realities and ask how realities are constructed" (2019: 233–4). Stephenson urges viewers to move beyond a sense of realities multiplying, exploding, and collapsing on the stage to question the genesis of what we think we know. When the matter in question is racial justice, the stakes for interrogating "how realities are constructed" are high. Rather than providing access to a stable and singular truth, documentary theater, like *Twilight: Los Angeles, 1992*, makes viewers conscious of the gestures that invoke our credulity or doubt, destabilizing our certainties.

Smith's work gains power from her claim to revoice verbatim witness testimony as she heard it; yet Smith has published multiple and conflicting versions of the play, further underscoring the elusiveness of a stable, shared reality. She adapted *Twilight: Los Angeles, 1992* each time she performed it live in Los Angeles and New York, published two very different print versions, and starred in a film adaptation that diverges yet again. In each iteration, Smith selected different characters to perform, altered the sequence of monologues to reshape the dramatic arc, and even edited the transcription of monologues to change the dramatic emphasis. From the over two hundred interviews Smith conducted, endless versions of the play could be constructed. Smith's repeated claim that the language of the play is verbatim draws attention away from her creative activity of shaping and arranging that material. Through her artful sequencing and juxtaposition of witness testimonies, Smith heightens the tensions between witness perspectives on racial violence and thus dramatizes the discord of the divided communities she has visited.

Post-Truth Polarization

Based on recent studies, the Pew Research Center has concluded that "Americans have rarely been as polarized as they are today" and that our political divisions on matters like racial justice and law enforcement are becoming "increasingly stark" (Dimock and Wike 2020). Their research demonstrates that Americans inhabit strikingly disparate realities in terms of their perceptions of race and justice. In *Post-Truth*, Lee McIntyre argues that people refuse to accept facts "when we are seeking to assert something that is more important to us than the truth itself"

(2018: 13). This is to say, when a strongly held feeling or belief does not mesh with verifiable evidence, it becomes necessary to discredit those facts to maintain one's ideological framework. Interestingly, this sort of confirmation bias, which McIntyre identifies as symptomatic of a post-truth culture, is often seen among "police detectives, who identify a suspect and then try to build a case around him, rather than search for reasons to rule him out" (2018: 45). Thus, questions of truth and facts are intimately bound up with questions of crime, justice, and racial bias. If, to take a trivial example, "sports fans from opposing teams can look at the same piece of videotape and see different things" (McIntyre 2018: 46), what can we expect when viewers encounter grainy footage of police subduing a suspect?

In her plays, Smith creates confrontations among witnesses living in disparate racial realities through her strategic sequencing of monologues. These witnesses may never have met in real life but because of Smith's canny sequencing of monologues, they seem to hear and respond to each other. As theater critic Vinson Cunningham has noted, "editing is key to Smith's art; she makes distant world views sometimes painfully proximate" (2020). Smith's sequencing of the monologues initially suggests connections among characters, but ultimately reinforces the individual speakers' commitments to their irreconcilable views. Smith's juxtaposition of their monologues creates a set of "competing and contradictory narratives that make it difficult for the audience to take sides or to form a united community sure of where justice lies" (Jay 2007: 120). Characters are so deeply entrenched in their own racial realities that when Smith juxtaposes their monologues to create dramatic exchanges, they speak at cross-purposes, undermining themselves and each other.

False equivocation is a dangerous fallacy of the post-truth era, and one might think that by juxtaposing divergent witness perspectives without comment Smith engages in false equivalence. As McIntyre documents in *Post-Truth*, the insidious ubiquity of false equivocation arose from corporate lobbyists for industries like tobacco and coal. They supplied their own "experts" to undermine critics and promote the false idea that we do not know for sure whether these industries are harmful to the public. When the news media presented these industry-funded experts on the same level as independent researchers, their false claims were given credence, leading to public misconceptions about what is known about the fault of those industries and the harm they cause. In presenting witnesses on this kind of level field of debate, Smith may be making a sly comment on the role of the news media in creating controversy and confusion rather than supplying truthful information. Indeed, she challenges the supposed objectivity of the news media through her monologue as reporter Judith Tur, who provides her helicopter film footage of the beating of white truck driver Reginald Denny. Tur admits that "each time I see this / I get angrier" and she refers to one of the rioters as an "animal" (Smith 2003: 85). As Tur walks Smith through the video footage, her objectivity burns away and her profound racial and class-based grievance as a white woman is laid bare.

At the same time, Smith's theater operates under a definition of truthfulness different from what the news media or legal sphere claims to uphold. She amplifies and perhaps even tacitly celebrates the unreliability and bias of her witnesses rather than smoothing it over. Smith is interested in the voices of witnesses who are openly partial, fallible, and emotional, insofar as they reveal perspectives not validated by the news media or in the legal sphere. One of her signature monologues portrays Josie Morales, a bystander who witnessed the Rodney King beating but who was not called to the stand during the Simi Valley trial. Morales vehemently declares that her testimony offers insights that the videotape taken of the incident cannot provide, and she is frustrated by being unheard. Smith errs on the side of voicing perspectives like that of Morales rather than adjudicating the credibility of witnesses, because, simply by juxtaposing marginalized voices with those of law enforcement authorities and political leaders, she is destabilizing the unearned credibility of those in power.

While Smith does not overtly endorse or refute any speaker's claims, she sets up stark contrasts between their realities, thus allowing them to cross-examine each other and to incriminate themselves. For instance, in the film adaptation, Smith intercuts the monologue of former LAPD chief Daryl Gates with that of former commissioner Stanley K. Sheinbaum and of June Park, whose husband was shot point-blank during the riots. Gates bloviates about why he attended a fundraiser rather than dealing with the civil unrest developing in the city after the Simi Valley verdict. He glibly claims that he did not even want to attend the event, but his supporters compelled him. Smith suddenly becomes June Park and exclaims: "Why!? Why he has to be shot?" (*Twilight: Los Angeles* 2000). Smith turns back into Gates and continues to ramble about his obligation to attend the event. Park breaks in again with her lament, demanding to know why her husband was killed. Finally, Sheinbaum interjects with mounting hysteria, screaming: "He's the *chief* and this thing / very well / may be falling apart!" (*Twilight: Los Angeles* 2000, emphasis mine). Smith undermines Gates's self-vindication with Park and Sheinbaum's grievances. If there is truth, Smith suggests, it is found in the friction between oppositional perspectives.

Likewise, in the case of witnesses Elaine Young and Keith Watson, in the act titled "Rocked," their opposing monologues are not merely juxtaposed, but violently fused together, as Smith transforms from Young into Watson. Smith could not have picked two witnesses whose perspectives differed more. While Elaine Young is a naive mouthpiece for white privilege and racist paranoia, Keith Watson gives vent to "black rage" (Smith 2003: 81). Through the merging of these antipodal characters, Smith brings together two familiar stereotypes: hysterical white lady and angry Black man. Watson is Young's worst nightmare and Young is what Watson despises. Smith yokes together their divergent racial realities in her single person and through the stark contrast of their perspectives, she embodies American disunity.

The stage directions describe Elaine Young as "a white woman who has had thirty-six plastic surgeries. Platinum blond hair. Jewelry. Flashy, expensive, designer glasses" (Smith 2003: 34). As Young, Smith's voice becomes nasal, childlike, and emphatic. Young earnestly describes herself as "such a victim!" because of her botched plastic surgeries

(Smith 2003: 37). She recounts how she went to the luxurious Beverly Hills Hotel for dinner during the riot. She recalls guilelessly that the hotel was "*mobbed*" by Hollywood businesspeople because "it was like a fortress!" (Smith 2003: 78–9; emphasis in the original). Young seems to see herself as someone hunkered down waiting out a war behind the castle walls and she evinces no awareness of her own privilege and complicity in the very Hollywood culture that Keith Watson wants to explode (Smith 2003: 66). At the conclusion of Young's monologue, the stage directions read: "If possible, the same actor playing Elaine Young should become Keith Watson and turn the desk over" (Smith 2003: 80). In the film adaptation, Smith concludes Young's speech, rips off her glasses and earrings, shoves a porkpie hat on her head, stares deadpan at the viewer, stands up, and flips Young's desk forward with a powerful shove. As Watson, she moves to another area of the stage jumbled with props and begins his monologue *in medias res*: "It was rage, black rage" (Smith 2003: 81). Her virtuoso expression of Watson's rage is riveting: "Yes! I was upset. / I was *highly* upset! / That could've been *me* out there getting my ass whooped! / And these four officers could a walked away for whoopin' my ass / like that? / *I'm-afraid-not*" (Smith 2003: 82; emphasis in the original). Smith repeatedly screams "*I'm-afraid-not*" and lunges about the stage, picking up objects and throwing them to the ground. She rips open a bag of packing peanuts and scatters them through the air, laughing gleefully.

Of course, viewers familiar with Smith's interview method will realize that it is very unlikely that Keith Watson behaved this way during his conversation with Smith. In her performance, Smith dramatizes and heightens his rage using the props and gestures of the theater, but this undermines her claim to replicate witness testimony exactly as she heard it. In pushing her portrayals of Young and Watson into the realm of caricature, Smith risks playing into and confirming racial stereotypes her readers may bring to their viewing. Although her stage directions urge actors to avoid parodying witnesses (Smith 2003: 7), her deliberate juxtaposition of hysterical white privilege and uncontrolled Black rage do make a mockery of them—but more so, of her captivated audience.

Smith strains credulity perhaps to see how far we will stay with her and take her portrayals at face value as credible. In doing so, she risks having the joke rebound painfully, if audiences accept absurd stereotype as reasonable truth. Smith takes this risk in her hyperbolic performance conjoining Elaine Young and Keith Watson to dramatize the vast gulf of understanding between their worlds, and to demonstrate the obstacles to achieving any meaningful reconciliation, let alone a shared reality.

Documentary footage from the film further underscores the unbridgeable gap between realities, as Smith gathered some of the witnesses together for a real-life reunion dinner. Right away, it becomes clear that they cannot even agree on a shared vocabulary to discuss what happened. The conversation breaks down very quickly because basic questions of language are so fraught. Activist Paul Parker begins by saying, "Let me make something perfectly clear. It's not a riot, it's more, it's a civil unrest. Or, as a lot of us call it, a revolution" (*Twilight: Los Angeles* 2000). Former LAPD chief Daryl Gates, who is sitting across the table, chooses not to acknowledge Parker's distinction between riot, civil unrest, and revolution. He immediately demands to know whether Parker was involved. Parker refuses to accept the premise of the question and responds defensively, "Well, first of all, like I say, I don't consider it no riot" (*Twilight: Los Angeles* 2000). As Gates continues to press his point, Parker stammers in frustration, trying to make his voice heard. Gates asks more pointedly: "Do you steal in a revolution?" (*Twilight: Los Angeles* 2000). They begin to talk over each other, and their heated words become indecipherable. Gates and Parker appear to be speaking two different languages, because they cannot agree on what to call the events of 1992 let alone parse what those events signified. Both resort to generalizations and accusations, perhaps to avoid acknowledging their own culpability in the violence. Other guests at the table chime in, and the din grows louder, until Smith interjects reproachfully, "Let me suggest one possibility here. As much as we all are gonna talk, is just to make sure that we're listening [sic]" (*Twilight: Los Angeles* 2000). The footage ends abruptly after her attempts to mediate their agitated exchange, suggesting that her call for more thoughtful listening failed. *Twilight: Los Angeles, 1992* challenges the viewing audience to be receptive to contradictory views that the playwright voices and embodies. Nevertheless, her own failed attempt to model dialogue around the reunion table demonstrates the near impossibility of achieving consensus about what is factual truth when the language we have for race and justice is so emotionally charged. This discord may be very familiar from the vantage point of a post-truth America, but it gives the lie to any nostalgia we may feel for an earlier time of shared reality.

Repetition and the Fallacy of a Post-Race Era

Following the election of President Barack Obama in 2008, some commentators proposed that we had entered a new post-racial era. They suggested that the election of the first African American president signified that a majority of Americans were able to overcome racial bias in the sense of looking beyond race in the voting booth. In this spirit, television commentator Chris Matthews remarked after President Obama's 2010 State of the Union address: "It's interesting, he is post-racial by all appearances. You know, I forgot he was black tonight for an hour" (Phillips 2010). His peculiar formulation suggests that racial progress is simply a liberating form of amnesia or colorblindness, and, indeed, the phrase "I don't see color!" has become an emblematic obfuscation of the so-called post-racial era. While the inauguration of President Obama was a remarkable watershed moment, it was not a remedy for entrenched racism in all its subtle and myriad forms. In his piece "There Is No Post-Racial America" Ta-nehisi Coates argues that as long as Americans view Blackness through the lens of criminality, it will take much more than the election of the first Black president to usher in a post-racial era (2015). In her Introduction to the 1994 edition, Smith recounts the series of events in the Rodney King incident, which have become almost a blueprint or plot archetype: an incident of police brutality takes place and is videotaped by onlookers, there is "an immediate outcry from the community," the officers are tried and found not guilty, "and the city explode[s]" (xvii). A period of reckoning and recrimination follows, incremental changes are made, and business as usual resumes until the next incident. After the dawn of the post-racial era was declared, this cycle repeated again and again, making matters of race, policing, and justice in America profoundly unresolved. The past is not past when the same pattern continues repeating. As Brian Norman observes in *Neo-Segregation Narratives*, "the nation continues to be haunted by a racial past" (Norman 2010: 169). Moreover, as cultural commentator Touré emphasizes in his piece "No Such Place as 'Post-Racial' America," the delusion that we have entered a post-racial era "feeds the notion that it's O.K. to be somnambulant about race or even aggressively dismissive of it" (2011). To believe that racism is "over" enables complacency, disinterest, and even a sense of injury among whites who feel attacked when systemic racism is criticized. This is all to ask, who gets to determine when something is "post-" in the sense of being in the afterward of what is over, completed, and resolved?

Smith's play is full of characters who are haunted by incidents of police brutality and racial injustice that occurred years, decades, and even centuries before. Her play is a snapshot of a particular time and place (as indicated by its title), but characters voice injustices from long ago with a raw and stinging immediacy as if they just happened. The play reveals how people view racially charged incidents through the lens of their prior experiences, creating narratives of cyclical repetition. Character Katie Miller, bookkeeper and accountant, asserts: "And it was the same thing with the sixty-five riots / same thing!" (Smith 2003: 68). Korean American store owner Jay Woong Yahng sees the killing of teenager Latasha Harlins through the lens of his own experiences with African American shoplifters: "You don't understand that situation! / Maybe I understand / because I have a similar situation in my store" (Smith 2003: 47). Activist Paul Parker sees the uprising in Los Angeles through the lens of American slavery, seeing the destruction wrought by the insurrectionists as a tribute to the characters in Alex Haley's *Roots*: "This is for Kunta! / This is for Kizzy!" (Smith 2003: 140). Beliefs about race relations deepen with each repetition, becoming calcified and habitual. Smith's dramatic technique of repeating her interview subjects' fumbling, often repetitive words enacts stylistically the play's theme of racial grievance as a harm that reverberates through time.

The opening monologue of the 1994 edition, titled "My Enemy," does not even mention Rodney King but rather focuses on police brutality in Los Angeles decades prior. The speaker, Rudy Salas, a Mexican American artist, begins by recalling how his grandfather hated "gringos" (Smith 1994: 1). In her performance as Salas, Smith begins the play at a fever pitch, not only tired and cynical and furious about a nation of "enemies" but also frightened by the historical déjà vu of intergenerational encounters with white supremacism. His "insane hatred / for white policeman" took hold in 1942 when he was a teenage zoot suiter. He recounts how the police arrested him and four officers kicked him repeatedly in the head until "they fractured my / eardrum" (Smith 1994: 3). Salas's hearing is permanently damaged from his encounter with the police, and his perception of white law enforcement is likewise irreparably harmed. Salas's monologue establishes a pattern of intergenerational racial grievance, as he begins his story with his grandfather, then speaks of his own initiation in racial violence, and then talks about how the police threaten his sons: "One night / cop pulled a gun at his head. / It drove me crazy— / it's still going on, / it's still going on. How you think / a / father feels, / stuff that happened to me / fifty years / ago / happened to my son?" (Smith 1994: 6). He describes with helpless fury watching as his sons grow up navigating the same treacherous territory as him. His opening monologue establishes a pattern of violent encounters with the police that repeats across generations within families, and his aggrieved recollections give the lie to the promise of a fresh new post-racial era.

The testimony of Rodney King is conspicuously absent from the play. King's story is told indirectly by his aunt, Angela King, and by other witnesses like Salas who recount their own experiences with police brutality. Angela King begins by remembering her parents' courtship and the generations in her family that led to her nephew, establishing her relationship with him. Smith could have eliminated this genealogical preamble, but it reminds us that their lives are more than that singular, brutal incident. When Angela King begins to talk about Rodney, she recalls a time that they went fishing together and he caught a fish in his hands when he was sixteen, an intimate detail that reminds us that he was once a beloved boy. She then abruptly changes course, as if her family memories were interrupted or punctured: "Um, um, um … /He—Glen, / Rodney— / went through three plastic surgeons / just to look like Rodney again" (Smith 1994: 54). She reflects that when she saw Rodney on the television news, "he looked just like his father" (Smith 1994: 54). Like Rudy Salas, she evinces a fundamental sense of intergenerational interchangeability and identification. The harm done to Rodney is harm done to his father is harm done to her.

President Obama's public remarks following George Zimmerman's killing of African American teenager Trayvon Martin in 2013 speak to the intergenerational trauma of racism and the impossibility of healing from wounds that are reopened anew. In strikingly personal terms, Obama expresses his recognition and identification with Trayvon Martin:

> You know, when Trayvon Martin was first shot I said that this could have been my son. Another way of saying that is Trayvon Martin could have been me thirty-five years ago. And when you think about why, in the African American community at least, there's a lot of pain around what happened here, I think it's important to recognize that the African American community is looking at this issue through a set of experiences and a history that doesn't go away. (Obama 2013)

The kinship and the loss that Obama articulates here transcend time. As a lesson in empathy, Obama's remarks serve to educate Americans who may struggle to appreciate the grief and anger of African Americans, as well as to convey that he understands the deeply felt hurt of "a history that doesn't go away."

Smith's play is full of Cassandras who warn that violence will flare up once again unless radical changes are undertaken. Congresswoman

Maxine Waters declares: "Today, as we stand here in 1992, / if you go back and read the [Kerner Commission] report / it seems as though we are talking about what that report / cited / some twenty years ago still exists today" (Smith 1994: 160). Otis Chandler, former editor of the Los Angeles Times notes: "this whole thing cannot be allowed to lapse / back into business as usual" (Smith 1994: 220). He admits that such vows have been made before. For viewers who encounter Smith's play almost thirty years later, when the same conversations continue to be rehashed, these clichéd declarations take on another layer of tragic irony.

Conclusion

In his farewell speech, President Obama connected the fallacy of the post-racial to the insularity of post-truth culture, noting: "For too many of us, it's become safer to retreat into our own bubbles … surrounded by people who look like us and share the same political outlook and never challenge our assumptions" (Obama 2017). At this point, when friends and relatives are "unfriending" each other right and left on Facebook because they cannot stand each other's political beliefs and do not share a basic factual vocabulary to discuss the news of the day, it is hard to imagine how we are to rekindle civility, let alone empathy. In 2019, political scientists James Fishkin and Larry Diamond of Stanford University organized a weekend conference for a diverse group of 526 Americans from across the political spectrum (Badger and Quealy 2019). At the event, titled "America in One Room," they gathered for small group conversations about controversial political issues central to the 2020 presidential election. Meeting in person and listening to other people sharing personal stories helped participants to gain a more nuanced appreciation of opposing views. While the weekend did not change the political position of many participants, a larger number did come away feeling more understanding and civil toward differing views. This experiment in civic engagement suggests a possible way forward in our deeply polarized post-truth era, and one that could be taken up in the realms of theater and the arts. *Twilight: Los Angeles, 1992* anticipates the partisan polarization of our post-truth era, and it gives the lie to any nostalgic fantasy we might entertain about an earlier time of shared consensus. And yet, the encounters with diverse and discordant voices of witness that Smith stages have the potential to unsettle viewers' fossilized beliefs. Smith's performance challenges viewers' assumptions by confronting us with voices and perspectives that may be unfamiliar, uncomfortable, and irreconcilable with the view from inside our own bubbles.

Smith has continued to create new works of verbatim theater that interrogate matters of truth, race, and justice, and in 2016 she performed her latest work, *Notes from the Field*, at the Second Stage Theater in New York. The play has since been adapted as a film that is available on HBO, but unfortunately this means that it is not widely accessible especially to low-income viewers. Critic Vinson Cunningham rightly observes that our nation needs "hundreds of Smith-style projects, inviting communities around the country into a more complete understanding of themselves" (2020). In 2020, in the face of continuing police brutality as well as the degradation and distortion of facts by the White House, *Twilight: Los Angeles, 1992* received renewed attention. In June, PBS made the film adaptation available for free streaming online, citing "the national crisis in the aftermath of the murders of Ahmaud Arbery (Brunswick, GA), Breonna Taylor (Louisville, KY), and most recently George Floyd (Minneapolis, MN)" ("Great Performances" 2020). The play was scheduled to be staged with new actors at the Signature Theatre in New York with Smith as playwright-in-residence, but production has been delayed by the Covid-19 pandemic until the 2021–2 theater season (Cunningham 2020).

In the spirit of theater as community-engagement, the encore presentation of *Twilight: Los Angeles* available on the PBS Great Performances website begins with a message from Smith that she recorded after the death of Freddie Gray in a police transport van in 2015: "As I read the headlines of 2015 from my hometown of Baltimore and around the country, my mind went back to the year that I spent in Los Angeles after the 1992 riots … In light of the challenges facing our country right now, I hope that this encore presentation of *Twilight* offers some lessons learned in Los Angeles." For millennial viewers who have witnessed the grainy footage of the killings of Eric Garner, Alton Sterling, Philando Castille, Ahmaud Arbery, Breonna Taylor, and George Floyd, the incidents surrounding the police beating of Rodney King will look sickeningly familiar, suggesting our repeated failures to learn lessons from the past. If Rodney King's famous question—often phrased as the beseeching "Can't we all just get along?"—is the unsaid subtext of *Twilight: Los Angeles, 1992*, Smith's performance of oppositional witness testimonies offers a negative answer: "No, we can't."

References

Badger, E., and K. Quealy (2019), "These 526 Voters Represent All of America: And They Spent a Weekend Together," *New York Times*, October 2. Available online: https://www.nytimes.com/interactive/2019/10/02/upshot/these-526-voters-represent-america.html (accessed January 13, 2021).

Coates, T. (2015), "There Is No Post-Racial America," *The Atlantic*, July/August. Available online: https://www.theatlantic.com/magazine/archive/2015/07/post-racial-society-distant-dream/395255/ (accessed April 10, 2021).

Connor, K. (2001), "Negotiating the Differences: Anna Deavere Smith and Liberation Theater," in E. Goldener and S. Henderson-Holmes (eds.), *Racing and (E)Racing Language: Living with the Color of Our Words*, 158–82, Syracuse: Syracuse University Press.

Cunningham, V. (2020), "The Urgency of Anna Deavere Smith's 'Twilight: Los Angeles,'" *New Yorker*, August 24. Available online: https://www.newyorker.com/magazine/2020/08/24/-the-urgency-of-anna-deavere-smiths-twilight-los-angeles (accessed January 13, 2021).

Dimock, M., and R. Wike (2020), "America Is Exceptional in the Nature of Its Political Divide," *Pew Research Center*, November 13. Available online: https://www.pewresearch.org/fact-tank/2020/11/13/america-is-exceptional-in-the-nature-of-its-political-divide/ (accessed January 12, 2021).

Garde, U., and M. Mumford (2016), *Theater of Real People: Diverse Encounters at Berlin's Hebbel am Ufer and Beyond*, London: Bloomsbury.

"Great Performances: About the Production" (2020), *PBS WNET Thirteen*, June 8. Available online: https://www.pbs.org/wnet/gperf/twilight-los-angeles-about-the-production/1329/ (accessed January 21, 2021).

Jay, G. (2007), "Other People's Holocausts: Trauma, Empathy, and Justice in Anna Deavere Smith's *Fires in the Mirror*," *Contemporary Literature*, 48 (1): 119–49.

McIntyre, L. (2018), *Post Truth*, Cambridge, MA: MIT Press.

Norman, B. (2010), *Neo-Segregation Narratives: Jim Crow in Post-Civil Rights American Literature*, Athens: University of Georgia Press.

Obama, B. (2013), "President Obama Speaks on Trayvon Martin" [Video], *The Obama White House*, July 19. Available online: https://youtu.be/MHBdZWbncXI (accessed January 13, 2021).

Obama, B. (2017), "Farewell Address to the American People" [Video], *The Obama White House*, January 10. Available online: https://youtu.be/QDyjUIsD-wQ (accessed January 12, 2021).

Parenteau, A. (2017), "How Do You Solve a Problem Like Documentary Theatre?," *American Theatre*, August 22. Available online: https://www.americantheatre.org/2017/08/22/how-do-you-solve-a-problem-like-documentary-theatre/ (accessed April 10, 2021).

Pellegrini, A. (1997), *Performance Anxieties: Staging Pyschoanalysis, Staging Race*, New York: Routledge.

Phillips, K. (2010), "MSNBC's Matthews: 'I Forgot He Was Black,'" *New York Times*, January 28. Available online: https://thecaucus.blogs.nytimes.com/2010/01/28/msnbcs-matthews-i-forgot-he-was-black/ (accessed April 10, 2021).

Smith, A. D. (1994), *Twilight: Los Angeles, 1992*, New York: Anchor Books.

Smith, A. D. (2003), *Twilight: Los Angeles, 1992*, New York: Dramatist's Play Service.

Stephenson, J. (2019), *Insecurity: Perils and Products of Theatres of the Real*, Toronto: University of Toronto Press.

Touré (2011), "No Such Place as 'Post-Racial' America," *New York Times*, November 8. Available online: https://campaignstops.blogs.nytimes.com/2011/11/08/no-such-place-as-post-racial-america/ (accessed April 10, 2021).

Twilight: Los Angeles (2000) [Film], Dir. M. Levin, USA: Corporation for Public Broadcasting.

Wright, D. (1992), "Theater; A Séance with History," *New York Times*, May 10. Available online: https://www.nytimes.com/1992/05/10/theater/theater-a-seance-with-history.html (accessed January 13, 2021).

2

Knowing Not What It "Seems": Re-Viewing Caryl Churchill's Post-Truth World in *Glass*, *Kill*, *Bluebeard's Friends*, and *Imp*

Mamata Sengupta

Theoretically for us, "knowledge" and the "world" seem to exist in a harmonious relationship where the former supplies explanations for and information on how the latter operates while the latter chiefly plays upon the chain of causality provided by the former. Practically, however, there is often an enormous gap between the truth that constitutes the human world and the information that constitutes the knowledge of it. Knowledge, which is presumed to be unbiased, verifiable, and true, often gets mediated through the human wish to control and represent the realities that might seem alarming, disturbing, or simply unpalatable. While misappropriated knowledge has a long and varied cultural/philosophical history, the 2016 US presidential election has rekindled worldwide critical interest in the "truthiness" of truths that constitute the human knowledge of the world. This chapter rereads four short plays (viz. *Glass*, *Kill*, *Bluebeard's Friends*, and *Imp*) by the British playwright Caryl Churchill to demonstrate how the playwright grapples with the divergent pulls of a world where misrepresented realities, politicized data, and misappropriated reportage loom large. Efforts will also be made to understand how this post-truth world reproduces its own culture of "counterknowledge," not merely to infiltrate our day-to-day existence but actually to supplant the very basis of that existence—the knowledge that constitutes our world, both theoretically as well as practically.

In 2008, the British journalist Damian Thompson defined "counterknowledge" as "misinformation packaged to look like fact—packaged so effectively, indeed, that the twenty-first century is facing a pandemic of credulous thinking" (Thompson 2008: 1). In the years that followed, the word "counterknowledge" has only become increasingly relevant. In 2016, the *Oxford English Dictionary* (*OED*) declared "post-truth" to be the word of the year, which it defined as an adjective "relating to or denoting circumstances in which objective facts are less influential in shaping public opinion than appeals to emotion and personal belief" (*OED* 2016: n.p.). Definitely, "appeals to emotion" and "personal beliefs" that might or might not have some objective facts and verifiable data to their support only justify Thompson's suspicions regarding the twenty-first-century "pandemic of credulous thinking" (Thompson 2008:1). As the world witnessed the flood of manufactured data, misleading claims, and fictitious realities that led to the election of Donald Trump as the forty-fifth US president, post-truth officially became a politico-philosophical reality. Apparently, post-truth has almost all the properties of "truthiness" such as logicality, veracity, and justifiability. Post-truth, however, differs from Truth only on one ground; that is, whereas the basis of Truth's "truthiness" is natural and obvious, post-truth needs to create false and, therefore, unstable fields of reference in order to anchor itself and justify what it claims. These "false fields of reference" enter the world of reality as truths and thereby supplant what we construe and count as knowledge. What we encounter in these short plays of Churchill is such a world of false realities.

The four short plays, *Glass*, *Kill*, *Bluebeard's Friends*, and *Imp*, were first performed in London at the Royal Court Theatre Downstairs, on September 18, 2019, under the direction of one of Churchill's longtime collaborators, James Macdonald. The first piece of the series, *Glass* is about an anonymous, see-through, fragile young girl who, in spite of being very much human, has a body of glass. While this glass body itself is problematic enough for the girl to cope with, the precariousness of her existence is further heightened by Churchill's strategic placement of the girl on the mantelpiece of the house, a place that she shares with a talking clock, an empty, old vase, and a red, plastic dog. In the world of the play, therefore, the glass girl finds herself suspended somewhere eternally between the throbbing human world of flesh and blood and the cold, static world of puppets and showpieces. She can neither participate fully in the human family that she originally belongs to and wants to be with nor can communicate meaningfully with the showpiece world of the mantelpiece that she has been forced to inhabit. The girl's crisis is further aggravated by Churchill's stage direction that "there should be no attempt to make the glass girl look as if she is made of glass. No effects making her seem invisible, etc. She looks like people look" (2019a: 4). Undoubtedly, this "humanness" of the glass girl alienates her further from both her human and nonhuman surroundings. If, on the one hand, her practical human body sets her apart from the inanimate world of the mantelpiece, then, on the other hand, the theoretical "see-through"-ness with which Churchill has constructed her denies her successful socio-familial acceptance and/or accommodation.

Complete in seven short scenes, *Glass* opens with a rhetorical question regarding the nature and form of a particular visual object that ultimately turns out to be the glass girl. The brother of the girl asks one of his friends whether he can "see" his sister by the window. The friend, however, is unable to see her and, therefore, responds negatively to the query. But the list that he provides of things that he can "see" underlines the haunting existential crisis that plagues our post-truth existence. The fact that the friend of the brother is able to see the window, the window panes, the film of dirt and grime on them, and even the shiny, spontaneous world that lies outside the window but not the glass girl highlights how realities are increasingly becoming invisible to modern human eyes, which have grown more accustomed to see and seek fabricated stories and false edifices. It is only after a clear instruction from the brother that the friend is finally able to identify "a thickness" by the window that he takes as the girl (2019a: 5). That in a post-truth world, realities have been reduced to mere formless, invisible "thickness" and, even after discovering them, it is hard to find them convincing, points up an alarming tendency of the twenty-first century that Thompson had identified years ago as the "pandemic of credulous thinking" (Thompson 2008: 1). In fact, in many ways, the glass girl is Churchill's symbol for Truth in a post-truth world. The girl's proneness to accidents, her dependence on bubble wraps, and the number of dents and cracks that she has developed on her glass frame signify the fragility that Truth has to suffer in a culture of counterknowledge. The near-transparent existence that the glass girl showcases sharply contrasts with the opaque and oblique ways in which the post-truth world operates.

While reviewing the play, Paul T. Davis calls attention to the latent gender politics of *Glass*. According to Davis, "The notion of a girl made of glass allows us to question female image and the gaze, and the invisible woman" (Davis 2019: n.p.). In fact, the glass girl is marginalized in, what we may call, a post-truth world on more than one score. On the surface level, it is her fragile, "glass"-like existence that physically alienates her from the sturdy, opaque, and therefore "normal" world (both animate and inanimate) that surrounds her. This fragility is a product of both her age and gender. Therefore, the glass girl is further marginalized as a *child*, on the one hand, and as a *female* child, on the other. Churchill hints at the glass girl's strained existence in school in scenes four and five wherein she is first bullied by a gang of her schoolmates and then is seen to warn one of her friends about something really horrific. The glass girl, however, is not the only one in the play to suffer abuse and bullying as a child. As she falls in love with her brother's friend who was initially unable to see her, she comes to know some dark truths about the boy's past. Though Churchill does not allow her audience to know exactly what the boy whispers into the ear of the glass girl, yet the horror with which she responds to his confessions clarifies that what his father did to him was neither pleasant nor parental, "Seven? From when you were seven?" (2019a: 10). The boy's next words that he does not want to report the incident to the police at once signals a compulsive silence that society has programmed him with and highlights his need to escape realities that he can neither forget nor forgive. His ardent wish to leave his parental house reiterates the same wish. The glass girl senses a similar kind of repression in one of her anonymous school friends who desperately wants to change her life even at the cost of pain and suffering. Though the play does not spell out the exact nature of the act through which the girl is about to bring this "change," the repeated warnings of the glass girl about the "pain" and "soreness" highlight a self-harming tendency on the part of the friend:

> GIRL: Why do you want to? It won't fix anything.
> G FRIEND: No, but it'll be different.
> GIRL: It'll be more pain.
> G FRIEND: It'll be different pain. (2019a: 9)

In *Glass*, Churchill presents her audience with a world where expectations collide with reality, where reality crashes on representation, representations refract, and it is this refracted representation or simply misrepresentation that constitutes the knowledge of the world for those who inhabit it. In the play, sociocultural institutions exist but not to accommodate or protect the individuals but to assert and exercise their own power and control over their members. The glass girl, her morbid school friend, and her abused boyfriend, therefore, all are bullied by their own families and societies that were meant to protect them. Unfortunately, however, the realities of these protector-turned-abuser families/societies do not get recorded, and instead a fictitious history of socio-familial bonding supplants the reality. In that supplanted reality, the glass girl continues to feature as a dear member of the family in which she is but an alienated presence. No matter how much concern the glass girl's family shows for her, she is barred from the core familial space, forever stationed on the dirty mantelpiece and fated to be erased from everyday memory just like the clock that has lost its relevance since "Time's on the phones" or the plastic dog that has not been touched in "three years" (2019a: 7). Similarly, the other schoolgirl and the abused boy too are virtual outsiders in their respective social surroundings. If the schoolgirl's dissatisfaction with her life combined with her urge to feel "different" gets drowned in the peer pressure to perform normalcy, then the boy's experience of parental abuse gets overwritten by his compulsion to "be" and "remain" obedient to the paterfamilias. Though these three young adults try their best to accept the constructed reality with which they have been forced to cope, Churchill makes her audience increasingly aware of the dangers of such a normative acceptance. At the final scene of the play, the abused boy commits suicide by jumping under a train and the glass girl throws herself from her window and thereby gets shattered into myriad fragments. The Truth that the glass girl and her boyfriend come to experience through living their respective lives stands in sharp contrast to the official truth of the world, which attempts to misappropriate their own tales. Their age, gender, and uncorrupted nature—all become their vulnerabilities in the post-truth world that operates on refraction instead of reflection. However, it is at the end of the play that the glass girl learns to turn her prime vulnerability into her agency to assert herself and her worth. As she smashes herself on the open street, the glass girl physically deconstructs herself into splinters to finally recover her once-erased ability to register her presence and power. The closing assertion of the play, "And they need to sweep the street well," records the girl's answer to the opening question of *Glass* regarding her visibility: "Look at the window, what do you see?" (2019a: 12, 5). Undoubtedly, the glass girl now is very much visible, and people who had not noticed her ever would now definitely take care to "see" her and stay away from her.

The second play in this collection, *Kill*, presents the audience with the narrative of a "plural" god whose experience and knowledge of life has only made him increasingly suspicious of his own existence and validity in a world order that harbors little or no godly values.[1] Churchill's god is also doubtful of the authority and the power that he, theoretically, has on his "inferior" human "subjects." The playwright clarifies in her stage directions that though *Kill* has two different groups of characters, the "gods" and the "people," the performance of the play should have only one actor for each of the categories performing as singular identities "as if (they are) just one person, i.e. don't assume different voices and characters" (2019b: 14). In fact, on the stage of *Kill*, the singular god and the solitary human being function in two different ways. First, they operate as representative members of their respective communities, voicing forth their collective uneasiness in a violent and dark world. On another plane, however, they function as multiple personalities having to coexist in one single frame, each fighting and clamoring for their own voice, yet none is able to extract him/herself from a compulsive collectedness or to exist peacefully with others. If the incoherent muttering of the person and his/her confused scribbling are visible signs of this existential crisis, then the studied logic of the god and the composure of his voice document a similar tension.

This authorial stress on the need to maintain a singular and indivisible presence of the human and the divine order, however, serves another important purpose. It is, in fact, Churchill's way of drawing attention to the alienated existence and utter helplessness of both the "gods" and the "people" in a post-truth world. What sets off the plot of *Kill* is the eternal problem regarding the role of fate in human life. The answer to this elemental query and the explanations that such answers entail, however, are neither simple nor brief. They need to encompass the entire human history, both mythical and historical. The singular "gods" who is entrusted with such an enormous duty appears to be too insignificant to carry out the task. However, it is this very "insignificance" of the "gods" that highlights how in a post-truth world fiction and fabrication usurp the rightful place of facts and realities. As the lonely god of Churchill's play desperately attempts to disclaim responsibilities for a series of human crimes and brutalities committed putatively under divine instructions, a hapless human being is seen sitting on the floor, scribbling on a piece of paper, and listening to the "gods" half-heartedly, with a half-uttered murmur. The crisis of the situation is further heightened in three different ways. First, the god of the play is made to occupy a position not on the stage proper but on a highly perched "cloud" that symbolizes both his superiority to and distance from the human world. The human being of *Kill*, then, is positioned on the floor of the stage to signify the inferiority and insignificance of the human beings as compared to the divine order. Finally, the authorial instruction that a child should perform the role of the "people" makes the divide between the divine and the human all the more prominent.

According to Michael Billington, the play *Kill* gives the audience "a potted version of the Greek myths reminding us that western civilisation is founded on horrific stories of homicide, incest, cannibalism and cyclical revenge" (Billington 2019). *Kill* opens with a reference to the crimes of Orestes who killed his mother Clytemnestra in order to avenge the murder of his father Agamemnon, whose killing was actually a revenge for the murder-sacrifice of his own daughter Iphigenia. While narrating this story, the god rejects the idea that Iphigenia's sacrifice was demanded by the gods and that in murdering Clytemnestra what Orestes did was to set the pattern right, "They sacrifice their children quite easily when there's a war to be won" (2019b: 16). The god then shifts his attention to other such violent episodes of heinous crimes wherein human decisions were justified as divine injunctions. Among the other disparate narratives of violence that the play records are the stories of Tantalous, the son of Zeus, who killed and served his own son Pelops to the gods as food and of the sorceress-princess Medea who first killed her brother to get the golden fleece for her lover Jason, and then murdered her own children to avenge herself on Jason when he betrayed her in love. It is at this precise point of, what we may call, his "confession" that the god breaks down into desperation. As Hannah Greenstreet observes, "The god grows desperate, imploring in a rush, 'and we say no don't do that it's enough we don't like it now don't do it we say stop please stop'. How do we make it stop?" (Greenstreet 2019). This is indeed a dark world order where the omnipotent self, that is, the god, has no power over what is being communicated to the person he theoretically controls, while that very person continues to operate on what he/she assumes to be the messages of the gods, without trying to verify the real origin of those messages. Churchill gives a last try at making her audience aware of the false claims of this world through the final cry of the god, "We say stop please stop" (2019b: 18).

The third short play in this collection, *Bluebeard's Friends*, attempts to retell a modernized version of a folk narrative regarding a psychopath wife-murderer. An early version of the tale can be found in Charles Perrault's *Histoiresou contes du temps passé* (1697), while the twentieth-century British writer Angela Carter offered a modern rendering of the Bluebeard story in her collection, *The Bloody Chamber and Other Stories* (1979). In the past narratives, Bluebeard appears as a wealthy, powerful, and handsome widower who marries one of the daughters of his neighbor. After the marriage, Bluebeard leaves for his castle outside the town with his young wife. Once in the castle, he warns her not to open a particular underground chamber which she, later on, finds to be a bloody room where the mutilated corpses of his murdered wives are kept. Bluebeard is finally killed by the brothers of the young wife. Churchill's play opens at the particular point when Bluebeard has been severely wounded by his brothers-in-law. The audience is presented with a number of anonymous voices belonging to Bluebeard's friends gossiping about his wives and his murderous instinct. While most of these friends are horrified to find Bluebeard as a serial killer, others are surprised at their own inability to see through his gentlemanly exterior. As the time passes, their discussion shifts from expressions of utter shock—"What did you say?" (2019c:23)—to performative condemnation—"Horrified to learn that my friend Bluebeard is a serial killer" (2019c: 23)—and finally, to shrewd assessments regarding the probability of monetizing this rare occurrence—"I got the dresses" (2019c: 24).

According to Paul Taylor, "Churchill's approach here [in *Bluebeard's Friends*] has her distinctively inspired stamp in its almost laconic outrageousness" (2019). She names the play, not after the hero, but after his "friends" for a specific reason. As Taylor further elaborates, "The full title of the play is *Bluebeard's Friends*; the focus is on his erstwhile moneyed intimates, seen foregathering in his castle for a postmortem over a few bottles of wine" (2019). In fact, in a post-truth world order, it is the marketability of things that is counted as their key virtue. Denizens of such a world, Bluebeard's friends are more interested in exploring the murders from a commercial point of view than in trying to understand their legal, social, or moral significance. Resultantly, Churchill too in the play is more interested in analyzing the shameless materialism and the self-serving psychology of Bluebeard's friends than in discussing a famous, half-dead, psychopath who is not expected to survive the assault. Since, as a serial killer, Bluebeard and people like him can easily be controlled and punished by society's power apparatuses such as the police and the judiciary, Churchill takes it upon herself to talk about something that has seldom been documented and/or analyzed before. Therefore, in *Bluebeard's Friends*, what the playwright offers us is a dark, inverted folktale wherein qualities like goodness, sympathy, and humanity are either nonexistent or have lost their fields of reference and what truly controls the world is a crude capitalist culture that revolves round manipulation and misrepresentation.

The more the friends of Bluebeard engage in discussing the murders, the more they seem to be interested in capitalizing on his crimes. As the initial shock at Bluebeard's monstrosity gives way to some "practical," worldly thoughts, one of the female characters bemoans her past rejection of Bluebeard as a prospective suitor. The lady is evidently more regretful than relieved to find out that in rejecting Bluebeard's advances she has actually robbed herself of the opportunity to feature in the latest list of celebrities, albeit dead. Another bunch of friends discuss whether the castle's history of having a psychopath murderer-owner would increase or decrease its market price, "Does murder put the price up or down?/Either way it's going to be foreign money" (2019c: 30). Yet another group of friends engage in analyzing the problems and prospects of incorporating the bloody chamber as a theme for a new business or a successful Halloween party, "There'll be miniature copies of the dresses/a little present/and then there'll be the actual clothes copies" (2019c: 30). The fact that these friends actually plan to use some of the bloodied clothes recovered from the corpses to "sell" them "as the women unharmed, victims no longer, power dresses" and their hope that these clothes "might be the bestseller" underline the crude commercialism that dominates today's world (2019c: 31).

In the Royal Court Theatre production of the play, the set designer Miriam Buether highlights the cruelty of the situation through making the bloodied, torn gowns of the dead wives of Bluebeard dangle indefinitely in the air on the stage. Taylor defines this as a metaphorical representation of both the psychopath husband's "perverted collecting habit" and of "the meaty marketing" opportunism that his shrewd friends showcase (Taylor 2019). The only saving grace in the play is the frenzied lady who is seen holding "scissors" and busy "cutting" and then "burning" the books written by male authors wherein "women get harmed and it's not condemned" (2019c: 31). Evidently for this woman, this act of cutting and burning books by male authors is both retaliation and mimicry. "Cutting" (disfiguring and fragmenting) an object is an attempt to destroy the unity of its being, and "putting" it to fire is to extinguish its very existence. Historically, both these have been patriarchy's highly preferred strategies to tackle and tame women who dare or desire. They have either been cut off from each other, and thereby cut out from society, or been burnt down for their deviance or defiance. Therefore, in *Bluebeard's Friends*, the woman's act of cutting and burning the books becomes the female counterstrategy to dismember and discard what patriarchy promotes as the only official narrative of female suffering. The act becomes all the more subversive when we remember that scissors is a phallic symbol and fire is mythically associated with Prometheus (a male). By wielding scissors and lighting the fire, the woman here comes out of a normative existence and thereby takes authority of selecting what defines and becomes her. Needless to say, it is her "frenzy" (the rejection of the social codes of "normalcy") that gives her the freedom and the excuse to "cut" and "burn" the world of male knowledge and logic as represented by the books.

In fact, in *Bluebeard's Friends*, it is through this frenzied woman that Churchill attempts to show her audience the way to deal with a post-truth condition. Since the post-truth world operates primarily through misappropriated knowledge, it is important to see through that knowledge in order to understand the "true" reality. The books that the woman destroys are all written by male authors and none of them condemn either the victimizer or the process of victimization. Evidently, what they offer is a biased representation of what "is" and what "ought to be." Here, the destruction of these books becomes the woman's rejection of the post-truth situation that surrounds her. The dark world of the play, however, soon interrupts her with questions that attempt to dissuade her from what she is doing, "You can find books by all the baddies, Books by bankers? Books by generals? … Books by dangerous drivers?" (2019c: 32). True that it is practically impossible for the woman to destroy all misogynist texts single-handedly, but she can at least make the other women aware of such politicized knowledge. Her claim that she will "get to" all such books highlights her confidence both in herself and in those other women whom she hopes to inspire through her ceaseless efforts (2019c: 32). Her resolution frightens the society to such an extent that it ultimately resorts to physical abuse:

> Ow you cut my finger.
> Get your hands out of the scissors then. (2019c: 32)

The woman's resolute answer to this abuse, "So I will have decluttered," marks her decision to continue with her work in spite of all odds (2019c: 32). Since, "decluttering" is the process of choosing what to keep and what to reject, it becomes our only means of navigating through a post-truth world that hinges on misappropriated claims and politicized information. To "know" in that world is to know "how to select," and to "select" is basically to "declutter."

The last play of the series, *Imp*, is divided into twelve different scenes that narrate the story of the old and irritable couple Jimmy and Dot, both of whom are in their late fifties or early sixties. Whereas Dot is a former nurse who was discharged of her duties and punished with imprisonment when she was found guilty of abusing a patient, Jimmy is perennially depressed and in the habit of recounting tragic narratives of Greek or Shakespearean heroes who died of their own faults of judgment. The apparently boring and uneventful life of the couple is soon disturbed first by their distant relative Niamh, a girl in her twenties, who comes to meet them after the death of her father, and, then, by Rob, a homeless and dyslexic man in his thirties, who occasionally visits their house and tells stories of his many adventures around the world.

The play opens with the picture of Jimmy narrating a modernized version of Shakespeare's *Othello* to Dot and Niamh. This simple session of storytelling, however, soon turns sour as Dot starts expressing some serious reservations about how the story progresses and what makes Jimmy choose the story for the evening: "It would be ok to kill her … You're still making excuses for him" (i.e., the husband) (2019d: 37). Evidently, both Jimmy and Dot are estranged from each other and their mutual uneasiness becomes visible from Dot's accusations about Jimmy's story, "Yes you're saying she'd have deserved it" (2019d: 37) and from her half-mocking reference to the "non-sexual" nature of their marriage, "We're not a couple, Niamh … we live together and there's kissing cousin but no kissing here" (2019d: 38). On second reading, Dot's need to clarify her stance actually shows her inability and unwillingness to trust the human capacity to assess real-life situations in a world full of fictitious realities. Just as Othello could neither understand Desdemona's innocence nor suspect Iago's plotting nature, each and every person in our society, for Dot, runs the risk of falling victim to appearances. Therefore, when Jimmy praises Niamh or Rob claims not to have secured an accommodation for himself and Niamh show signs of falling for Rob, Dot has a reason to suspect all their intentions and decisions, "Speak for your own, thank you very much" (2019d: 39), "Stop right there … You were going to say how all these people are getting housesd [*sic*] before you" (2019d: 45), and "Does he sleep at your place … He's not even that beautiful" (2019d: 52–3).

In fact, the world of *Imp* is built around the twin pillars of human beliefs and age-old superstitions. And it is Dot who functions in the play as an agent of both these apparently warring elements. If, on the one hand, she continuously questions everyone around her about every point they make and every argument they present, then, on the other hand, Dot keeps with herself a bottled-up spirit, the "imp" of the play's title, whom she firmly believes to be an inverted edition of Aladdin's Genie. Whereas Aladdin's spirit could easily perform everything that his master would want him to do, Dot's imp can only grant malevolent wishes. When Rob decides to part his ways with Niamh and wants to leave for Dubai in search of a suitable employment, Dot has an opportunity to utilize the evil powers of the imp, "We want total doom …I'm going to try it. I could do something to the son, he'd mind that" (2019d: 66). Nothing bad, however, happens to Rob or to his son other than that Rob is simply unable to go to Dubai, while Niamh finds a new boyfriend and moves to Paris on an assignment for a period of three months. When Dot learns that Jimmy and Rob had earlier opened the bottle to see if there was anything inside it, she is convinced that the imp must have escaped from captivity and that it must be waiting somewhere inside the house to avenge itself on the inhabitants.

According to Jessie Thompson, the play *Imp* is a "poignant look at how our beliefs can comfort and trap us" (2019). Both Jimmy and Dot, finds Thompson, try to ward off their "anxieties about the universe in different ways" (2019). While Jimmy works hard on developing his athletic abilities or simply tells stories, Dot either quarrels with him or secretly seeks solace in the imp that she believes to have captured in a wine bottle. The play ends with the picture of all the four characters Jimmy, Dot, Niamh, and Rob gathering together once again in Jimmy and Dot's living room and gossiping about the absent imp. Niamh, who is now visibly pregnant, expresses her fears that she might not be able to love the child appropriately following which Dot mysteriously declares that she would now place the imp's bottle on the shelf "quietly" (2019d: 82). Churchill leaves the issue of the presence or the absence of the imp inside the glass bottle undecided not only to increase the drama of the situation but also to underline the impossibility of knowing or controlling one's own life in an obfuscated post-truth world.

In his book *Post-Truth and Political Discourse*, David Block makes an interesting list of the kinds of statements that we randomly come across in a post-truth condition. According to him, the post-truth world is full of six kinds of information:

(i) The "esoteric" truths ("conspiracy theorising")
(ii) The "creative" truths ("the imaginative social construction of factual universes")

(iii) The "lies" ("saying something one knows or believes to be false")
(iv) The "misleading" statements (saying something to create "a false interpretation")
(v) The "bullshit" ("intentional" and "deceptive misrepresentation"), and lastly,
(vi) The "deliberate propagation of ignorance." (2019: 70)

All these sorts of "mis"information taken together is what constructs the infamous "alternative facts," which the US advisor to the president, Kellyanne Conway, famously referred to during her January 22, 2017, press meeting, a phrase that the US television journalist Chuck Todd mockingly explained as mere "falsehood": "Look, alternative facts are not facts. They're falsehoods" (Blake 2017). What the audience of Caryl Churchill experiences in the four short plays under discussion is a dramatization of the internal crisis of people who are forced to inhabit such a post-truth world of "alternative" realities. Since the facts that make and unmake the lives of Churchill's characters are themselves constructed by concealed, misrepresented, and supplanted information, they can hardly sustain the megamyths that they produce. Resultantly, the characters of Churchill's play are forced to inhabit a void from where there is no easy escape. It is this all-pervasive void that makes the glass girl fragile and the "gods" powerless. The same void is responsible for the unfeeling commercialism of the friends of Bluebeard and the silent sufferings of people like Jimmy, Dot, Rob, and Niamh, who perennially place their hope on people, situations, or spirits that do not either exist or are absent. Churchill, however, is not a pessimistic playwright. Almost all her characters in *Glass*, *Kill*, *Bluebeard's Friends*, and *Imp* have an indomitable will to mark their presence in the world. It is this will to seek the Truth and to find out what really works that enables the glass girl to break free from her static, fragile existence, to fall in love, to live life on her terms, and finally to transform her weakness into her agency. When the "god" tries to dismantle his "omnipotence" or the female friend of Bluebeard tears apart the books, we notice a similar effort of registering one's voice against the official narrative of the post-truth world. Similarly, in *Imp*, the four sad and lonely people never stop looking forward to the future. George Orwell is popularly believed to have said, "In a time of universal deceit, telling the truth is a revolutionary act" (qtd. in McIntyre 2018: 1). Definitely, these four plays by Churchill perform a similar revolutionary act by stressing the indomitable human will to survive amidst every crisis and void; for this is not merely the only Truth that "matters" but also the only Truth that "needs to matter" in our day-to-day post-truth life.

Note

1 The play *Kill* mentions the dramatis personae in the plural as "gods" and "people." In this chapter, however, they are referred to in the singular as "god" and "person" for the clarity of discussion.

References

Billington, M. (2019), "*Glass, Kill, Bluebeard, Imp*: Churchill's Compelling Quartet," *Guardian*, September 26. Available online: https://www.theguardian.com/stage/2019/sep/26/glass-kill-bluebeard-imp-review-finding-fascination-in-bloodshot-fables (accessed December 20, 2020).

Blake, A. (2017), "Kellyanne Conway Says Donald Trump's Team Has 'Alternative Facts.' Which Pretty Much Says It All," *Washington Post*, January 22. Available online: https://www.washingtonpost.com/news/the-fix/wp/2017/01/22/kellyanne-conway-says-donald-trumps-team-has-alternate-facts-which-pretty-much-says-it-all/ (accessed January 14, 2021).

Block, D. (2019), *Post-Truth and Political Discourse*, London: Palgrave Macmillan.

Churchill, C. (2019a), *Glass* in *Glass, Kill, Bluebeard, Imp*, 3–12, London: Nick Hern Books.

Churchill, C. (2019b), *Kill* in *Glass, Kill, Bluebeard, Imp*, 13–19, London: Nick Hern Books.

Churchill, C. (2019c), *Bluebeard's Friends* in *Glass, Kill, Bluebeard, Imp*, 21–33, London: Nick Hern Books.

Churchill, C. (2019d), *Imp* in *Glass, Kill, Bluebeard, Imp*, 35–82, London: Nick Hern Books.

Davis, P. T. (2019), "Review: *Glass, Kill, Bluebeard, Imp*, Royal Court, London," *British Theatre*, September 26. Available online: https://british theatre.com/review-glass-kill-imp-royal-court-london/ (accessed January 21, 2021).

Greenstreet, H. (2019), "Review: *Glass, Kill, Bluebeard, Imp*," *Magazines*, September 30. Available online: http://exeuntmagazine.com/reviews/review-glass-kill-bluebeard-imp-royal-court/ (accessed January 11, 2021).

McIntyre, L. (2018), *Post-Truth*, Cambridge, MA: MIT Press.

"Post-Truth" (2016), *The Oxford English Dictionary*, abbreviated to *OED*. Available online: https://en.oxforddictionaries.com/word-of-the-year/word-of-the-year-2016 (accessed December 17, 2019).

Taylor, P. (2019), "*Glass, Kill, Bluebeard, Imp:* Caryl Churchill Quartet Is Haunting and Audacious," *Independent*, September 26. Available online: https://www.independent.co.uk/arts-entertainment/theatre-dance/reviews/glass-kill-bluebeard-imp-review-caryl-churchill-harvey-weinstein-scandal-hollywood-a9121181.html (accessed January 22, 2021).

Thompson, D. (2008), *Counterknowledge: How We Surrendered to Conspiracy Theories, Quack Medicine, Bogus Science and Fake History*, London: Atlantic Books.

Thompson, J. (2019), "*Glass, Kill, Bluebeard, Imp*: A Whirlwind Ride through Caryl Churchill's Relentless Imagination," *Evening Standard*, September 26. Available online: https://www.standard.co.uk/culture/theatre/glass-kill-bluebeard-imp-review-a-whirlwind-ride-through-caryl-churchills-relentless-imagination-a4246886.html (accessed November 17, 2020).

Part Two
Politics

3

The Alternative Realities of David Henry Hwang's *Soft Power* and Anne Washburn's *Shipwreck*

William C. Boles

The phrase "alternative facts" entered the political lexicon less than forty-eight hours after Donald J. Trump's inauguration as the forty-fifth president of the United States. Upset by photographs as well as crowd-size estimates suggesting that his inauguration was dramatically smaller than President Barack Obama's, Trump directed Sean Spicer, his press secretary, to assert that this comparison was incorrect. Spicer combatively stated that the Friday afternoon inauguration had been "the largest audience ever to witness an inauguration, period, both in person and around the globe" (Hunt 2017). The next day Kellyanne Conway, a political advisor to the president, went on NBC's *Meet the Press*, a Sunday morning political talk show. When pressed by host Chuck Todd why Trump sent Spicer to the Press Room of the White House to promote a lie, she memorably responded: "You're saying it's a falsehood and Sean Spicer, our press secretary, gave alternative facts to that" (Jaffe 2017).[1] Conway's use of the alternative facts defense, that Sunday morning, became one of, what would be, a continual trail of viral moments of post-truth posturing by the administration.

I reference this well-known moment to highlight another Conway alternative fact moment, which occurred only a few days later. However, whereas her first use of alternative facts was to placate the ego of a wounded president who throughout his administration always measured himself against his predecessor, she now created a fictional, alternative event to argue for a controversial administrative policy. In an interview about Trump's travel ban, Conway defended the administration's severe policy as a safety measure to protect American citizens. She then referenced a massacre that occurred in Bowling Green, Kentucky, carried out by two Iraqi refugees. The problem was that said massacre never happened.[2] The press quickly called out the erroneous nature of her claim and many noted, like *The Washington Post*, that Conway was now taking "'alternative facts' to a new level" (Schmidt and Bever 2017).[3] The true story that Conway had conflated to a terrorist attack was far less dramatic. Two Iraqi men were arrested in Bowling Green for attempting to raise money to send weapons to terrorists in Iraq. The subsequent arrest of the two individuals was entirely bloodless. While Conway's first declaration of "alternative facts" created a blizzard of commentators appalled at the administration's willingness to disavow factual, photographic evidence, this second incident had an unexpected viral response. Citizens of Bowling Green seized upon Conway's gaffe and quickly responded via social media in memorializing the "tragic" event. A Wikipedia page was created, covering the massacre (and still exists). Interviews with "survivors" began appearing on YouTube but, of course, these were "mock interviews with role-players giving their eye-witness accounts of the massacre. These varied in the seriousness of their tone and the degree to which the interviewee assumed an alternate identity" (Evans 2018: 462). Not surprisingly, the news media sought out these Bowling Green parodies, and CNN posted "several mock interviews … and thereby giving Bowling Green protests and role-players a national audience" (Evans 2018: 467). Kellyanne Conway's alternative reality of a horrific massacre gave birth to a community performance, which claimed her fiction, making it their own and responding to the "tragedy" through satiric humor. Ann Ferrell, a Bowling Green citizen, said, "This is Kentucky, and we are used to being the butt of the joke … So there's also some sense of pride that someone else blundered, and we get to take it and make it a joke on them" (Goldstein 2018: 477). *The New York Times* suggested the following about the mock massacre narrative: "Social media and journalistic scrutiny aligned with comedy to right a wrong pretty definitively. That it happened so organically showed that false 'facts' might not always be the stubborn things so many people fear they are becoming" (qtd. in Goldstein 2018: 473). A means to combat the Trump administration on its lies had been born, inspiring others to follow, including American playwrights.

Alternative facts proved to be too enticing an opportunity to miss for David Henry Hwang and Anne Washburn, whose Trump-inspired plays offer key moments where the espousing of alternative facts lead to striking ensuing alternative realities, one of a Trump-influenced world from the perspective of China in David Henry Hwang's *Soft Power* (2018) and another of an alternate version of Trump himself in Anne Washburn's *Shipwreck* (2019). Even though both pieces are diametrically different—Hwang's a self-described musical within a play, Washburn's an intimate, contemplative gathering of friends over a weekend—both offer stinging indictments of the post-truth world where alternative facts have become the tools of the victorious, while the truth has been laid bare, helplessly limp, only embraced by those who have no power to wield it. In both cases, the playwrights ultimately encourage their audience to recognize the incongruities of a post-truth world and reclaim the power embedded in truth and facts.

Soft Power: China Rewrites the United States

Trump actually was not the main influence when David Henry Hwang began working on *Soft Power*,[4] which had its world premiere in 2017 at the Ahmanson Theater in Los Angeles. In 2014, Michael Ritchie commissioned Hwang to write a play for the fiftieth anniversary of the Center Theater Group. Inspired by the Lincoln Center revival of Rodgers and Hammerstein's *The King and I*, which premiered in April of 2015, Hwang set to write a musical that reversed the Rodgers and Hammerstein musical's narrative as well as its power dynamics: "I always loved this musical but as I have gotten older I became aware of aspects of it that are questionable such as whether an English woman would come to Siam to teach the king how to run his country" (Stein 2018).[5] Assuming that Hillary Clinton would win the 2016 election, his early, unfinished version of *Soft Power* focused on Xuē Xíng, a Chinese businessman visiting America, who meets Hillary Clinton at a *King and I* fundraiser, and soon becomes her political advisor, echoing the same influence that Anna had over the King of Siam. He teaches her how the American system pales in comparison to the Chinese way, especially when it comes to democracy and gun control. As Hillary tells Xuē when they meet at the fundraiser, "We can learn a thing or two from China!" (Hwang 2019: 9).[6] Hwang explained that *Soft Power* is "a Chinese musical that celebrates the rise of China over America, and what a bad idea democracy is—it's an anti-democratic musical" (Tran 2018: 42). Ironically, Hwang held a staged reading of his half-finished draft on the day of the election. Needless to say, the next day Hwang's narrative no longer fit the reality of what the country had decided. Hwang's reaction to Trump's victory was complicated because he had two different reactions, one as a Hillary supporter and one as an artist. He told *The New York Times*: "I guess I felt like, oh, the election is terrible for the country, but maybe it'll be good for the show. Because it sort of shows the Chinese point of view is right. Democracy isn't a good system. It doesn't always elect competent people. It creates chaos" (Ito 2018). His desire for the direct parallel with *The King and I* was jettisoned but he maintained the advisory relationship between the two characters, and Xuē helps Hillary emerge from her funk after losing to Trump, who does not appear and is never named in the piece. Adding to the narrative wrench of Trump winning the election, Hwang also found himself struggling with the contemporaneous nature of the play's political material. Writing a piece that takes place in the current time period was problematic for him, admitting: "It's very hard to write about the moment that you're in" (Sheidlower 2019). However, he found a way out of the conundrum, by deciding that "the musical supposedly is written 50 years from now by a Chinese author … The show assumes that China has become the dominant power 50 years down the road, and that they therefore control the narrative. China stepped into the dominant role when America collapses after the 2016 election" (Stein 2018). This premise then, much like the alternative facts and realities offered by the Trump administration, allows for China to proffer an alternative view of the United States, highlighting its foibles and failures, while also claiming America's cultural creations as their own.

That latter point is played up to comical effect at the start of the second act, while also highlighting the power of the victor to convert alternative facts into an accepted reality. As the second act opens we are no longer in the musical world of Xuē and Clinton, but instead find ourselves witnessing a "Commentary Interlude," led by Yáo Tuō, a Chinese television presenter, of the fiftieth anniversary production of "Ruǎn Shílì" (which translates as "Soft Power"). Joining Yáo on stage is Lóng Kūn, the daughter of the musical's composer; Jū Míng, the son of the book's author; and two academics, Lǐ Bìyù, who is an expert on second-world countries and will be able to shed light on "exotic America" (Hwang 2019: 61), and Harry O'Hara (Hālǐ Àohālā), who is an adjunct professor from Columbia University. We quickly learn that "Ruǎn Shílì" is a seminal example of a new art form created by Lóng and Jū's parents, who had "a revolutionary idea to create a new kind of theatre show": the musical (Hwang 2019: 62). The experts expound on the birth of this previously unseen art form, demonstrating how the victor redefines facts for their own purpose and how easily others accept the newly created reality.

Jū: [My father] called it "shuō chàng jù"—literally "spoken and sung drama."
Lóng: This was a totally new form, which the world had never seen before.
Hālǐ: Actually ...
Yáo: Yes, the American perspective!
Hālǐ: Many scholars believe that shuō chàng jù was first invented in America. Perhaps your fathers simply appropriated an American art form to tell a Chinese story.

Bìyù: Actually, there were no American artists per se. Only native craftspeople. (Hwang 2019: 62)

When Hālǐ protests against the argument that America's great musical creators were merely "native craftspeople" and stresses that their works were "quite sophisticated," Bìyù corrects him by noting that the underdeveloped attempts were about cats and "talking lions," prompting Yáo to surmise that "they were children's shows" (Hwang 2019: 63). When Hālǐ continues to protest, Lóng accuses him of trying to change the facts of history and that his insistence on an alternative vision is far too political. She then threatens to bring his institution to the government's attention, suggesting that the United States has now become a Chinese territory. Hālǐ immediately offers a groveling apology for his disrespect, even though he knows the facts he cites are correct. China's alternative vision of America is maintained, and the expert and the truth are silenced.

The musical we are watching also rewrites our present-day America. "Ruǎn Shílì" depicts the United States as a violent, gun-obsessed, xenophobic, racist, and electorally flawed democracy. (The song "Election Night" comedically highlights the ridiculousness of the US electoral system, as Xuě's confusion increasingly grows the more he learns about the convoluted steps used to elect a president.) The musical presents an America that has fallen into despair and chaos after Trump's election, and since Chinese artists are now articulating the US story, they are free to offer their own version, no matter how skewed, meaning the Golden Gate Bridge now resides in New York City's harbor; McDonald's is where political candidates go to raise money for their campaign; Hillary Clinton is an energetic, tap-dancing, ballroom-gown-wearing thirtysomething woman; and the streets of New York are filled with gun-toting, xenophobic, rabble rousers, who go by the names of Tony Manero (a reference to *Saturday Night Fever*), Holden Caulfield, and Betsy Ross as well as bucolic monikers like Bobby Bob and Randy Ray. Even the life story of David Henry Hwang (Hwang is a character in the story and is called DHH) is altered. He was actually stabbed in Brooklyn on November 29, 2015, by an unknown assailant, but the musical changes the attack to election night and the attackers are Trump supporters, who, before stabbing him, tell him to return to the country he came from.[7]

And yet, while Hwang admitted the piece can be seen as a piece of Chinese propaganda, as can be seen by the examples above, Hwang does not let China have the final pronouncement on the state of the United States. Hwang revisits a technique from his revision of *Flower Drum Song*, where the final lines of the play were spoken not by the characters but the actors themselves as they were directed out at the audience. At the end of *Soft Power*, the stylized musical settings and colorful costumes disappear, leaving an empty theatrical space that stretches all the way to the back wall of the theater. The house lights come up, the cast enters, now dressed in their normal street clothes, and they proceed to sing a reprise of "Democracy," which was originally sung earlier by Hillary Clinton. No longer characters in the fictional Chinese musical, the actors sing to us, as Americans, who, like the audience, find themselves living in a Trumpian world. They call to us, acknowledging as follows: "Look, this country's a disaster/ In so many ways/But we have the power/ … /To change" (Hwang 2019: 92). As I previously wrote after seeing the world premiere in Los Angeles, Hwang's play and its powerful ending exhorts the audience "to remember and believe in the power of democracy as they exit into the fraught, controversial, and dangerous times existing outside the doors of the theatre" (Boles 2019: 215). In addition, by only having performers of Asian descent in the musical, except for the performer playing Hillary, Hwang highlights how far the country has to go in its relationship not only with China but also with the Asian faces that dot the American landscape. As Hwang has oft intimated in interviews over the past forty years, "I never experienced overt racism, but you always knew that you were not completely accepted … [and] the United States had been at war with practically every Asian country. So having this face means that you kind of look like the enemy, in history or in current events or in movies" (Chow 2019: 56). As the staging of the final song indicates, Asian American faces are not the enemy, as Trump railed during his campaign and after.[8] They are one of us. They share our similar concerns and wish the best for our country. The power to change, then, resides in each one of us and our reliance on one another, no matter the skin color.

Shipwreck: Trump Rewrites History

Shipwreck was not actually Anne Washburn's first foray in writing about Trump. Her adaptation of Rod Serling's *The Twilight Zone* (2017) has a moment where our contemporary world of Trumpian-inspired political disagreement between friends seeps into one of Serling's episodes. "The Shelter" depicts what happens to the bonhomie between neighbors when a threatened missile attack turns a dinner party of friends against one another as one family hides in their bomb shelter, while the rest violently argue outside the steel door, debating as to who is more deserving of being saved. After learning the attack is a false alarm, all must face the uncomfortable truth of their neighbor's political and moral character. Washburn added dialogue to Serling's script to echo the provocative and antagonistic discussions Trump's campaign had fostered throughout the country.[9]

While *The Twilight Zone* was slated to premiere in December of 2017 at the Almeida Theatre in London, she began writing *Shipwreck* in June of the same year, less than six months after Trump was inaugurated. Driving her desire to write the play were conversations she found herself having with friends about Trump, his actions, leadership, and controversial personality. She revealed that she "wanted to see what it would be like to write about the current time, because that was all I was thinking or talking about" (Williams 2019: AR 6). However, like Hwang, she also acknowledged the difficulty of writing about a contemporary political moment. "Whether art has a responsibility to be contemporaneous, whether it can be contemporaneous, is a huge question. I feel like the idea of an immediate political theater is very enticing and yet often disappointing. It's a hard nut to crack" (Williams 2019: AR 6). Unlike Hwang, who relied on the device of setting the play in the future, Washburn leaned into the contemporaneity of the moment by setting the majority of the action shortly after the infamous dinner between Trump and FBI director James Comey, where the president asked whether Comey was loyal to him. And, again, different from Hwang, Washburn not only names Trump but also makes him a character in the play.

The main narrative of the play alternates between a weekend gathering of liberal friends bemoaning the political state of the United States at an upper New York State farmhouse and flashbacks to the family that previously owned the house, a white couple who adopted a Black baby boy. However, the two scenes that overwhelm the rest of the play feature Trump at the center. Helen Lewis called them "nightmarish" (2019: 51), while Sarah Hemming thought them "wildly lurid" (2019). Each features alternative realities depicting the myth of Donald Trump, one is set on the eve of the Iraq War when President George W. Bush meets with the realtor in his office, and the other imagines the infamous dinner conversation between Trump and Comey.

Unlike Hwang whose *Soft Power* argues that the United States fell into chaotic destruction precisely because of Trump's leadership, Washburn wanted *Shipwreck* to provide a balanced perspective of Trump. She was not interested in crafting a hit piece or taking cheap shots against him, precisely because of the "electric point of division" that he fosters among friends, families, and co-workers (Trueman 2019). She acknowledged that she had her own biased political perspective about him, so she sought out "other viewpoints, visiting websites that I don't normally hang out at" (Williams 2019: AR 6). Washburn was aware that there would be audience members who would react like Lewis and Hemming to the Trump character, but she deliberately intended not to replicate the figure everyone knew. Instead, she made him into a representation of his own "idealization of himself" and that while it may be "an absurd scene" for anti-Trump audience members, for "a certain Trump supporter, that is the person they're imagining" (Marks 2020: E1). In a different interview she expounded further on this depiction of him. "People really love him and believe in him and they aren't stupid, you know? They have different information and they're operating from a different emotional base, so it was important to find a way to genuinely honour him, even if only in micro moments" (Trueman 2019).

The stimulus for the alternative reality surrounding Washburn's Trump is introduced by Yusuf, a New York City lawyer, who pinpoints "the *fundamental* Trump Lie" to a moment during the second debate in the course of the Republican primary, which was held at the Ronald Reagan Library (2019: 42). It is a lie, that like Conway's utterances discussed earlier, gives birth to an entire alternative reality, one that Washburn embraces in her Trump characterization. In that debate when the topic under consideration turned to international politics, candidate Trump found himself stymied, unable to participate because of his lack of experience. However, never one to be silent for long, he inserted himself into the foreign policy discussion by referencing the Iraq War, and how he was the only one vocally against the war. Yusuf proceeds to recite Trump's lies to his friends:

> I am the only person on this dais
> the only person
> that fought very *hard* against us … going into Iraq
> —that was in 2003 you can check it out
> I'll give you twenty-five different stories—
> twenty-five stories—
> in fact a *delegation*—
> the White House.
> a *delegation*—was sent to my office to ask me to "cool it." (Washburn 2019: 45)[10]

Yusuf protests greatly the myth that Trump created that night:

> If Donald J Trump, this gaudy would-be mogul Donald J Trump had actually had fought "very very hard" against the Iraq War and all the papers had written about his "fight" and he had gripped the nation and rallied the nation with his uncompromising stand against the war

such that the White House was motivated to send a "delegation" to *beg* him to "cool it" ... I would have *remembered* that ... right? ... No one can remember the past. (Washburn 2019: 46; emphasis in the original)

This moment where Trump redefines his past, providing an alternative set of facts about his position on the war, mirrors precisely his actions throughout his professional life, where facts were manipulated for his own best possible benefit. A case in point is the uncertainty over how much Trump is actually worth. He has admitted in a deposition that his worth is defined not by how much he owns and how much is in the bank, but how he feels that day. This moment of self-mythologizing at the Republican debate, his ease in recreating his history, and the blatant lie he offers forth is at the heart of Washburn's fascination with the character of Trump that she creates in *Shipwreck*.

At the end of act one, the anti–Iraq War Trump proffered to the viewing public on that California stage appears. Like Hwang's Hillary Clinton in *Soft Power*, Washburn's Trump is depicted as much younger, diligent, laser-focused, and an organized businessman. Her stage descriptions describe him as *"everything that is chiseled, square-jawed, dynamic, noble. He is Ayn Rand hero in a world in which that is actually a good thing"* (2019: 69). His broken, stuttered cadence, his incomplete, random thoughts, and hyperbolic statements are no longer present in this incarnation. Instead, his grounded comments show a man who is thoughtful and invested in America, rather than himself. He offers respectful contemplative advice: "Mr. President, with all due respect; I must tell you I think a war would be an enormous mistake. The Middle East is a tinderkeg right now; the last thing we need is a spark" (Washburn 2019: 72). He holds a high level of esteem for the nature of the office: "I'm not going to challenge a sitting president. I have too much respect for the office and what it represents" (2019: 74). Pro-Trump viewers will see a depiction that reifies their opinion that he is the right man for the job, suggesting that Washburn succeeded in her attempt to provide a more even-keeled depiction. However, to be honest, Trump supporters present in the audience will likely be in the minority. More realistic is the fact that the audience will tilt more liberal, and they will only see the sardonic humor in these pronouncements, recognizing that the Trump who is president would never say such things. Despite the disparate perspectives surrounding this representation of Trump, Washburn's scene zeroes in on exactly how Trump has benefited from a post-truth world that embraces alternative facts, when he shares with President Bush his secret to his success as a businessman: "Roy Cohn used to talk about the power of the bluff. What is a bluff? Not a lie, but a strategic re-imagining of the situation. How do you bluff? You create a reality" (2019: 75). That ability to not only create a reality, something Trump has done his entire public life, but also the ability to believe in it fully is exactly what is at the heart of his success and other post-truth figures. Whereas Hwang only presents failure and chaos associated with Trump, Washburn acknowledges that the savviness and adaptability to use alternative facts and the ensuing alternative reality is precisely why Trump has risen. As he tells Bush, this skill is "what gives me the cojones to summon a winning hand into existence from thin air" (2019: 75). Previously, Washburn had adapted Serling's *The Twilight Zone* for the stage; here she provides her audience with a glimpse into *The Trump Zone*. Whereas Serling's stories relied, for the most part, on science fiction narratives, Washburn's vision of Trump, despite its basis in a lie, demonstrates the reasons for Trump's rise: our ability to forget the past, our lack of interest in pursuing the truth, and the egotistical power of one man to create his own mythology.

While the first incarnation of Trump is a vision of a true leader looking out for the country, the second incarnation of Trump is not as positive. In the play's penultimate scene Washburn returns us to the world of Trump, jumping forward in time, and to another incident that the weekend friends discuss throughout the play—the dinner between Comey and Trump. The impeccably dressed businessman now appears sporting a cape, a glistening, oiled-up torso, and all-American tight shorts. Being honest, I have to admit that when this incarnation appeared on stage I thought Washburn was channeling him as a wrestler because of his numerous appearances at Vince McMahon–sponsored wrestling events. Shortly thereafter I realized my mistake. The vision was one of a godlike figure, completely in control of his surroundings and waited upon by a host of human-sized Ibises, who ominously surround Comey throughout the scene.[11] And yet, despite his godlike demeanor, the depiction is a fever-dream version of a leader on the verge of a mental meltdown. The present-day Trump who randomly spews off-topic comments is here (at one point he becomes distracted and riffs on Jimmy Stewart). His preoccupation with his predecessor, Barack Obama, is also foregrounded. At one point he repeats, almost word for word, part of a speech that Obama gave after winning the Iowa caucus in 2008 about the power of hope, even to the point of name-checking Obama's family members. Trump tells Comey: "Hope, as Michelle and I tell Sasha and Malia every morning as they set out for school, is the belief that destiny will not be written for us" (Washburn 2019: 124).

This alternative reality of Trump, which, in contrast to the first depiction, now parallels how many liberals may see him, highlights what was articulated in the introduction about the disruptive force of alternative facts and the rise of our post-truth times. We have always known Trump was a liar, but we have allowed his lies, and other lies, to proliferate to the point that we no longer take notice. Trump's assertion that he was against the war was disproven when an earlier interview with Trump by Howard Stern, a New York City radio host, was unearthed. The result of this discovery, as Yusuf explained, is as follows: "He makes himself up from thin air. *Nobody cares*" (Washburn 2019: 53; emphasis in the original). Daily, Trump mythically created himself, growing grander and more important with each passing alternative fact, and Washburn's second incarnation of Trump demonstrates what we made possible through our inaction, a godlike figure who is uncontrollable, expecting all to answer to him. Sarah Hemming was struck by the Trump scenes, noting they display "the alarming way myth outruns truth and stories replace history before our eyes" (2019). This final version of Trump shows exactly the result of allowing alternative facts to go unchecked. Self-mythologizing political leaders need to be challenged. Alternative realities cannot take hold. If we continue to allow them to proliferate, then the godlike, rambling, dangerous figure of Trump seen at the play's end becomes what we deserve.

Conclusion: Post-Truth, Hwang, and Washburn

Alternative facts and the alternative realities they create were used by Conway, Trump, and others to control the narrative and foster a vision of America that fit their political perspectives, personalities, and policies. They became the building blocks in the creation of a Trump Nation throughout his term in office. Hwang and Washburn both borrow the concept of alternate facts to explore the alternate realities that ensue and, in the process, challenge and question the administration's attempts to redefine truth. While Hwang's *Soft Power* is intentionally set up as a propaganda-like piece to call the audience to action, to believe (once again) in democracy, and hold faith in the United States despite the current administration, Washburn admits to a more limited influence her play can have upon her audience. After all, her play, for the most part, is "a group of people in a room, talking and listening"; however, within those moments "there's this possibility to carve out a space for reflection and complexity—even if only in the tiniest way. There's no solving this in one evening, but it's a start" (Trueman 2019). And yet, both, in their own way, aim for conversation. Both aim to make the audience question not only what occurs on stage but also what has occurred in the national news over the past few years. Both call the audience to question the lies that have been put forth due to the rise of post-truth politics. While Lee McIntyre's book on post-truth does not mention either play, his summation of our role in the post-truth era applies to the intention behind Hwang and Washburn's works. In essence,

> one must always fight back against lies ... The point of challenging a lie is not to convince the liar, who is likely too far gone in his or her dark purpose to be rehabilitated. But because every lie has an audience, there may still be time to do some good for others ... At the very least

it is important to *witness* a lie and call it out for what it is. In an era of post-truth, we must challenge each and every attempt to obfuscate a factual matter and challenge falsehoods before they are allowed to fester. (McIntyre 2018: 157–8)

It is worth ending with a recognition that neither David Henry Hwang nor Anne Washburn is known as political writers. While politics has crept in more recently, like *Yellow Face* (2007) in Hwang's case and *The Twilight Zone* for Washburn, their works have not articulated a strident politicization and didactic perspective that would be more at home in the works of Clifford Odets, Arthur Miller, or Tony Kushner. And yet, in this distinct moment, at this difficult time, the political rhetoric of the country impelled these two playwrights to engage and offer their audience the opportunity to explore, examine, question, and come to see, perhaps, in Washburn's case, the other side, however briefly. As Conrad Ricamora said, who played Xuē Xíng, about the power of theater during our distraught political era: "Theater can provide an escape, but it also should be a place where we all come to debate and think and keep our minds on when we're in our seats" ("Conrad" 2018). Both playwrights aim for the theater and its audiences to do exactly that, as we all navigate our ways through the lies, alternative facts, and deceptions, which have become commonplace in a post-truth world.

Notes

1 Ralph Keyes notes that Conway was not the first political figure to introduce the concept of "alternative facts." When asked about the conflicting testimony between Anita Hill and Clarence Thomas, Bill Clinton suggested that "neither Anita Hill nor Clarence Thomas was a liar; each simply told the truth as he or she saw it. What a layperson might consider a lie, said Clinton, a lawyer such as he might see as simply an 'alternative version of reality'" (2004: 119).

2 Conway's claim of a fictional massacre was not the first time the Trump administration cited a violent act that never occurred. On January 19,

2017, the day before being inaugurated, Trump made mention of a nonexistent terrorist attack in Sweden.
3 Conway discounted the pushback against her comments, citing that she had misspoken. However, later in the same month she referenced the Bowling Green massacre two more times, raising questions about the veracity of her excuse.
4 Hwang's title reflects what he saw in his travels. America wields soft power around the world and China desires to emulate that same success: "I think soft power has been the goal of China for a good 20 years now … there's a big desire [to] create a show that would get on our Broadway" (Tran 2018: 43).
5 This is not the first time Hwang has set about to rectify a problematic Rodgers and Hammerstein musical with Asian American characters. He reconfigured the story and songs for *Flower Drum Song*, which had its premiere on Broadway in 2001.
6 The quotes used from *Soft Power* are from the revised script of the Public Theater's production in New York City in 2019.
7 See Hwang (2016).
8 See Stracqualursi (2017).
9 See W. Boles (forthcoming 2022).
10 Much of what Washburn quotes from the debate is accurate, but there is one notable distinction, namely that Trump does not say that it was the White House that sent a delegation to see him. Here is what he said in the debate that overlaps with Washburn's script:

> I am the only person on this dais—the only person—that fought very, very hard against us, and I wasn't a sitting politician going into Iraq, because I said going into Iraq—that was in 2003, you can check it out, check out—I'll give you 25 different stories. In fact, a delegation was sent to my office to see me because I was so vocal about it. (Beckwith 2015)

11 While the godlike presence of Trump fits the way Trump carried himself in office, I still like my initial response of him being a wrestler.

References

Beckwith, R. T. (2015), "Transcript: Read the Full Text of the Second Republican Debate," *Time.com*, September 18. Available online: https://time.com/4037239/second-republican-debate-transcript-cnn/ (accessed August 31, 2021).

Boles, W. C. (2019), Review of *Soft Power*, *Theatre Journal*, 71 (2): 213–15.

Boles, W. C. (forthcoming 2022), "From Curator to Co-Author: Examining the Narrative and Political Choices of Anne Washburn's Stage Adaptation of *The Twilight Zone*," in R. Riekki and K. J. Wetmore, Jr. (eds.), *The Many Lives of* The Twilight Zone: *Essays on the Television and Film Franchise*, Jefferson, NC: McFarland Press.

Chow, A. R. (2019), "8 Questions: David Henry Hwang," *Time*, November 11: 56.

"Conrad Ricamora Lights Up New Musical *Soft Power*" (2018), *Variety*, June 1. Available online: https://variety.com/2018/legit/news/conrad-ricamora-soft-power-htgawm-1202828388/ (accessed June 25, 2020).

Evans, T. H. (2018), "The Bowling Green Massacre," *Journal of American Folklore*, 131 (522): 460–70.

Goldstein, D. E. (2018), "Never Remember: Fake News Turning Points and Vernacular Critiques of Bad Faith Communication," *Journal of American Folklore*, 131 (522): 471–81.

Hemming, S. (2019), "Anne Washburn's *Shipwreck* Wrangles with America, Liberalism and the Trump Presidency," *Financial Times*, February 20. *Proquest* (accessed June 25, 2020).

Hunt, E. (2017), "Trump's Inauguration Crowd: Sean Spicer's Claims versus the Evidence," *Guardian*, January 22. Available online: https://www.theguardian.com/us-news/2017/jan/22/trump-inauguration-crowd-sean-spicers-claims-versus-the-evidence (accessed May 23, 2021).

Hwang, D. H. (2016), "The Time I Got Stabbed in the Neck," *New York Times*, January 8. Available online: https://www.nytimes.com/2016/01/08/fashion/mens-style/the-time-i-got-stabbed-in-the-neck.html (accessed May 23, 2021).

Hwang, D. H. (2019), *Soft Power*, unpublished Public Theatre Opening Night draft, October 11.

Ito, R. (2018), "2 Tony Winners Try to Upend Rodgers and Hammerstein," *New York Times*, May 3. Available online: https://www.nytimes.

com/2018/05/03/theater/soft-power-david-henry-hwang-jeanine-tesori.html (accessed June 25, 2020).

Jaffe, A. (2017), "Kellyanne Conway: WH Spokesman Gave 'Alternative Facts' on Inauguration Crowd," *NBCnews.com*, January 22. Available online: https://www.nbcnews.com/storyline/meet-the-press-70-years/wh-spokesman-gave- alternative-facts-inauguration-crowd-n710466 (accessed May 23, 2021).

Keyes, R. (2004), *The Post-Truth Era: Dishonesty and Deception in Contemporary Life*, New York: St. Martin's Press.

Lewis, H. (2019), "Separate Circles of Hell," *New Statesman*, March 1–7: 51.

Marks, P. (2018), "How 2 Actors Strikingly Play Lightning Rods," *Washington Post*, March 1: E1.

McIntyre, L. (2018), *Post-Truth*, Cambridge, MA: MIT Press.

Schmidt, S., and L. Bever (2017), "Kellyanne Conway Cites 'Bowling Green Massacre' That Never Happened to Defend Travel Ban," *Washington Post*, February 3. Available online: https://www.washingtonpost.com/news/morning-mix/wp/2017/02/03/kellyanne-conway-cites-bowling-green-massacre-that-never-happened-to-defend-travel-ban/ (accessed May 23, 2021).

Sheidlower, N. (2019), "Tony Award-Winning Playwright David Henry Hwang Speaks of Chinese-American Relations, Fragility of American Democracy at Panel on *Soft Power*," *Columbia Daily Spectator*, December 5. Available online: https://www.columbiaspectator.com/arts-and-entertainment/2019/12/05/tony-award-winning-playwright-david-henry-hwang-speaks-of-chinese-american-relations-fragility-of-american-democracy-at-panel-on-soft-power/ (accessed June 25, 2020).

Stein, R. (2018), "Hwang's *Soft Power*—Part Play, Part Musical—Sparked by *King and I* Revival," *San Francisco Chronicle*, June 21. Available online: https://www.sfchronicle.com/entertainment/article/Hwang-s-Soft-Power-part-play-part-12994357.php (accessed June 25, 2020).

Stracqualursi, V. (2017), "10 Times Trump Attacked China and Its Trade Relations with US," *ABC.com*, November 9. Available online: https://abcnews.go.com/Politics/10-times-trump-attacked-china-trade-relations-us/story?id=46572567 (accessed September 4, 2021).

Tran, D. (2018), "David Henry Hwang; Backward and Forward," *American Theatre*, May/June: 40–3.

Trueman, M. (2019), "Can Theatre Keep Pace with Real-Life Political Drama," *Financial Times*, February 15. Available online: https://www.ft.com/content/81bf4472-2a2a-11e9-9222-7024d72222bc (accessed June 25, 2020).
Washburn, A. (2019), *Shipwreck: A History Play about 2017*, London: Oberon.
Williams, H. (2019), "After *Twilight Zone*, the Trump Zone," *New York Times*, February 10: AR 6.

4

Negotiating the Fifth Wall

Lynn Deboeck

People recognize that lies are bad; nonetheless, they pervade our social landscape. Both secular moral codes and religious dictates underscore the basic principles that lying is wrong and should be avoided. Speaking specifically of the US population, sociologist Erving Goffman goes further, explaining that

> lies have a uniquely corrosive impact on the creation of public policy. At the most basic level, they destroy public trust in our political systems, causing the American people to lose faith in their government. Lies also distract from real debate, bogging down lawmakers and regulators, sometimes for years as settled science is argued over. Finally, lies create balkanization in our political culture, making ideological consensus impossible. (2016: 4)

Yet, lies are not the only things building our post-truth era. Apathy, self-centeredness, disconnection, and exhaustion all play a role. The public stage sees the tools of misdirection and trickery used in the art of political deception. With or without direct or explicit lies, our public figures seem to actively push away truth and/or those seeking it. From a theatrical perspective, the players are almost constantly and aggressively dissociating themselves from the script provided in order to write their own. Control of their narrative (or their group's narrative) has become paramount in this age and with it, honing the use of performance conventions to manipulate audiences. Gregory Bateson, in his theory of play and fantasy, divides human verbal communication into two directions of abstraction: the denotative and the metalinguistic

(2016: 159–69). The latter involves the relationship between the speakers and listeners. When we use this form of abstraction to frame our consumption of post-truth, public performance, we complicate the relationship between the speaker and audience by understanding the starting point to be one of false denotation in the guise of truth-hood. In this chapter, I bring forward examples of public figures and their performances of this phenomenon. It should be noted that all the public figures referenced here are indeed performers, as all their activity has been "carried out with a consciousness of itself" (Carlson 2016: 74). Their activity includes usage of time-honored theatrical conventions audiences everywhere can recognize (center-stage focus, call-and-response, sidebars that "break" the imaginary fourth wall, etc.), as well as newer modes of manipulation. In particular, I highlight and label a frequently used convention, coining it the "fifth wall."

For centuries, the concept and practice of theatrically breaking the fourth wall have been utilized in a specific, revelatory fashion. An actor on a stage abruptly turns to the audience, addressing them with eye contact, facial expressions, and words. This choice, also seen in film and television, breaks the illusion that the performance is limited to the invisibly demarcated space behind the fourth wall. The essential idea behind the convention is that the spectator is finally seeing what is "true." The convention has also been used on our public and political stages. Our current post-truth moment reveals to us another convention, which I have termed the "fifth wall." Political performers wield this wall in a different manner. While the fourth wall is stationary, but always assumed to be between the spectator and performer, the fifth wall is mobile and intentionally employed and controlled by the performer, much like a riot shield. We see politicians, pundits, and leaders using this device to deflect, ricochet, and mirror challenging (or outright accusatory) questions and statements away from themselves and onto other targets to change the narrative. If the questions are not flattering or threaten their standing, the fifth wall saves them by forcefully removing truth from the equation. Former president Donald Trump developed a reputation as someone who did not just deflect truth, but actively ignored it. He lied about knowing (and paying off) Stormy Daniels; he told the public that he had stopped the family separation policy he put in place at the border when he had not; he claimed he had control over the Covid-19 crisis in early 2020; and he still claims he won the 2020 election—just to name a few. Onnesha Roychoudhuri, co-founder of social justice organization Speech/Act, elucidates the specious nature of Trump and other politicians like him, "Here's the thing about narcissistic ideologues: they don't respond to logic, or dissuasion in the name of facts or reason. We could fact-check him all day and night, but he wasn't playing by the rules of the game" (2018: xxxiii). The game, in this case, is performing as a leader. The rules include at least *appearing* truthful.

Political historian Heather Cox Richardson has been making a name for herself with her "Letters from an American" blog that contextualizes our current political moment. Asked in an interview by Bill Moyers about Trump's autocratic approach to leading, she offers insight into the motivations behind his frequent lies and distractions, while also showing that our current moment is not the only time lying to control one's narrative has been used. Citing Senator Joe McCarthy's use of the tactic in the 1950s, she explains, how by changing the subject continuously, these politicians stay ahead of the story and thereby control the narrative. Utilizing the fifth wall as they do to forcibly push away truth, they implicate other people, taking time and energy away from holding themselves accountable, while their audience and the press puts that momentum into fact-checking. Once the first lies are revealed to be false, the revelation is lost as pertinent because in the wake of the first lies more have already been offered that need to be debunked, creating a cycle of the politicians staying ahead of their untruths. Richardson goes on to explain the difference in Trump's use of these tactics, claiming his motivations to be even more reprehensible. She makes clear that when Trump fills the space with lies (his own and the alternative realities he creates using the fifth wall)

> you keep your audience off guard all the time. They never know what the truth is. They never know what's coming next, and they don't know

how to answer any of it. And it's a game of psychological warfare, if you will. But if you keep knocking people around enough, eventually what they do is simply say, "I don't care. It's too much for me. Everybody's lying. I don't know what's real. Just make it all go away." And when you do that, the way is pretty clearly open for an autocrat to step in. (Moyers 2020)

Use of the fifth wall, then, is not only disruptive but quite dangerous. Autocracies have and continue to thrive based upon the leader's unscrupulous use of false narratives to shape the world by which they want their subjects to be controlled. And, as Richardson lays out for us, exhaustion can be a valuable asset for despots. If you exhaust your public with so many lies, they soon stop caring enough to pay attention. Academic psychologist and science writer Ari Rabin-Havt, in examining particularly adept performers who lie to the public for gain, demonstrates the result of this: if you get your public to the point where they do not know whom to believe, you put them "in a position of ideological 'paralysis'" (2016: xvi). As we can see, while theatrical conventions such as the fourth wall, and indeed even breaking the fourth wall, are used to pull the audience into a relationship of trust and acceptance where they create a narrative together, the fifth wall is used to push people into doubt and mistrust, in an effort to one-sidedly control the narrative outcome.

One type of performance in which we see these attempts at narrative control is the press conference in the United States. Setting aside the troubling nature of Donald Trump's relationship with the truth, it is important to note that he is not the inventor of this approach. Multiple members of the American political establishment on both sides of the aisle and for long before Trump was even born have mastered their use of the fifth wall during press conferences. However, for the sake of this discussion my focus is on Trump's four-year presidency. From the bumbling Sean Spicer to the stern Andrew Cuomo, from the strained Nancy Pelosi to the disingenuous Paul Ryan, they have displayed fifth wall tactics that range from ignoring a major issue to directly casting blame on someone else, but usually to take any truth being directed at them and fling it away. Using a variety of examples from 2017 to 2020, up to and including the Covid-19 crisis, I will illustrate the usage of this particular convention, the benefits and harm to which its use can lead, and I offer a performance framework through which to understand its efficacy. For the sake of clarity, it is important to revisit the theatrical terms supporting and leading to my concept of the "fifth wall."

The "fourth wall" is a theatrical convention, largely attributed to theater theorist and philosopher Denis Diderot, which was established in nineteenth-century Europe to underscore the trend toward realism and naturalism in performance. The custom perpetuates the idea that there exists an imaginary or invisible wall between the spectators and the audience, typically at the edge of the stage or acting space. In other words, if viewing the interior of a room, you would be able to see three of the walls, but where the fourth should be would simply be the window through which the spectators watch the play. The performers react to each other, but not to the audience, who exist on the other side of the invisible partition. In addition, then, the audience views the performance as if peeking-in on an actual interaction, or slice-of-life, taking place. The convention grants the scene the weight of consequence due to the facade of uninhibited reactions as well as the assumption that intervention from the onlookers is impossible.

As realism and naturalism were challenged by other theatrical forms, performers then started manipulating the audience by selective and specific "breaking" of this fourth wall, creating an entirely new convention.[1] This departure from the normalized convention drew attention to moments or elements of the story or form. Spectators would tune in differently to those moments, presuming deeper commentaries or meta-narratives were being revealed. Tom Brown's look at breaking the fourth wall in cinema explores how directly addressing an audience serves to "intensify our relationship with the fiction" (2012: x). Challenging the prevalent notion that the convention of breaking the fourth wall destroys the illusion, Brown and others have found that spectators relish the connection made between them and the characters and, indeed, invest themselves more fully in the story being told. It stands to reason, then, that people wishing to *divest* their audience of a story would use a decidedly different tactic.

The suspension of disbelief refers to the spectator's willingness to suspend doubt and believe the piece of drama they are watching for the sake of deriving pleasure from the experience. There are a variety of conventions that manipulate this suspension. Breaking the fourth wall, as one, consciously reveals information that interrupts this suspension, while also providing a strong argument for the aside to be even *more* true than the mise-en-scène encapsulated behind the fourth wall. The broken fourth wall makes it seem as though the audience is receiving the "inside scoop" or a secret just for them. Despite the fictional nature of what is being consumed, there is a greater currency to the belief that there exists a truer truth, and therefore the shared secret is highly prized. But what happens when connecting with your audience means revealing parts of yourself you wish were left out of the narrative?

I posit the existence of a new (or, rather, unnamed) convention: the fifth wall. I name it such because it is yet another theatrical convention adopted by performers, and it also carries rhetorical significance as a barrier to truth (or at least access to truth). Over time, our relationship with what is fictional versus what is fictional*ized* has become strained. Our oversaturated media age grooms us for this development, desensitizing us with a constant barrage of broadcasts and overused conventions. For example, it has become much more difficult to make the experience of breaking the fourth wall a jarring one to the spectator. Shows such as *The Office* have made it a playful expectation to share jokes directly with their TV audience. And yet, the reason eye contact or facial expressions made directly to the camera (rather than toward the interviewer) create such a connection in *The Office* is due to the meta-commentary of the show's premise. *The Office* offers us an example of an intermediate between genuine use of the fourth wall as an established convention (i.e., there are no people watching us) and fifth wall execution (i.e., everyone is watching us, so we want to sculpt what they see). Other shows such as *Fleabag* or *Miranda* offer a similar transition, though with the focus being on the main character and her relationship with the audience, which makes those shows even closer to how public figures perform. In *The Office*, the recognition and relationship are communal ones, which take the possibility of controlling the narrative out of the story being told because the power is more equally distributed. The liminal transition space used in these shows acknowledges that people are watching without the power of shaping. In *The Office*, it is evident that the characters do not obey the fourth wall principle by virtue of their frequent nods to the camera in their "play within a play" mockumentary. However, as written characters, they do not have the same control as live players to change their own narratives in the production. The humor is controlled by the writers.

I argue that the fifth wall is employed in real life, surprising audiences with misdirection, to control the "joke" of how a politician's life is perceived. The control comes with the fact that the misdirection is packaged to look like fourth wall manipulation—something that their audience is more likely to understand and go along with since they have grown accustomed to it in popular entertainment. Conveniently hiding its use behind a fourth wall disguise makes the fifth wall an even more useful weapon. The earnestness of performing as though there is a fourth wall separating you from your spectators creates a false sense of security—surely someone would not act that way if they knew they were being seen, so one must interpret the performance as a performance. And yet, if viewed as a piece of fiction, we almost expect the people in this narrative to wink at the screen, breaking the fourth wall to connect with their supporters, and say, "Don't worry, I've got this—I'll send them in the other direction." The public figures I look at here use the fifth wall in three main ways: redirecting blows away from themselves, taking aim at others by using what is thrown at them, and distracting their assailants with incomplete or incorrect reflections of the situation. Since the fifth wall is not a new convention, my examples are not in chronological order but included to illustrate these main ways that the fifth wall presents itself: as redirection, as aiming at a target, and as distraction.

Traditions of both performance and viewership have evolved over time to influence not only live theatrical performance but live political performance as well. Much of the bombastic, declarative and oratory styles of earlier-eighteenth-century European drama, which developed largely from religious oration, bled into how leaders addressed their publics. What resulted was a highly intricate system of communication between those in power and those they led. As we see today in the United States, politicians and those in the public arena perform for the people, at times informing them and, at others, seeking to sway them. All public figures have an additional job requirement to manage their image, and this leads to an intense desire to obsessively control their own narrative. These are largely theatrical goals, which I argue are the ultimate ends pursued by the performers on the public stage who are using the fifth wall.

Baz Kershaw investigates the politics of radical theater performance from the 1960s to the 1990s. He claims that changes to the theater during this period had specific, political ends (Kershaw 1992). I posit the mirror image of this argument, looking at our current public figures' performances as having specific, theatrical ends. Agitprop theater is one branch of political theater that demonstrated how the artist could agitate the public with their art. The various performances of public figures from press conferences to television interviews to even State of the Union addresses demonstrate how the performer in the spotlight diverts the public with their manipulative and intentional use of known theatrical conventions and contributes to the development of newer ones. Perhaps unsurprisingly, it has developed that the figures who excel at manipulation also seem to be the most frequently seen. As author Ralph Keyes explains in his book, *The Post-Truth Era*,

> a key source of this transformation is twenty-four-hour news cycles that put public figures always on call. The better looking and better spoken they are, the more frequently they're placed before cameras. With its penchant for politicians who perform well, TV gives the nod to those who are good at the deceptive arts. As a result, such politicians are a much bigger, more ubiquitous, and influential presence in our lives. (2004: 128)

As with the other "deceptive arts," what I am calling the fifth wall was not developed overnight. Scores of leaders and political figures have used their platform in a two-faced way for centuries, convincing the voting public that they are to be trusted while weaving narratives that do not match the facts. All of this affects how we consume news media since "fake news mimics the form and function of standard news, leveraging our collective notions of what news is or should be to its advantage" (Brotherton 2020: 18). In the 1970s, the nation witnessed Richard Nixon being caught in multiple lies, most notably regarding the Watergate scandal. In the 1980s, Ronald Reagan used his actor charm to distract from his controversial stance in the Iran-Contra affair. The 1990s saw Bill Clinton perjure himself about a sex scandal. Barack Obama pushed attention away from his drone strikes. Donald Trump continuously lied to the public about the state of our union, erroneously claiming everything from the country having the highest employment numbers to describing his call to Ukrainian President Zelensky (the reason for his first impeachment) as "perfect." And those are just the presidents. Donald Trump was not the first, nor will he be the last, to wield the fifth wall in deflecting criticism and weaponizing his lies. However, though he continued a long history of such presidential deceitfulness, he was arguably one of the most active and unscrupulous liars—even when it came to the Covid-19 pandemic.

As an example, when Trump was diagnosed with Covid-19 in October of 2020, he was asked pointed questions at several press conferences, asking when he last tested negative before the positive diagnosis. These questions were intended, no doubt, to establish how long the president had been infected. For months before the announcement of his diagnosis, there had been several headlines when the president had tested negative, so this should have been an innocuous question, as it had been readily answered before. However, the threat it posed (presumably due to the fact that it might implicate the president in infecting others) was great enough to warrant his use of the fifth wall to deflect the question and refuse to answer. Trump used the fifth wall by both manipulating his image into one of a "man of the people" to proactively elicit sympathy and afterward lying to distort the narrative of his diagnosis. First, before his diagnosis, he spoke publicly about how difficult it was to avoid interacting with people and maintain social distancing measures. Despite it eventually coming out that it was his staffer, Hope Hicks, who had infected him and the first lady, while speaking to the press to let them know that he just went for a test and would "see what happens," he made a more explicit comment about whom it was difficult to avoid: "It's very hard when you're with soldiers, when you are with airmen, when you're with the Marines, and the police officers, I'm with them so much. And when they come over to you, it's hard to say, 'stay back, stay back'" (Fox, Gumbrecht, and Christensen 2020). This statement pushes blame onto others were he to test positive, while also using them as a shield by self-branding as too kind and diligent of a commander in chief to back away from military and law enforcement members, even during a pandemic. By expressing how "very hard" his experience is, he is redirecting the negative attention directed at him as a potential infector and instead casting himself as the ever-present and conscientious head of the military, who must shake hands with his troops. By specifically naming the branches of military and service people whom he was apparently constantly surrounded by, he aims any blame at those very groups or ones who support them, essentially pointing the finger back at them as if to say: "How could I say no to your boys and call myself an American?" The military has often been used indiscriminately in this way by presidents seeking legitimacy and Trump was no exception. It poses a false dichotomy—either a patriot who supports our troops and leads the military by example, or an anti-American coward who does not deserve the title of president. Trapped in this dichotomy, the question of his potential to threaten others by infecting them with a deadly virus is concealed behind what is considered more important— nationalistic fervor. Additionally, Trump distorted the order of events as he announced shortly after midnight on Friday, October 2, 2020, that he had received his positive Covid test that night. Yet later confusion arose around statements Dr. Conley (the former president's physician) made on the morning of October 3 that Trump was seventy-two hours into his diagnosis. This use of the fifth wall highlights the tactic of distraction—by deliberately muddying the waters of when he was actually diagnosed, he buys himself time as people scramble to do the math and see how long he was infectious. But of course, before it can be resolved, Trump has another distraction ready.

Other people who have used the fifth wall have done so in distinctly similar ways. In December of 2019, prior to Trump's first impeachment, but after articles had been put forward, when asked if she hated President Trump, Nancy Pelosi responded by returning to the press conference podium and saying:

> I think the president is a coward when it comes to helping our kids who are afraid of gun violence. I think he is cruel when he doesn't deal with helping our dreamers, of which we are very proud. I think he is in denial about the climate crisis. However, that's about the election. Take it up in the election. This is about the constitution of the United States and the facts that leads to the president's violation of his oath of office. And as a Catholic, I resent your using the word "hate" in a sentence that addresses me. I don't hate anyone. I was raised in a way that is a heart full of love and always pray for the president. And I still pray for the president. I pray for the president all the time. So don't mess with me when it comes to words like that. ("Nancy Pelosi Tells" 2019: 00:23–1:15)

In this thirty-second statement, Pelosi handles the fifth wall in two of the ways previously delineated: redirection and aiming at a target. By redirecting the negative attention that stemmed from the word "hate" and aiming criticism at both President Trump for things she feels he does that might be more representative of one who "hates" and at the journalist who used the word "hate," she paints herself as a pious victim. Cleverly using "I" statements, Pelosi takes a performative (and psychological) approach, giving the appearance she is responding for only herself. In addition, framing her accusations as merely stating her own thoughts ("I think") creates distance from the phrases she is using, which are heavy indictments of the president and his actions.

Then using the word "we" to express pride, Pelosi aligns herself with Congress and what the American people "should" be and differentiates that from Trump. Essentially, she is calling him un-American in the same way that he casts himself as extra-American. After establishing Trump as the appropriate target for criticism, she makes a masterful pivot with her riot-shield fifth wall that effectively removes her from any culpability by claiming that this is all about the constitution of the United States. In this case, her hands are tied—she must move forward with impeachment because she is impelled to by this document to which she has taken an oath. Much in the same way that Trump uses his office to hide behind when inculpating military officers in his contraction of Covid-19, Pelosi too uses the fifth wall to deflect negativity, leaving her standing as a dutiful Speaker of the House. Not only is the impeachment unavoidable but, in her last sentences, Pelosi makes it the only moral choice. Aligning herself with Catholicism and prayer, she has rhetorically flipped the script handed to her by the reporter who asked the question. This is not to say she used lies. She may very well be Catholic, and she might pray for Donald Trump. But what she was being asked—if she hated him—was something that detrimentally affected her image and narrative and a simple "no," to her mind, would not have deflected the word "hate" away from her with enough force. Though Trump and Pelosi sit on opposite sides of the political aisle, their use of the fifth wall is quite similar.

Another fifth wall example—this time being used for redirection and distraction—was during the confirmation hearings for Brett Kavanaugh to the Supreme Court in September of 2018. Dr. Christine Blasey Ford's accusations of prior sexual assault caused not just the accused, Kavanaugh, to deflect but also many other Republicans who were in favor of his appointment. Instead of the focus remaining on the candidate being scrutinized, senators such as Lindsey Graham sidetracked the issues being raised, instead placing the focus on how "destructive" the questions were, as in this exchange in which Graham speaks mainly to the Democrats but the sentences in emphasis below indicate when he speaks directly to Kavanaugh:

> **Lindsey Graham:** If you wanted an F.B.I. investigation you could have come to us. What you want to do is destroy this guy's life, hold this seat open and hope you win in 2020. You said that, not me. *You've got nothing to apologize for. When you see Sotomayor and Kagan, tell them Lindsey says hello because I voted for them.* I would never do to them what you've done to this guy. This is the most unethical sham since I've been in politics. And if you really wanted to know the truth, you sure as hell wouldn't have done what you've done to this guy. *Are you a gang rapist?*
> **Judge Kavanaugh:** No.
> **Lindsey Graham:** I cannot imagine what you and your family have gone through. ("Lindsey Graham Erupts" 2018: 00:49–1:38, emphasis added)

Note how Graham uses pronouns and the vague label "this guy" to reference Judge Kavanaugh. Rhetorically, Graham creates distance between the accusations made and the judge by reimagining them applying to just "some guy," as opposed to Judge Brett Kavanaugh. Then, he reframes the entire discussion around making Judge Kavanaugh the victim in the situation, inflating the harm caused during the question-asking with the clever use of inflammatory, yet still vague, wording. Instead of claiming the *questions* are unethical or unfair, he refers to "what you've done to this guy," implying of course that deep, unspeakable harm has been perpetrated by the Democrats and that we should pity their target—Kavanaugh. Once Graham establishes whom he wishes to be the victim, he then exaggerates the impact by asking an over-the-top, rhetorical question, "Are you a gang rapist?" What this effectively does, as a fifth wall maneuver, is to blast all the questions back onto the questioners in a sarcastic but accusatory manner. Graham's maneuvering carries weight because such loaded language scares the accusers and backs them into a corner, effectively asking them: "Are you calling this man a gang rapist?" He finishes by underscoring his emphasis on Kavanaugh being the victim by bringing in more sympathetic bystanders, Kavanaugh's family. Regardless of what position you take on the hearings and the outcome, this is a perfect example of the fifth wall—using one's position in a performance to pander to a lie with all the appearance of being passionately truthful. In addition, Lindsey Graham manages an incredible feat by juggling—quite deftly—at least three separate audiences with his wall. Though he presumably is speaking directly to Kavanaugh and his family, that is merely a pretense and a part of the fifth wall manipulation. The audiences for whom he truly performs are the Democrats he attacks, the Republicans he seeks to stoke, and the television audience he wishes to sway. His goal is to discredit the Democrats by labeling their questioning "shameful," and thus make the Republicans "the honest and fair ones." But he does so in the guise of standing up for a man he paints as upright (though, to be fair, the only direct answer he receives in this exchange is that Kavanaugh is not a self-proclaimed gang rapist—a pretty low bar).

Two more prime examples of using the fifth wall for distraction include remarks made by Sean Spicer and Donald Trump about events in 2017. In April of 2017, Sean Spicer, then White House press secretary, infamously made the statement that Syria's leader, President Bashar al-Assad, was worse than Hitler, who he erroneously claimed had not "stooped to use chemical weapons" ("Spicer Says" 2017). This moment has been balked at since it happened for its inaccuracy. Adolf Hitler is notorious for using chemical weapons on millions of people. It also positioned al-Assad as a good person, since a good person would not "stoop" to do anything. But viewed as a tactic instead of a gaffe, we can see there was utility in Spicer's distraction. He distracts his questioners with an incorrect reflection of the situation. In the end, the critique of his mistake ended up taking precedence in the narrative constructed about the connection between the United States and Syria, instead of al-Assad's crimes and the consequences thereof. Sean Spicer had already established himself as a distracter earlier in 2017 by warping many other stories and events, including incorrectly characterizing the Women's March. He referenced the event in his regular press conference covering the top events of the day in the United States by bringing up "the protestors" only once in his lengthy speech about "coverage of the last twenty-four hours." The focus then shifted away from the march itself (decidedly the most consequential event on that day, being recorded as the largest single-day protest in US history) by making it an inferior piece of news in the scope of those twenty-four hours and then by refusing to answer follow-up questions about the march. Roychoudhuri describes her own reaction to Spicer's misrepresentation:

> The narrative of the day, despite the largest protest ever seen in a single day in the United States, was the debate over the size of the crowd who had watched Donald Trump's presidential inauguration. I watched slack-jawed from my friend's couch as Spicer wrapped his bizarre speech, and members of the press lobbed questions at his back as he swiftly exited the briefing. In that moment, I realized we were up against something formidable: where we turn our attention constructs the fabric of our reality. (2018: 6)

Roychoudhuri's realization is why the fifth wall works. In essence, it does not matter what is happening if no one is looking. And if people are busy contemplating one person's mistakes, they can miss a lot.

Months after his inauguration, in August of 2017, Trump would find himself at the pointed end of questions surrounding his defense of people at a Nazi rally in Charlottesville, Virginia, and his own response mirrored the one Spicer gave concerning al-Assad. At a press conference after the Charlottesville incident, a reporter stated to the president, "You're putting what you're calling the alt-left and white supremacists on the same moral plane"; Trump responded with his now infamous view that both sides in the riot were to blame and that the rioting white supremacists "had some very bad people in that group, but you also had people that were very fine people, on both sides" ("President Donald Trump" 2017: 00:00–00:04, 01:01–01:09). Using ambiguous phrases such as "some people," "that group," and "both sides" dissociates whom Trump is talking about from the actual riot and the specific, white supremacist groups involved. After all, "people" can be described as fine, while you would be hard-pressed to do the same with white supremacists. When confronted about his statement in the days following the press conference, he was asked to publicly condemn white supremacists, to which he claimed he had already done so in the past. By shifting the blame onto the reporters not accurately reporting his words, Trump made the issue *about* his words, rather than having the focus be on the Nazi rioters themselves and the threat they posed. In this situation, Trump behaved like other high-profile individuals who lie and deflect the truth, even though it may seem like the wrong choice for a leader to make. As Ralph Keyes asserts, "doing something that could get them in trouble meant they were no longer passive life livers. They'd taken charge. The same thing is true of liars. Lying can convey a sense of mastery" (Keyes 2004: 92). While it seemed plain that Trump's choice to defend the Nazis was not only unethical, but hurtful to his own image, Keyes's perspective would understand the situation differently—that enacting the breadth of his power being president (through saying what he wanted instead of what should have been said) granted more control to Trump than the immorality of his words took away.

Erving Goffman, in his look at cynicism within the performer, explains that those who put on a part, as all on the public stage must, "may be moved to guide the conviction of his audience only as a means to other ends, having no ultimate concern in the conception that they have of him or the situation" (2016: 61–2). In other words, while all performers intend to convince the audience of something—and to emphasize that the something is true—there are those who do not care what their spectators end up believing but have "other ends" they wish to pursue. Those ends include, but are not limited to, usurping control over a narrative by *redirecting* time and energy away from people investigating their flaws, *aiming at targets* outside of the point of focus, and *distracting* detractors with lies and disinformation.

The fifth wall, as a mode of performance-deception used by politicians and other public figures, evolved out of theatrical practices. The same type of deception is used fictionally on our stages and screens, but it also establishes a new horizon for where theatrical walls could be built or torn down. At this point, it is difficult to be prescriptive, but as we have seen in staged performances throughout history— most recently the 2016 performance of *Hamilton* that Vice President

Pence attended and was publicly addressed by the cast and booed by the audience—theatrical performance has been and will continue to be a practice that can easily become politicized and used to make statements. Whether those statements will affect the political process as much as performance tactics have remains to be seen.

As the examples I have used here show, many of our public figures, particularly in politics, push truth away when it does not serve the narrative they wish to display. If we allow this to continue, we run the risk of our institutions no longer serving us. In other words, "if we're led to believe that the political realm isn't a legitimate place where we can seek relief and remedy for these concerns, politics remains an abstract game—one in which we understand our primary roles to be spectators placing their bets on the outcome rather than actors who have the power to directly impact that outcome" (Roychoudhuri 2018: 42). While it may take more effort to fact-check, hold public figures accountable for their words and actions, and call them out for their fifth wall manipulation, we must stay on stage if we wish to have a say in how our play ends.

Note

1 While direct address existed prior to the nineteenth century (as with Shakespearean soliloquies), the convention of direct address took on different meaning after the fourth wall had become the established custom of theater audiences.

References

Bateson, G. (2016), "A Theory of Play and Fantasy," in H. Bial and S. Brady (eds.), *The Performance Studies Reader*, 159–69, New York: Routledge.

Brotherton, R. (2020), *Bad News: Why We Fall for Fake News*, London: Bloomsbury.

Brown, T. (2012), *Breaking the Fourth Wall: Direct Address in the Cinema*, Edinburgh: Edinburgh University Press.

Carlson, M. (2016), "What Is Performance?," in H. Bial and S. Brady (eds.), *The Performance Studies Reader*, 71–6, New York: Routledge.

Fox, M., J. Gumbrecht, and J. Christensen (2020), "President Donald Trump Has Covid-19: How Serious Is His Risk?," *CNN Health*, October 2. Available online: https://www.cnn.com/2020/10/02/health/trump-melania-coronavirus-risk-factors-bn/index.html (accessed December 10, 2020).

Goffman, E. (2016), "Performances: Belief in the Part One Is Playing," in H. Bial and S. Brady (eds.), *The Performance Studies Reader*, 61–5, New York: Routledge.

Kershaw, B. (1992), *The Politics of Performance: Radical Theatre as Cultural Intervention*, New York: Routledge.

Keyes, R. (2004), *The Post-Truth Era: Dishonesty and Deception in Contemporary Life*, New York: St. Martin's Press.

"Lindsey Graham Erupts: Kavanaugh Hearing an Unethical Sham" (2018) [TV program], CNN on YouTube, September 27. Available online: https://www.youtube.com/watch?v=RTBxPPx62s4 (accessed October 14, 2020).

Moyers, B. (2020), "Heather Cox Richardson and Her Daily Letters," *Moyers on Democracy Podcast*, July 29. Available online: https://billmoyers.com/story/bill-moyers-and-heather-cox-richards-on-her-daily-letters/ (accessed October 14, 2020).

"Nancy Pelosi Tells Reporter Who Asks If She Hates Trump: 'Don't Mess with Me'" (2019) [TV program], CBS News on YouTube, December 5. Available online: https://www.youtube.com/watch?v=hh5Tobcv51M (accessed October 16, 2020).

"President Donald Trump on Charlottesville: You Had Very Fine People, on Both Sides" (2017) [TV program], CNBC on YouTube, August 15. Available online: https://www.youtube.com/watch?v=JmaZR8E12bs (accessed March 15, 2021).

Rabin-Havt, A., and Media Matters for America (2016), *Lies, Incorporated: The World of Post-Truth Politics*, New York: Anchor Books.

Roychoudhuri, O. (2018), *The Marginalized Majority: Claiming Our Power in a Post-Truth America*, Brooklyn, NY: Melville House.

"Spicer Says Hitler Didn't Use Chemical Weapons" (2017) [TV program], CBS News on YouTube, April 11. Available online: https://www.cbsnews.com/news/spicer-says-hitler-didnt-use-chemical-weapons/ (accessed October 16, 2020).

5

When the Play Is Not the Thing: The Mueller Report and the Limits of Documentary Drama

Victoria Scrimer

Long before the recent rise of post-truth politics, theater artists, theorists, and audiences have been variously probing, worrying over, and making claims about the nature of truth, where it can be found, and how it can be made known. From Hamlet's *Mousetrap* to realism's minutely detailed box sets to the unscripted provocations of avant-garde experiments, theater in all its unreality has often promised to show us a transcendent glimpse of truth. In particular, documentary drama—also sometimes called "theater of fact" or "theater of witness"—has, since the agitprop "Living Newspapers" of the Soviet Blue Blouses, laid unique claim to a particular kind of activist truth-telling that takes its aesthetic cues from news media. The form was refined and popularized by Erwin Piscator in the 1920s as a way to "speak the truth" (Innes 1972: 62) and show audiences an "absolute [political] reality" (Piscator [1963] 1978: 96). By the 1930s, documentary drama was exerting artistic and political influence in the United States as a centerpiece of the Federal Theatre Project. But as Stephen Bottoms (2006) observed, Americans' "profound distrust of the news media in general" seems to have tempered a sincere revival of this type of documentary theater in the twenty-first century (57). Considering Americans' distrust of media has only increased along party lines over the last several years,[1] it should follow that a form of theater which trades in "truth" and "witness" would find little purchase in a political landscape many have labeled "post-truth."

Yet, the sheer volume of staged readings that emerged from Robert Mueller's 2019 "Report on the Investigation into Russian Interference in the 2016 Presidential Election" tells a different story. Despite its intimidating length and what many have characterized as a total lack of narrative, there is something about the Mueller report that begs to be performed. Prior to Mueller's own July 2019 testimony in front of Congress, dozens of Democratic lawmakers gathered on May 16, 2019, in the House Rules Committee room to conduct a marathon live reading of the report. On June 24, Law Works produced a one-night performance of Pulitzer Prize-winning playwright Robert Schenkkan's (2019) adaptation of the Mueller report, starring A-list celebrities including Annette Bening, John Lithgow, and Kevin Kline. This was followed in early July by live readings hosted by activists and theater makers in New York, Seattle, Cleveland, West Hollywood, and Washington, DC, among many other towns and cities. The popularity of these performances suggests many Americans are as desperate for dramatic theater's assurances of "truth" and resolution as we are suspicious of drama's incursion into the real.

As a piece of judicial rhetoric, the Mueller report seemed to promise a conclusive legal accusation or defense of Donald Trump's behavior as it pertained to Russian election interference. According to the report, pursuant to 28 C.F.R § 600.8 (c), upon the conclusion of his investigation, Mueller was *expected* to provide the attorney general with "a confidential report explaining the prosecution or declination decisions reached" by the special counsel (Mueller 2019: 8). The report, however, failed to deliver any legal conclusions, citing Department of Justice guidelines regarding the criminal prosecution of a sitting president (Mueller 2019: 202–4). Rather, Mueller begins section II of the report with a tormenting nonconclusion, stating "while this report does not conclude that the president committed a crime, it also does not exonerate him" (2019: 205). The many subsequent stagings of Mueller's text, including Mueller's own testimony, are an attempt to use dramatic theater to wring a conclusive truth from a fallible text.

Looking specifically at Schenkkan's stage adaptation of Mueller's report alongside his testimony a month later, we can see how these performances draw from documentary theater's discourse of political activism and are presented as an act of civic duty intended to inform citizens and enact democracy, but these performances also demonstrate that using drama to carve out a satisfying narrative truth can become an end in itself, offering audiences surrogate emotional satisfactions. In *The Empty Space*, Peter Brook (1968) warned of a type of deadly theater that we are convinced is good for us—"important" and "worthwhile" for reasons that privately elude us. The deadly theatergoer "in his heart sincerely wants a theater that is nobler-than-life and he confuses a sort of intellectual satisfaction with the true experience for which he craves" (9). Similarly, political scientist Eitan Hersh has written about the recent rise of political hobbyism, "a catchall phrase for consuming and participating in politics by obsessive news-following and online 'slacktivism,' by feeling the need to offer a hot take for each daily political flare-up, by emoting and arguing and debating" in a way that is not intended to influence our communities or our country but to "satisfy our own emotional needs and intellectual curiosities" (2020: 3–4). Most political hobbyists believe their voracious appetite for national political news is a matter of "staying informed" and they mischaracterize their behavior as dutiful participation in civic life (2020: 6–7). As Hersh argues, hobbyism distracts well-meaning citizens from the difficult, long-term, and comparatively boring work of politics that necessitates changing hearts and minds across party lines. Political hobbyism highlights large ideological issues on a national stage, allowing many citizens to regard them (as they would in a conventional theater) at a safe remove. Like political hobbyism, deadly theater does not challenge us; it lacks the "vitality of new invention" and relies instead on that which is predictably satisfying, self-evident, or even boring (Brook 1968: 16). There are echoes of Brook's deadly theater and Hersh's political hobbyism in live readings of the Mueller report insofar as they draw spectators into self-affirming communities of shared outrage that perpetuate rather than challenge existing social and political norms.

First, consider how Mueller's report and testimony limn the sociopolitical anxieties over the truth-value of theater. On July 24, 2019, special counsel, Robert Mueller—gaunt, grim, and impossibly stoic—stood before the House Judiciary and Intelligence Committees to answer questions about his 448-page report on Russian interference in the 2016 election. Four months earlier, on March 29, 2019, Mueller had submitted the text of his report to Attorney General William Barr, retired as special counsel, and officially closed the investigative office. Mueller's testimony before Congress was supposed to fill in the narrative gaps and finally put a cap on the public uncertainty surrounding his inconclusive report. In his opening gambit to the House Intelligence hearing, however, the Republican representative from California and chair of the House Intelligence Committee, Devin Nunes, opined, "Today's hearing is not about getting information at all." Rather, Nunes claimed, it was a desperate attempt by Democrats to "bring the Mueller investigation to life and create a 'television moment' through ploys like having Mr. Mueller recite passages from his own report" ("Robert Mueller Testifies" 2019: 13:50). "In other words," Nunes spat, "this hearing is political theater" ("Robert Mueller Testifies" 2019: 13:58). Indeed, it is hard to dispute Nunes's point. Just days before, Democratic representative from California and ranking member of the House Intelligence Committee, Adam Schiff, did, in fact, tell CBS's *Face the Nation* that he suspected most Americans had not read the report. Schiff described the report as "a pretty dry, prosecutorial work product" and unabashedly announced, "We want Bob Mueller to bring it to life" ("Interview" 2019: 3:03).

In the standoff between Nunes and Schiff it is easy to see the perennial debate over the uses and abuses of theater. Nunes holds down the age-old opinion of all anti-theatrical dogmatists since Plato: theater is manipulative, dangerous because it appeals to the peoples' base emotions. Theater is code for "false" and anything that has the look of theatricality is not to be trusted. Schiff, on the other hand, expresses the sometimes naive optimism to which all theater lovers and theater artists are prone—a vision of theater as alchemy, a magical combination of liveness and presence that can transform a broom handle into a sword, a 448-page redacted legal document into a smoking gun. More specifically, Schiff, the other Democrats in Congress, and the approximately thirteen million American viewers who tuned into the two-and-a-half hour hearing were, in many respects, following in a long tradition of documentary theater as political activism, hoping, and believing, that the simple act of having someone embody and represent a text on a public stage might reveal truths that were otherwise obscured.

We now know, of course, as a piece of theater—political or otherwise—Robert Mueller's testimony was destined to be a flop. *The New York Times* hailed Mueller's performance as "The Blockbuster That Wasn't" (Baker 2019). Far from breathing life into the text, Mueller's testimony was as insistently dry as the pages of his report. Not only was his performance distinctly *unlively* but, as one *Politico* staff reporter stated, the public learned "very, very little [new information]. Mueller refused to answer dozens—if not hundreds—of questions" ("Here's What Surprised" 2019). Amidst his numerous nonresponses and deflections, the gray-faced lawyer refused to depart from the text of his own report, repeating his statement from May 29, 2019, that "the report is my testimony, and I will stay within that text" ("Robert Mueller Testifies" 2019: 19:30). Even before his testimony, it seemed inevitable that Mueller's insistent commitment to the text was bound to disappoint an attentive public that had, since the report's release, been staging attempts to rescue Mueller's report from the page.

The most technically dramatic of these rescue missions took place one month before Mueller made his appearance before lawmakers, when a live audience assembled in the nave of New York City's historic Riverside Church and thousands logged onto their computers to watch Law Work's live performance of Robert Schenkkan's *The Investigation: A Search for Truth in Ten Acts*. As its lofty venue and title suggest, Schenkkan's play takes full advantage of documentary theater's discourse of truth and revelation to build a sense of urgent, "real world," public responsibility, seeming to implicate the audience in the titular search for truth. There is, however, an interesting mechanism at work in this piece by which the search for truth and the search for dramatic satisfaction become confused. Given Schenkkan's well-known political perspective, the progressive history of the Riverside Church, and the left-leaning politics of New York City theatergoers in general, it is difficult to imagine that any audience member attending this production did not already have a firm grasp on their own opinion of Trump's guilt or innocence. In this sense, the play's "search" for truth is disingenuous and consequently disengaging.

More accurately, *The Investigation* could be characterized as a search for the narrative satisfaction we are denied in the Mueller report. Spurred, as it was, by the Mueller report's failure to conclusively accuse Trump of a crime, *The Investigation* is designed to reaffirm a shared recognition of Trump's apparent guilt among audience members whose attendance at the performance marks their tacit agreement on the matter. *The Investigation* effectively uses documentary theater's long-standing aesthetic strategies to simulate political engagement while providing the closure and catharsis missing from the Mueller saga. Indeed, if we look at the production's creative choices along with Schenkkan's decisions in editing the performance text we see clear efforts to satisfy dramatic convention in ways that make the performance easily surveyable and more conclusive than the text of Mueller's sprawling report and subsequently more popularly entertaining. Rather than question the authority of Mueller's text, the production seeks to amend it, ultimately reifying its authority. While this social imaginary may make for a satisfying ritual, it makes for deadly theater and even deadlier activism.

The immediacy with which Schenkkan was able to bring the Mueller report to the stage imbues the endeavor with an import and authenticity upon which documentary theater often capitalizes. Impressively, *The Investigation* went from conception to production in just under four weeks (Sherman 2019). The production's expediency says, "You know this is true because you see we've no time for sets and illusion." This production shows that the truth-value of dramatic representation can be derived not only from its relationship to official documents but also from its chronological proximity to the original event. The aesthetic simplicity and directness of documentary theater that emerged out of necessity among the Blue Blouses also serve the rhetorical purpose of assuring audiences of the production's commitment to transparency. Like much documentary theater, *The Investigation* capitalizes on the public's double-edged interest in and suspicion of theatrical spectacle. Implicitly denying the antecedent, it reasons, "If theatricality is false, then the rejection of theatricality is a marker of truth."

The performance keeps theatricality at arm's length from the outset by self-aligning with journalism. For example, well-known journalist and political commentator, Bill Moyers, introduces the play. Invoking Jürgen Habermas's notion of the public sphere, Moyers directly addresses the audience as "serious citizens" and characterizes their participation in the proceedings as an "enriching communion," suggesting that they are "searching for truth" through discourse and discussion (though, Habermas's model arcs toward consensus rather than "truth" per se) (Schenkkan 2019: 4:10). Moyers refers to the stage as the "public green," where we can observe and participate in the "continuing drama of democracy" (Schenkkan 2019: 4:14). Yet, Habermas's notion of the public sphere has been widely critiqued for supposing a particular (masculinist) style of rational argumentation,[2] and the public sphere has been radically altered by new media in ways that do not necessarily foster deeper political engagement. Moyer's introduction to *The Investigation* serves as a perfect example of the way documentary theater and its alliance with news media feeds into the misleading discourse of civic duty characteristic of political hobbyism.

Despite the show's own emphasis on seriousness and civic duty, *The Investigation* is not entirely without spectacle. Framed by the church's soaring neo-Gothic windows, the show's eighteen actors appear on the altar behind simple individual podiums draped with American flag bunting. Taken together, the entire scene is authoritative but without frills, walking the aesthetic line between grand religious rite and community theater—borrowing on the promises of truth and authenticity associated with both modes. The church setting itself invokes a sense of holy truth that, like the patriotic bunting, preemptively wraps the contents of the performance in the suggestion of unassailable moral and traditional ideals. The pared-down set, consisting of simple podiums, notebooks, and a single projection screen borrows from historical examples of documentary theater and is suggestive of transparency and urgency—everything is visible; we have no time for a theater of illusion here.

The performance, however, is overdetermined by its historic venue and celebrity cast. To borrow a concept from Marvin Carlson (2003), the stage is "haunted" by the historic church's well-known history as a staging ground for social justice activism. The Riverside Church is not only comfortably familiar as one of the most recognizable religious structures in New York City but it has also long served as a site of progressive organizing. Since its founding in the 1920s, the church has maintained a sometimes radical commitment to nondenominational, interracial, and international worship and has continued to facilitate a number of progressive ministries, hosting LGBTQ activists, environmentalists, and racial justice activists. To wit, the Riverside Church is a public symbol of the many progressive values the Trump administration has seemingly worked tirelessly to undermine. The play's recognizable cast, featuring several outspoken Trump critics, are haunted in much the same way, lending the general sense of trustworthiness that celebrity endorsements seem to engender but also giving a much more specific tone and tenor of political activism to the performance. In this sense, the performance space and the cast both appeal to audience members who already feel the report's findings are a foregone conclusion, but they do little to draw in audience members who might genuinely be newly informed or persuaded by the proceedings.

I must also mention that *The Investigation* is haunted by its titular twin, Peter Weiss's 1965 documentary theater piece, *The Investigation: Oratorio in 11 Cantos*, which is a restaging of the Frankfurt Auschwitz trials. An observer at the trial, Weiss drew the text of his minimalist script largely from the German journalist Bernd Naumann's notes and his own observations on the trial (Cohen 1993: 84). The trial took place nearly twenty years after the Soviets liberated Auschwitz; so

Weiss's recreation of the trial, like Schenkkan's play, looks for truth not necessarily in the original historical events, but in the documentation of their legal aftermath. In its use of verbatim facts and documents to disrupt traditional modes of realistic dramatic representation, Weiss's *Investigation* "is a descendant of the revolutionary Proletcult and Agitprop movements of the Soviet Union of the 1920s and their Weimar versions propagated by Erwin Piscator, among others" (Cohen 1998: 51). There are a number of significant differences between Weiss's play and Schenkkan's that are worth exploring, but by referencing Weiss's play in his title, Schenkkan positions his own play in a powerful lineage of politically charged documentary theater.

In invoking Weiss's piece, Schenkkan's title also draws an implicit (and controversial) comparison between Trump's crimes and the crimes of Nazi war criminals. On one hand, this lends Schenkkan's performance some serious political import. On the other hand, it too easily capitalizes on the outrage fueling the popular and polarizing meme equating Trump and his fascistic tendencies to Hitler. Beyond the argument that comparing Trump's presidency to the genocide of six million people is irresponsibly reductive, this *reductio ad Hitlerum* functions rhetorically as a broadly construed ad hominem attack that effectively ends all discussion by equating any counter-discourse to Nazism.[3] This framing undermines Moyer's vision for the performance as a utopic dialectic on the public green and suggests, rather, that the appeal of these readings is to bring like-minded people together in mutual outrage.

Shared outrage, of course, is not always a negative thing. As Hersh notes, outrage can be "a way to energize yourself and others to translate values into concrete actions" but "the problem arises when emotion and anger are the end rather than the means to the end" and outrage becomes "a shortcut to feeling engaged" (2020: 126). This is all to say that the set, cast, location, and title of *The Investigation* attracts a like-minded audience and prepares them for a specific type of performance whose trajectory is predictable. Far from a revelation, the performance is an invitation to affirm that which the audience already knows. This predictability is heightened and extended by the dramatic structure Schenkkan carves out of Mueller's text.

In an effort to appeal to theatergoers who, by and large, are conditioned to expect a comprehensible story, coherent meaning, and resolution and catharsis Schenkkan distills Mueller's sprawling documentation into a performance text of roughly one hour and ten minutes. Significantly, Schenkkan does this by dispensing entirely with volume I of Mueller's report and jettisoning Mueller's legal analysis. Following Horace's age-old dramatic advice, Schenkkan passes by untold what will not turn to gold and hurries us to the action. He begins his play not *ab ovo* with Russian interference, but *in medias res*. This has the effect of reducing the text down to a length more familiar and palatable to the average American audience and it moves instances of direct dialogue to the forefront, making for a performance that feels much more like a conventional play than a public reading of a legal document. Importantly, it also narrows the focus onto one clearly delineated story line—Trump's obstruction of justice.

In terms of dramatic structure, Schenkkan's choice is imminently logical. Conflict is an enormously influential structuring element of Western dramatic theater. It is the mechanism by which dramatic theater makes visible important non-concrete themes, allowing dramatists to actualize ideas on stage. Volume I of the report, which deals with Russian interference in the 2016 election, contains no such conflict. It begins with Mueller's unambiguous bombshell that the "Russian Government interfered in the 2016 presidential election in sweeping and systemic fashion" (Mueller 2019: 8). One of several active measures taken by Russia that is revealed in Mueller's report is the social media campaign enacted by the Internet Research Agency, LLC (IRA), a Russian organization, that "conducted social media operations targeted at large U.S. audiences with the goal of sowing discord in the U.S. political system" (213). Using social media like Facebook, YouTube, and Twitter, the IRA was able to reach hundreds of thousands if not millions of unwitting Americans, capitalizing on our political hobbyism and attraction to dramatic conflict. For years the IRA posed on social media as activist groups from both sides of the aisle to manufacture a greater sense of partisan animosity. Recognizing and acting against this finding is quite frankly a *big deal* in terms of our civic duty but Mueller's finding is also, by and large, uncontested. The revelation of Russian efforts to undermine the US democratic system by sowing seeds of discord is ironically perhaps one of the very few issues that should stand to unify Americans rather than set us against each other in antagonistic conflict, but for this very reason it lacks an appealing dramaturgy.

Trump's behavior during the investigation and Mueller's failure to officially condemn it, however, contains an unresolved partisan conflict with which Schenkkan's audience already holds a well-established stake. Schenkkan's choice to focus his performance text only on volume II casts the audience as knowing, informed, responsible, citizen-activists empowered to intervene in an unfolding drama. Dramatically speaking, this is a much more interesting (and flattering) role than that which the audience would have to play if Schenkkan staged volume I in which the left and right are united as dupes, the unwitting pawns in a game of international politics. The irony, of course, is that at the same time it avoids directly addressing it, Schenkkan's play capitalizes on the same strategy Russia used, relying on our predictable interest in and tendency toward partisan conflict to fuel *The Investigation*'s emotional engine.

In this respect, *The Investigation* expertly fosters the affective recognition and solidarity among audience members that is paradigmatic of dramatic theater. This is what makes the play interesting and enjoyable. Much of the play is performed with a wink and a nod in humorous recognition of the absurd obviousness of Trump's villainy juxtaposed against Mueller's understated reportage. For instance, early in the show, John Lithgow, as Trump, erupts onto the stage shouting, "What the HELL is this all about?!" swiftly following Kevin Kline's raised eyebrow and deadpan delivery of Mueller's no-nonsense narration, "The President expressed anger" (Schenkkan 2019: 7:17). This comic dynamic, in which an unwitting and characteristically bombastic Trump blunders away to the chagrin of those around him, repeatedly earns laughs throughout the show. For instance, in one of the biggest laughs of the show, Alfre Woodard as Hope Hicks describes her reaction to Trump's infamous unscheduled interview with *The New York Times* in which Trump criticized Jeff Sessions's recusal. She recounts trying to stop the train wreck, but states, "[Trump] loved the interview" (Schenkkan 2019: 32:24). This pattern suggests the play is a farce rather than a tragedy and that the show's cathartic qualities emerge from the audience's shared laughter.

In this staging, Mueller comes across as significantly more likeable and trustworthy than he does in real life precisely because Kline's performance gives the audience the extratextual confirmation that we long for—Kline is our dream-Mueller, our coconspirator. In fact, all the performers' dry deliveries and frequent deadpan asides draw the audience into a reassuring world in which everyone involved in the political drama recognizes the president's corrupt buffoonery. The fantasy that this performance perpetuates is that Mueller is on the audience's side, that we are allies in his investigation despite all evidence to the contrary. What we do know about the inscrutable special counsel is that, in writing his report, Mueller went out of his way to avoid conclusively condemning Trump on paper, going to almost comic lengths to sidestep the special counsel's responsibility to offer a decisive resolution on the "difficult issues" of law and fact (2019: 213). Whatever motivations we assign to Mueller's inconclusivity, it seems reasonable to assume that this document, despite all the aesthetic bells and whistles announcing its authority, is not the most likely place to go mining for conclusive legal evidence of Trump's guilt.

Despite this, Schenkkan borrows the structure for his play from Mueller's text. The "ten acts" referenced in the play's title is a dramatic pun on the ten potential acts of obstruction Mueller lays out in volume II of his report. This setup figures each of the president's potentially obstructive actions as a play act, contributing to the conflation between news and entertainment, blurring the lines as to whether the search for truth occurs in Trump's real-world actions or in the acts of the play.

Even while borrowing Mueller's structure, though, the production must work to instill the sense of conclusion missing from the text of Mueller's report. For instance, in the text of the report, Mueller states that the investigation "focused on" or "examined" a "series of actions" that are organized into ten "key issues or events" (2019: 206). Schenkkan alters the semantics of this framework at the beginning of the play by having Annette Bening as narrator definitively state that the investigation "found ten, *TEN* (emphasized) possible acts of obstruction of justice" while the text of the overhead projection eliminates the "possible" altogether, simply showing "TEN ACTS OF OBSTRUCTION OF JUSTICE" (Schenkkan 2019: 6:26). Changes like these seem slight but they are significant because they foster the illusion that Mueller's report is more conclusive than it is. Rather than question the report itself or the judicial apparatus that empowers such a report, this performance clings to it as the sole vestige of truth. To "search" for truth in a dramatic reading of the Mueller report is to assume that the report contains some fundamental kernel of truth to begin with.

In the end, *The Investigation* doubts its own ability to deliver a satisfying sense of truth from the text of the report alone, falling back on a heavy-handed stab at resolution. In the last minutes of the performance, Bening walks the audience through the nonconclusion of the Mueller report stating that the special counsel "did *not* have confidence that [Trump] was innocent" (Schenkkan 2019: 1:12:50). Lithgow then breaks character, stands, and reads, speaking presumably for the audience, "But if they thought he was guilty and had committed any one or all ten acts of obstruction, why didn't they charge him?" (Schenkkan 2019: 1:12:59). Citing Mueller's own excuse, that a sitting president cannot be tried for a crime, Bening pedantically and all-too sympathetically informs the audience, "If he wanted to charge the president, he couldn't. Mueller's hands were tied by regulation" (Schenkkan 2019: 1:13:54). Bening then directs us to article II section IV of the US Constitution, which outlines the procedures for impeachment. After a brief history of impeachment proceedings in the United States, she concludes with a vague but strident call to action: "Our forefathers fought a bloody war against a tyrannical king. When they framed the Constitution, they did so fully aware of the potential dangers of a powerful executive ... Robert Mueller did his job. The question is, will we do ours?" (Schenkkan 2019: 1:17:00). Presumably intended to inspire, this final salvo leaves me wondering who the "we" is that Bening addresses and what our "job" or duty is considering that Trump's impeachment would be a federal-level procedure ultimately decided by a Republican-led Senate.

The distillation and animation of Mueller's lengthy text does not magically reveal otherwise-obscured facts originally contained in the text but, as one might imagine, Schenkkan's editing *does* go a long way toward making the Mueller report easily surveyable, more present, more conventionally interesting. This is, at least part of, the job of the documentary theater maker. Like all art, documentary theater seeks to heighten the sensation or enliven the thrum of the everyday so we might better see things for what they are—to quote Viktor Shklovsky "to make the stone stony"—or perhaps to make the truth truer. In this way we mistake entertainment for truth. The strategies dramatists have for drawing our interest (conflict, action, linearity) heighten our emotions to sometimes distracting, impotent, or even destructive ends—in the case of readings of the Mueller report, they do so at the risk of contributing to the ever-deepening sense of animosity we foster for that other half of the population we believe to be our political enemies. This sense of anger and animosity is evoked especially when we feel the events in question are contemporary and close to our lived experience, as in the case of documentary theater.

The Investigation strikes me as a dangerous form of political hobbyism and a piece of deadly theater because it does not, as Brook says, instruct or educate, illuminate, or elevate but cheapens its important subject matter in predictable ways. At the end of the day, *The Investigation* is not intended to help anyone rethink or remediate those fissures in our democracy created, in part, by the very Russian strategies of polarization the play casually edits away. It appeals, rather, to the left's sense of outrage, easily invoking our favorite villain *du jour* and allowing the audience to comfortably maintain its self-conception as dutifully informed citizens whose truths are self-evident. Perhaps worst of all, the play provides us with the placating illusion that we are supported by and effectively participating in the very government apparatus we most desperately need to be questioning.

Eager to bring Trump's misdeeds to light, many on the left seemed to forget that Robert Mueller is the grim face of the political establishment interested primarily in maintaining the status quo. Mueller's somnolent performance incited widespread confusion and dissatisfaction among viewers across party lines. In general, audience members disagreed on how to interpret Mueller's behavior. Critics, of course, saw his failed performance as evidence of the illegitimacy of the investigation and a vindication of Trump's innocence, supporters saw it as Mueller's attempt to rise above the political fray, and friends and former colleagues suspected that health issues, old age, or a decline in mental acuity were to blame. For instance, tweeting during the testimony, David Axelrod the former top Obama White House strategist while Mueller was FBI director, wrote, "This is delicate to say, but Mueller, whom I deeply respect, has not publicly testified before Congress in at least six years. And he does not appear as sharp as he was then" (2019). Former federal prosecutor, Glen Kirschner, echoed this sentiment on Twitter, suggesting that "Bob Mueller is struggling. It strikes me as a health issue. We need only look at his earlier congressional appearances to see the dramatic difference in his demeanor and communicative abilities" (2019).

Mueller's failure to perform as expected extended beyond behavioral into narrative dimensions. Immediately following the testimony, CNBC criticized Mueller as "no storyteller" and reported that his "uncharismatic, sometimes halting stage presence ... left even some of his supporters wanting" (Breuninger 2019). For instance, on NBC's *Meet the Press*, Schiff admitted he wished Mueller had testified in a "more narrative fashion" (Schiff 2019). In other words, what the audience wanted was a clear story that fulfilled conventional narrative expectations acted out by a vigorous and confident man of authority.

It is telling that, as a public, we are so socially conditioned to expect such a performance that a failure to perform in this way can only be explained by physical or mental illness. Mueller's performance may have failed to reveal extratextual information about the investigation, but the public disappointment that attended his performance reveals a great deal about the extent to which the American public relies on dramaturgical structures to understand and cope with our current political moment.

Ostensibly, the public hoped, in reading between the lines of Mueller's performance, they could learn more about the Russia investigation and Trump's alleged obstruction of justice but, of course, all that lies behind Mueller's performance is information about Robert Mueller himself. Despite his protestations, Mueller *did* perform. The scriptocentrism that Mueller modeled and his stalwart refusal to appear theatrical in any way is its own kind of performance shaped by what we could easily call the Western patriarchal aesthetics of truth. Mueller's self-conscious and performative adherence to the script of his own report follows what Dwight Conquergood (2013) identifies as a long-standing habit of white Western colonialism in which only that which is in the written record has authority and those who control the archive of documents determine what constitutes truth. Completely in keeping with Mueller's history as an old-school-establishment civil servant, Ivy league–educated Marine, and registered Republican who spent twelve years of his career as director of the FBI, Mueller's no-nonsense stoicism is carefully cultivated to communicate not only impartiality but also absolute detachment. His performance plays into sexist, racist, and classist aesthetics of truth as unemotional, official, restrained, and not coincidentally performed by a man. Given the friction between these values and progressive political ideals, it is a wonder to me so many well-meaning people on the left would turn to Mueller *or* his report in the hope that either would willingly undermine the very establishment that empowers them.

To echo Adam Schiff's ambition for Mueller's testimony, documentary theater aims to bring documents to life. But, like

Frankenstein's monster, it is perhaps worth asking what energy animates this particular transformation. What do we bring to life when we give body to Mueller's text? As an audience member at more than one reading of the Mueller report, these performances engender outrage, frustration, and, if we are lucky, a vague sense of self-satisfaction for having done *something*. To expect theater to magically transform the Mueller report from an ambivalent document to a smoking gun is to willfully ignore, at our peril, the intransigence of a text like the Mueller report and the shortcomings of the system that produced it. As Mueller warned us, the report speaks for itself. We want many things from the Mueller report that it is not willing to give us, that it does not contain (linear narrative, clear conclusions, resolution), and our various attempts to evoke these things on stage, whether through drama or ritual, inevitably ring false both artistically and politically. Many a director will tell you sometimes there are readings that a text will not support. Perhaps these examples can inform the future of documentary drama more broadly. Live readings of the Mueller report spend all their energy trying to transform a document, rather than trying to transform their audience. The fact that nothing is transformed by these performances should serve as a litmus test that, in our search for truth, we are either looking for the wrong things or looking in the wrong place.

Notes

1 Gallup's annual Governance Poll for 2020 showed the percentage of Americans who had no trust at all in mainstream media was up five percentage points since 2019 at 33 percent. The poll also revealed that there was a record-setting disparity between Democrats' and Republicans' trust in news media (Brenan 2020).
2 See McKee (2004) for a general overview of this critique or van Zoonen (2005) for a feminist critique of Habermas.
3 See Godwin (1994) for the influential description of this "rhetorical hammer" that has come to be known as Godwin's Law.

References

Axelrod, D. (2019), (@davidaxelrod), Twitter, July 24. Available online: https://twitter.com/davidaxelrod/status/1154017858168508416 (accessed February 10, 2020).

Baker, P. (2019), "The Blockbuster That Wasn't: Mueller Disappoints the Democrats," *New York Times*, July 24. Available online: https://www.nytimes.com/2019/07/24/us/politics/trump-mueller-democrats.html (accessed February 9, 2020).

Bottoms, S. (2006), "Putting the Document into Documentary: An Unwelcome Corrective?," *TDR: The Drama Review*, 50 (3): 56–68.

Breuninger, K. (2019), "Here Are 5 Big Takeaways from Robert Mueller's Testimony," CNBC, July 24. Available online: https://www.cnbc.com/2019/07/24/here-are-5-big-takeaways-from-robert-muellers-testimony.html (accessed February 12, 2020).

Brook, P. (1968), *The Empty Space*, New York: Simon & Schuster.

Carlson, M. (2003), *The Haunted Stage: The Theatre as Memory Machine*, Ann Arbor: University of Michigan Press.

Cohen, R. (1993), *Understanding Peter Weiss*, Understanding Modern European and Latin American Literature, Columbia: University of South Carolina Press.

Cohen, R. (1998), "The Political Aesthetics of Holocaust Literature: Peter Weiss's *The Investigation* and Its Critics," *History & Memory*, 10 (2): 43–67.

Conquergood, D. (2013), "Beyond the Text: Toward a Performative Cultural Politics," in E. P. Johnson (ed.), *Cultural Struggles: Performance, Ethnography, Praxis*, 32–46, Ann Arbor: University of Michigan Press.

Godwin, M. (1994), "Meme, Counter-Meme," *Wired*, October 1. Available online: https://www.wired.com/1994/10/godwin-if-2/ (accessed February 10, 2020).

"Here's What Surprised Us during the Mueller Testimony and 4 Other Takeaways" (2019), *Politico*, July 24. Available online: https://www.politico.com/story/2019/07/24/mueller-testimony-1432264 (accessed February 23, 2020).

Hersh, E. (2020), *Politics Is for Power*, New York: Scribner.

Innes, C. (1972), *Erwin Piscator's Political Theatre: The Development of Modern German Drama*, London: Cambridge University Press.

"Interview Rep. Adam Schiff" (2019), *Face the Nation*, July 21. Available online: https://www.cbsnews.com/news/transcript-rep-adam-schiff-on-face-the-nation-july-21-2019/ (accessed August 12, 2021).

Kirschner, G. (2019), (@glennkirschner2), Twitter, July 24. Available online: https://twitter.com/glennkirschner2/status/1154015466572005382 (accessed February 10, 2020).

McKee, A. (2004), *The Public Sphere: An Introduction*, Cambridge: Cambridge University Press.

Mueller, R. (2019), *The Mueller Report*, Jackson, MS: Thirteen Colonies Press. Kindle.

Piscator, E. ([1963] 1978), *The Political Theater*, Hugh Rorrison (trans.), New York: Avon Books.

"Robert Mueller Testifies before Two House Committees" (2019), C-SPAN, June 24. Available online: https://www.c-span.org/video/?462628-1/robert-mueller-congressional-testimony (accessed August 12, 2021).

Schenkkan, R. (2019), "The Investigation: A Search for Truth in Ten Acts," Law Works, The Young Turks, YouTube, June 24. Available online: https://youtu.be/8zUblhfv6GI (accessed August 12, 2021).

Schiff, A. (2019), "Interview with Chuck Todd," *Meet the Press*, July 28. Available online: https://www.nbcnews.com/meet-the-press/meet-press-july-28-2019-n1035481 (accessed December 21, 2021).

Sherman, H. (2019), "Robert Schenkkan: 'I Looked to Shakespeare When I Wrote My Lyndon Johnson Plays,'" *The Stage*, October 14. Available online: https://www.thestage.co.uk/features/robert-schenkkan-i-looked-to-shakespeare-when-i-wrote-my-lyndon-johnson-plays (accessed February 28, 2020).

van Zoonen, L. (2005), *Entertaining the Citizen: When Politics and Popular Culture Converge*, Critical Media Studies, Lanham, MD: Rowman & Littlefield.

Part Three

Performance

6

Australian Biographical Theater on the Post-Truth Stage

Stephen Carleton and Chris Hay

In the epilogue of Tommy Murphy's *Holding the Man* (2005), a stage version of the 1995 memoir by Timothy Conigrave, Tim reads a letter to his recently deceased lover John Caleo. Tim and John's love story, and its tragic conclusion at the height of the AIDS crisis in Australia, has formed the narrative spine of the play, and the letter has been imported verbatim into the stage version from the memoir. It ends:

> **Tim:** Life is pretty good at the moment. I have my health and seem to be doing most of the things I want to do before I die. I guess the hardest thing is having so much love for you and it somehow not being returned. I develop crushes all the time but that is just misdirected need for you. You are a hole in my life, a black hole. Anything I place there cannot be returned.
> *The actor playing JOHN leaves the stage.*
> I miss you terribly. *Ci vedremo lassù, angelo.* (2006: 161)

Conigrave's memoir ends with this same declaration ([1995] 2009: 286). The stage version, however, continues for a final beat:

> **Actor Playing Tim:** Timothy Conigrave died in October 1994.
> *Holding the Man* was published in 1995: a gift to John. The End.
> (2006: 161)

As the change in dialogue attribution suggests, in this final moment of the stage version of *Holding the Man* the actor playing Tim steps out of character and delivers his final lines "as himself." This creates a prototypical distancing effect, not only taking the audience out of the action of the play just as their emotional investment is highest, but also authenticating the events of the play as true.

Holding the Man premiered in Sydney in November 2006, in a production directed by David Berthold for the Griffin Theatre Company. That same production then toured the east coast of Australia, with three return seasons in Sydney in 2007 alongside one each in Brisbane and Melbourne in 2008. With some cast changes, Berthold's production was presented on London's West End between March and July 2010. Subsequent revivals have been presented in Australia—directed by Rosalba Clemente for the State Theatre Company of South Australia in 2011, and again by Berthold for La Boite Theatre in Brisbane in 2013—as well as overseas, including high-profile productions in San Francisco and Los Angeles. As recently as 2019, the play has been performed as far afield as Nashville, Tennessee, and in translation in Florence, Italy. We include this roll call to emphasize the play's impact and reach: according to the records of AusStage, the Australian Live Performance Database, it is the most widely performed Australian play of its decade on the professional stage. Its international reach, too, is unusually wide for a contemporary Australian play: *Holding the Man* joins only Joanna Murray-Smith's *Honour* (1995) and Andrew Bovell's *When the Rain Stops Falling* (2009) in finding recent success on both sides of the Atlantic.[1] This success is particularly notable given Murphy was at the time an emergent playwright, with only two previous professional productions, both in 2005—the premiere of *Strangers in Between* (2006: 1–62) and a revival of Murphy's student play *Troy's House* ([1999] 2005).

Any analysis of Murphy's subsequent plays, including the two that we take as our case studies in this chapter, must be framed by this early success; Murphy's work will inevitably be introduced to audiences with some variation on "from the playwright of *Holding the Man*." In turn, Murphy's subsequent career can be viewed in terms of his role as a biographer: even though *Holding the Man* is a stage adaptation of Conigrave's memoir written a decade after his death, Murphy insists that "although I could never meet him, I somehow sought to collaborate with Tim" (2010: 76). That collaboration can be understood as foregrounding the emotional narrative of Conigrave's memoir; Berthold writes in his preface to the Australian edition of the published text:

> Tellingly, in early letters to his publisher Tim calls sections of the book "scenes." This observation suggested a way to tell the story, but what story? Part of Tim's reason for writing the book was to educate about HIV/AIDS, but this was not our purpose here. We wanted the love story. (2006: xi)

This observation highlights both the theatrical potential of the source material, and Murphy's role in editing and shaping the material of Tim's life. These two are interdependent: "Tim adjusted the raw material of his life to meet his story-telling needs, and Tommy has adjusted the source material to meet his theatrical needs" (Berthold 2006: xii). Murphy is here understood as a more or less traditional biographer, who takes the raw material of his subject's life and gives that life theatrical form through creative mediation.

Murphy's rise to prominence with *Holding the Man* places him at the vanguard of contemporary Australian biographical theater, a term we borrow from Ursula Canton to refer to plays that feature "the presence of either a recognizable subject of biography or the portrayal of the search for such a life story" (2011: 23). After a trio of plays that explored different forms,[2] Murphy returned to biographical theater in the 2010s with two plays: *Mark Colvin's Kidney* (2017) and *Packer & Sons* (2019). We distinguish biographical theater from the narrower category of verbatim and documentary theater, while acknowledging the potential similarities in dramaturgical approach identified by Katherine Lyall-Watson:

> Verbatim theater, biographical theater and literary biographies all rely on the eye of the author/playwrights to choose which part of the mountain of information to represent. The author/playwright as editor is able to paint a picture of characters by choosing what to include and, perhaps more importantly, what information to exclude. (2013: 16)

Biographical theater, we argue, offers greater inherent creative license to paint this picture than the adherence to strict verisimilitude and facticity that verbatim and documentary theater demand. We began this account with a moment in Murphy's *Holding the Man* that made a clear truth claim—a borrowing from verbatim and documentary theater practices, where "the link to the truth claim" is paramount (Reinelt 2006: 83)—and we will consider similar moments in these later plays. This, in turn, requires us to consider the historical circumstances of their production, as Carol Martin highlights:

> Complicating and questioning truth claims in order to interrogate the real is indicative of the ways in which what is deemed real can be understood and determined in diverse ways in different historical circumstances. (2013: 9)

In other words, the nature of truth claims made on stage must be considered in light of the status of truth in the world outside the theater.

Unlike *Holding the Man*, *Mark Colvin's Kidney* and *Packer & Sons* are written in what Murphy calls "the era of 'fake news'" (2017: "Writer's Note" n.p.), a phrase that has come to be seen as a constituent feature of the post-truth era, where "reality is now so elusive and our perspectives as individuals and groups so divergent that it is no longer meaningful to speak of, or seek, the truth" (d'Ancona 2017: 98). The post-truth era thus presents particular challenges for biographical theater, which are pointed to by Canton's study: "instead of asking whether the elements in a production are factual or fictional, we have to ask how the distinction is made and why it matters" (2011: 41). Alice Rayner further draws attention to the way the curatorial choices of the biographer inflect notions of truth, arguing that "the very acts of selecting, combining, and theatricalizing dissolve the terms of the real and put them into the terms of the imaginary" (1995: 12). The capacity of biographical theater to speak to the post-truth age has been recognized by other lauded Australian playwrights too—including David Williamson (*Rupert*, 2013),[3] Murray-Smith (*Switzerland*, 2016),[4] and Alana Valentine (*Letters to Lindy*, 2017)[5]—but we focus solely on Murphy here, as we assert that his wider body of work is inseparable from his success as a theatrical biographer.

In this chapter, we will use an analysis of *Mark Colvin's Kidney* and *Packer & Sons* to argue that the post-truth age has altered the form of biographical theater on the Australian stage, by replacing an appeal to facticity with an appeal to visceral emotion as the primary authenticator of biographical truth. This argument finds support in Mathew d'Ancona's polemic *Post-Truth: The New War on Truth and How to Fight Back*, where he argues that post-truth represents "the triumph of the visceral over the rational, the deceptively simple over the honestly complex" (2017: 20). We argue that in *Mark Colvin's Kidney* and *Packer & Sons*, as in the post-truth era more broadly, "the objective is to trigger emotions" (d'Ancona 2017: 121)—and, crucially for our purposes, that emotional appeal is positioned as no less true than the factual one it replaces. We trace the impact of these ideas on Murphy's work through close analysis of the text of both plays, as well as the commentary around their premiere productions. In so doing, we contend that there is a developmental movement toward an appeal to the emotional across Murphy's biographical oeuvre. *Mark Colvin's Kidney* represents a stylistic departure from the more literal biographical adaptation of Conigrave's *Holding the Man*. The former, however, still relies heavily on the tropes of fact-based biographical theater writing: references to personal interviews with the subjects; screen projections of actual televised footage and/or radio reports; and other techniques we will discuss shortly. With *Packer & Sons*, however, we argue that Murphy moves further again along a continuum toward emotional truth-based storytelling. It is a more wholly conjectural and imaginative retelling of episodes in the Packer family's lives. Finally, we suggest that this developmental shift in Murphy's recent plays index an alternate route for Australian biographical theater, recognizing as d'Ancona does that "in a post-truth world … it is not enough to make an intellectual case. In many (perhaps most) contexts, facts need to be communicated in a way that recognizes emotional as well as rational imperatives" (2017: 127). Even as the documentary sources are cloaked by the appeal to emotion and imagination, Murphy's biographical theater retains "a measure of efficacy; it is a way of knowing" (Reinelt 2009: 23) his subjects.

Mark Colvin's Kidney

The link between biographical theater and the phenomena of fake news in a post-truth world is highlighted by Murphy's thematic and generic preoccupations in these plays, as both deal with media scandals in the post-truth era. Premiering at Belvoir Street Theatre in March 2017, and again directed by longtime collaborator David Berthold, the titular character in *Mark Colvin's Kidney* is a high-profile investigative journalist in Australia, who made his name as a fearless pursuer of truth as a foreign correspondent during the 1980s. Colvin rose to fame as a young reporter covering the Iranian-US hostage crisis in 1980 and presided over Australian radio's flagship current affairs program, *PM*, from 1997 through to his death in 2017. The play's dramatic arc centers around his need for a kidney transplant in the early 2010s, and the unexpected (certainly by Colvin!) altruistic offer of an organ donation from Mary-Ellen Field, who is referred to in Murphy's dramatis personae as "an Australian businesswoman living in the UK" (2017: n.p.). She was a PR agent to the famous and Colvin interviewed her when she testified against the Murdoch empire for the phone-hacking scandal that unfolded in the UK in the late 2000s. The two formed a subsequent friendship of sorts.

Of particular interest to us here is Murphy's choice to position Field as a co-protagonist of a play named after Colvin. Indeed, the image used to market the production is of Sarah Peirse, the actor who played Field, and the advertising copy centers her narrative:

> Mary-Ellen Field is a successful Australian business consultant in London—until she's accused of betraying the secrets of her clients to the press. Her life comes crashing down, and she starts to wonder if she's losing her mind. Then it emerges that her phone was being illegally tapped by reporters, and she sets out on a campaign to restore

her reputation. But along the way, her ideas of redemption change—she's been interviewed by a journalist on the other side of the world, and his story puts everything into a new perspective. (Belvoir n.d.)

In his Writer's Note in the published text of the play, Murphy confirms that *Mark Colvin's Kidney* dramatizes Field's experiences: "Here is a story that makes claims of truth. It is about a woman who sought to correct falsehoods" (2017: "Writer's Note" n.p.). This insistence on truth is of course a dangerous business in a post-truth world, with its catch-cry of "who is to say what is false?" (d'Ancona 2017: 92). Murphy's opening stage directions declare:

The following is based on actual events.

The play makes use of surtitles to display the source of quoted material, the translations of lines spoken in foreign languages and occasional scene settings.

The authors of the quoted correspondence have approved its use in this script. Messages, emails, transcripts, and tweets are unabridged unless stated otherwise. (2017: n.p.)

From the outset, then, *Mark Colvin's Kidney* mirrors Field's insistence through its commitment to staging truth claims.

Beyond the core premise of the play being based on real events, *Mark Colvin's Kidney*'s wider context is imbricated in the rise of the post-truth Murdoch world. Field was a victim of the Murdoch empire phone-hacking, itself a symbol of the ethical vacuity of one of the world's largest proponents of the post-truth, fake news paradigm. Field's altruistic kidney donation mirrors her determination to testify at the Leveson Inquiry into the culture, practices, and ethics of the British press (which specifically considered the phone-hacking scandal), in order to pursue justice and reveal truth there. Field is the victim of "fake news" herself, as depicted in the opening scenes of the play, and she refuses an out-of-court settlement that would greatly assist her parlous financial situation in order to testify. She is the first character we meet in *Mark Colvin's Kidney*, initially in interview with the surgeon who will go on to perform the organ transplant, but then in flashback in Scene Two we witness the moment of discovery of the phone-hacking scandal. We see her in conversation with her celebrity client, supermodel Elle Macpherson, who accuses Field of leaking private details to the press—details we soon realize have in fact been sourced through hacking of Macpherson's private calls. Macpherson wrongly accuses Field of alcoholism and forces her into rehab to demonstrate her commitment to truth and client loyalty.

While based on true events, the play is not a polemical investigation of media integrity, nor one that seeks to portray a factual interrogation of organ donation or the lives of the rich and famous. It is not verbatim or documentary theater—though it does employ some of those traditions' tropes and techniques. Some scenes (like the first with Macpherson, and those in the Arizona rehab facility) are obviously writerly and conjectural. Others, like the first telephone exchange between Field and Mark Colvin where he approaches her for an interview, smack of authenticity in detail because they are based on Murphy's personal research with both subjects. Verbatim techniques in that scene that enhance its appeal to facticity include naturalistic dialogue effects where characters interrupt or apologize for talking over the top of each other:

> **Mary-Ellen:** Yes, well, nobody has ever … /You know I—
> **Mark:** You know I—Sorry, I cut you off.
> **Mary-Ellen:** No no. That's alright. What were you going to say?
> **Mark:** Ah …
> **Mary-Ellen:** It has been traumatic, like you say. My health has suffered. The doctors have only just managed to diagnose this thing going on in my brain where my heart forgets to circulate blood. It is a complete nightmare and nobody seems to care. I cut you off again. (Murphy 2017: 26)

The scene then segues into a "live" recorded section of Colvin's *PM* radio news program reporting the Murdoch phone-hacking scandal, introducing the interview with Field that she has evidently agreed to provide, on condition of anonymity. This is accompanied with a surtitle: "Mark Colvin reported this story on Wednesday, February 9, 2011. 18:29:00" (Murphy 2017: 27).

In another scene, the BBC radio program *Today* (at least partly scripted by Murphy, as the original has not been retained) underscores a conversation between Field and her husband Bruce to provide a sense of veracity (Murphy 2017: 13–19). Later, there are three "News" scenes that act as visual transitions, providing televised footage of celebrities, journalists, and editors entering court to testify in the Leveson Inquiry. The play is a mélange, then, of speculative narrative drama based on interviews with the key players and verbatim theater techniques, which combine to add veracity or authenticity to the claims being presented in the clearly fictional scenes. As Canton writes, "both a general desire for authenticity in an increasingly mediatized world, and the perception that official media are restricted to politically opportune representations have led to a search for untainted, more authentic perspectives on reality" in the theater (2011: 3). Murphy is searching for authenticity here, but, despite the incorporation of the verbatim-like techniques outlined above, he never pretends that the play is not theatrical artifice, even when *Mark Colvin's Kidney* veers toward the intimate and personal.

The second act focuses more on this interpersonal relationship dimension—the decision to donate the kidney, and the time it reportedly took to persuade Colvin of the altruism of Field's intent. In Act Two, Scene One, Field unnerves Colvin with personal detail she knows about him that she has gleaned through their conversations—his blood type, recounts of childhood scarring (physical and psychological) in boarding school, his relationship with his mother. This mirrors the type of detail that the Murdoch tabloids have acquired about others via phone-hacking and triggers Colvin's doubts about Field's intent. When Colvin finally agrees to the transplant, the scene in the surgery is interspersed with actual recorded voice-over of an unusually contrite and vulnerable Rupert Murdoch, "secretly recorded by a *Sun* journalist in the newspaper's headquarters":

> **Rupert Murdoch:** *I don't know, you know in my heart, I'm not going to ask you now but I would have thought a hundred percent—but at least ninety percent—of payments were made at the instigation*

> of cops, saying, "I've got a good story here. It's worth five hundred quid," or something. And you would say, "No, it's not," or "We'll check it out," or whatever. And they'd say, "Well, we'll ring the Mirror ..." [Whispering] *It was the culture of Fleet Street.* (Murphy 2017: 69; emphasis in the original)

As the audience watch actors portraying the real characters of Field and Colvin undergoing both parts of transplant surgery, they hear a recording of a media mogul discussing the confection of fake news.

During Colvin's recovery from a dialysis session in Act One, Scene Thirteen, a verbatim exchange of surtitled tweets between Field and Colvin is interspersed with a scene where Field is in a confessional in a medieval French Catholic church. There is a comic turn with a priest trying to administer confession while Field is on the phone with Colvin, followed by the surtitle: "This encounter with a priest never happened" (Murphy 2017: 41). Even as the play's "real life" story draws to its heart-warming conclusion about the triumph of altruism in the era of fake news, Murphy is still offering sly winks to the audience to remind us it is a play, and that the story has been embellished in service of entertainment—possibly the sort of claim those tabloid proponents of fake news would make about their own reportage. Indeed, this moment of acknowledgment of Murphy's invention serves to reinforce the connection to facticity of the reminder of the play, which carries no such disclaimer.

As Canton describes it, "the terms of biographical theatre, the challenge to Empiricist history and to the belief in a clear dichotomy of factual Truth and fiction was expressed in the playful use of historical and biographical references" from the advent of postmodernism and its intrusion into the Western European and American stage from the early 1970s onward (2011: 9). Murphy's work is not 1970s-styled theater "happening" or performance art experiment; nor is it postdramatic pastiche freed of the constraints of narrative felty. He is a theatrical storyteller attempting to dramatize real lives in fiction on stage. In *Mark Colvin's Kidney*, he embellishes his dramatic storytelling with the tropes of investigative journalism: tweets, media grabs, live footage, and so on. With *Packer & Sons*, however, he leaves these quasi-documentary techniques aside in pursuit of a more mythic portrayal of the lives of another set of characters deeply implicated in Australian media and politics in the post-truth era. Emotion is more obviously triumphing fact in this later work, marking a more complete immersion in what we argue is a new kind of post-truth biographical Australian playwriting genre.

Packer & Sons

Packer & Sons was first produced at the Belvoir Street Theatre in Sydney in November 2019, directed by Belvoir's Artistic Director Eamon Flack. Drawing inspiration from journalist Paul Barry's books, *The Rise and Rise of Kerry Packer* and *Rich Kids*, Murphy's play interweaves time periods to examine three generations of Packer men at the helm of the family's Australian newspaper, magazine, television, and casino empire: from founding grandee Frank Packer, to his sons Kerry and Clyde, to current inheritor James (son of Kerry). The "*& Sons*" in the title would imply that Frank is the titular Packer being depicted here, and that the sons are the intergenerational progeny of the family patriarch, but Murphy's Playwright's Note to the premiere production frames the family's "fourth monarch" James as the central character, and Kerry as "the father." He points out from the very outset that he intends reading his very real historical/political characters through the prism of mythos:

> This is not Kerry; this is the Roman god, Saturn, tormented by a prophecy that he would be overthrown by his offspring ... He reminds us that the competition between father and offspring is a crisis of masculinity. (Murphy 2019: "Playwright's Note" n.p.)

This offers evidence of our earlier assertion that Murphy's biographical theater is consciously appealing to emotion over facticity, and indeed we argue that this is a feature of his later work, dealing as it does with media figures imbricated in the manipulation of "story" and of fact in order to appeal to an ever-widening readership. In *Packer & Sons*,

Murphy as storyteller is finding the story of the Packers' lives through the guise of antiquity and classical mythology, and expressing it in contemporary theatrical form that poses a "trade places" (Murphy 2019: "Playwright's Note" n.p.) question to the audience.

The spine of the play is based on biographical detail and an incident that is widely known and in the public domain, at least in Australia. Most informed observers of Australian politics and media will remember, for instance, that Kerry and Clyde Packer inherited the family empire from Frank, who viewed the latter as the likelier heir; that Kerry was sent off for a stint in the Australian outback to work for a time as a jackaroo[6] to "grow up"; that Kerry (in middle age) had a heart attack on his horse playing polo that left him clinically dead; that Kerry had a loose rivalry-allegiance with Rupert Murdoch (himself the similarly aged son of a media baron, Keith) in the 1970s; and that their sons, James and Lachlan, joined forces to launch themselves into the digital era and famously brought about financial damage to their fathers' respective empires. It was the men's fathers who effectively steered them through the ill-judged One.Tel "dot com" investment crisis[7] of the new millennium.

Those main dramatic events are all reasonably well-documented biographical details—perhaps we can call them "facts." The interpersonal weaving of them into family drama, though, is writerly conjecture (even if sourced from Barry's books), and their theatrical realization the most liberal of Murphy's post-truth interventions. This inventive theatricality—skipping between time periods in the blink of an eye, having actors swap roles and portray multiple characters—is established from the outset, illustrated by the transition from Scene One to Scene Two. An ageing Kerry Packer has the famous heart attack while playing polo, and son James rushes to the rescue and orders a helicopter to whisk him to a private surgeon. Through casting decisions, the son transforms into his father at a younger, vulnerable point where he is being bashed by criminal syndicate henchmen for unpaid gambling debts (Murphy 2019: 3). The physical pummeling he receives mirrors the pounding paramedics have provided the same character (Kerry) in the previous scene, that of his famous heart attack. His mythic flaws—gambling, poor diet, alcohol abuse, vulgarity, misogyny—the markers of the "crisis of masculinity" Murphy says he is exploring—are all laid out in these establishing sequences. Gone, in this play, are the verbatim quotes, the tweets, the media projections and surtitles explaining historical facticity or otherwise, the accoutrement of biographical research that marked *Mark Colvin's Kidney*. Here, we are being asked to take leaps of faith and *imagine* what might have been said, what characters might have looked like, and how thematic resemblance is reechoed through canny casting and doubling.

In Act One, Scene Seven, where the brothers (Clyde and Kerry) discuss how they'll divide up their dead father's empire, Clyde wears a caftan for a meeting with lawyers while Kerry defecates in the next room with the toilet door open. The creative license in imagery here is liberal, a theatrical exaggeration of their personalities. We hear Kerry "grunting" and "wiping his arse" and then reenter the room as the adult Kerry, now played by the older actor who had until now been playing the brothers' father (in the original production, Josh McConville becomes John Howard) (Murphy 2019: 24–5). He is now the man of the family, ready to take on the mantle of the family business:

> *The toilet flushes. KERRY washes his hands.*
> **Clyde:** You think you can be him?
> *KERRY re[e]merges, now played by the SENIOR PACKER actor.*
> **Kerry:** No, I think I can be better than him. You can't hack being Packer, Clyde. I can.
> **Clyde:** You think you can shit me out, Kerry?
> **Kerry:** You want to be liked. That's what Dad did to you. I don't care.
> (Murphy 2019: 25)

Drawing on Murphy's notion of Roman myth to tell the Packer family story, Clyde augurs a family curse at this key transformational point.

> **Clyde:** The thing I know about being a tycoon, the more a person gets involved in being a tycoon, it chews up so much of him that there is less of a real person left. … Four million dollars. I don't

need the Packer life for me or my son. It's a curse. (Murphy 2019: 26)

This family curse—the moral weight of ill-gotten gains—passes from generation to generation, and Act Two switches focus from Kerry to James. Theatrical sleight of hand aside, the conceptual shift in central character here is disorienting.

Act Two suffers dramaturgically as the plot becomes bogged down in researched detail and verisimilitude over the details of the Packer/Murdoch sons' botched One.Tel bid. The play's rhythm stutters a little as if it is caught between Murphy's previous and present ways of telling a biographical story. Indeed, this was highlighted in John Shand's review for *The Sydney Morning Herald*, which compared *Packer & Sons* unfavorably to *Mark Colvin's Kidney* by observing that in this play "Murphy has stayed too glued to history, while—in dramatic terms—the episode is overly repetitive" (2019). Act Two, Scene Four, though, offers a striking post-truth theatrical image as it uses faltering technology—a lousy dial-up internet connection at a climactic shareholders' meeting—as a comedic *lazzo* satirizing the failed vision of the sons' millennial reinvention of their fathers' ambitions:

> **James:** You still with us there, Lachlan?
> *Silence.*
> **Lachlan:** I'm here. Yep.
> **James** Think you dropped out ... First thing—
> **Lachlan:** No, I'm here.
> **James:** 'Kay, first thing, ah, Jodee has promised that there will be seventy-five million—
> **Lachlan:** Sorry. Yep.
> **James:** It's cool. A lag on the ... (Murphy 2019: 57)

Here are a group of ambitious young speculators wanting to make billions in new digital technology, and they cannot even get a clean speakerphone connection to plot their coup.

As James's online venture goes down the proverbial toilet, and he unravels in private conversation with Lachlan—the stage directions tell us that he "blubbers tears" at the prospect of the One.Tel venture losing hundreds of millions of dollars (Murphy 2019: 61)—the family curse referenced earlier manifests and threatens to bring this Roman myth to its tragic conclusion. Murphy deploys the theatrical technique of a ghost appearing to presage doom:

> *A MAN appears in a crisp shirt and black tie from another era. He could be Clyde Packer's ghost. He is more likely to be a member of Lachlan's household staff. He is invisible to them. As they talk, he wipes a bench and leaves a bowl of nuts for them. He disappears.* (Murphy 2019: 60–1)

It is unclear why it is Clyde Packer's ghost who appears here—and only here—and not that of his father Kerry, or even the original patriarch, Frank. Perhaps it is because Clyde was the family's conscience and the one who identified the curse in the first place. Either way, Kerry intercedes, cleans up James's mess, and steers the empire back to safe ground, and the play ends on a rare father-son moment of vulnerability—they hug for the first time—but ultimately it is a note of failure and doubt as Kerry leaves his floundering child to face the company board:

> **James:** I'm sorry I've done this to you.
> *JAMES gets himself a cigarette.*
> I know. I have to front up there today. Just me. To be my own man. My own man. By myself. To own it. I owe you that. And I think I need it because … I want it.
> *KERRY puts on his hat to leave. JAMES' hands are shaking.*
> I want that. I want it. I want. I want.
> *His father, his grandfather, is his shadow. JAMES smokes the entire cigarette.* (Murphy 2019: 71)

The reference to James being shadowed by both his father and grandfather is presumably referring to the acting double—the fact that actor John Howard has played both characters in the play.[8] The family saga concludes in the terrain of Roman myth—ghostly hauntings, fortunes lost and restored, and the father prevailing over the usurping son—that Murphy invites us to read the story through in his Playwright's Note. We are not necessarily in the domain of fake news and sheer invention of fact in this mythic rebranding of Australian biographical theater, but we are, as d'Ancona suggests, being invited to interpret truth through the lens of emotion, in service of a larger truth about family legacy, masculinity in contemporary crisis, and the psychological toll of unchecked human greed.

Conclusion

To return to the question of truth claims with which we began this chapter, the comparison of *Mark Colvin's Kidney* with *Packer & Sons* illustrates a shift in Murphy's writing with regard to how truth claims are performed and presented on stage. Both plays are based on extensive documentary research and interviews—the published script of each reveals a long list of interview subjects and source materials. However, it is only in *Mark Colvin's Kidney* that this documentary material is authenticated on stage, through the use of not only surtitles to cite sources in real time but also verbatim material including the recording of Rupert Murdoch quoted above. In *Packer & Sons*, though, this appeal to facticity is replaced by an appeal to emotion, illustrated most clearly through the physical transformations the cast undergo to theatricalize the play's thesis about generational trauma. The most affective of these was described in *The Guardian*'s review:

> McConville is responsible, too, for an unforgettable early scene. He is playing young Kerry, muscular and shirtless, and hauling himself from hospital bed to ashtray where a cigarette smolders. He inhales—and transforms. His chest caves, his shoulders slope, he smears his wig off and his belly billows out. The flesh of his face seems to actually droop. McConville becomes the bullish businessman of legend literally before our eyes.[9] (Hennessy 2019)

Instead of turning to the documentary record to authenticate the events of the play, in this later play Murphy "looked for opportunities to bring bright flashes of theatricality to bear" (Shand 2019).

We might view this progression as a theatrical version of what former US president Donald Trump called "truthful hyperbole" (qtd. in d'Ancona 2017: 15)—or perhaps, to take the *Oxford English Dictionary* as a more authoritative source, "appeals to emotion and personal belief" (2016). In looking at *Mark Colvin's Kidney* and *Packer & Sons* side by side, we can identify that the later play replaces an appeal to facticity with an appeal to exaggeration, emotion, and belief. This is not to say that *Packer & Sons* is any less true; indeed, even if "the shards of the document are tattered and thin" (Reinelt 2009: 23), the truth claim of the play still "functions as at least partially persuasive" (Reinelt 2006: 83). In other words, the audience knows this likely is not the true story of the Packers, but we also know that we will never be able to know the truth, and so what we see on stage is close enough to be persuasive. This is an important lesson for biographical theater in the post-truth era— an era in which the tenets of biography itself are under siege: even as we write, Australia's Deputy Prime Minister Michael McCormack declared that "facts are sometimes contentious, and what you might think is right somebody else might think is completely untrue" (qtd. in Farr 2021). A truth claim need not be presented in exhaustive, documentary detail in order for a play to function as effective biography. Instead, by eschewing the authentic source material of Mary-Ellen Field and Mark Colvin and in its place offering audiences access to the emotional truth of the Packers, Murphy is remaking and offering a future pathway for biographical theater on the post-truth stage.

Notes

1 *Honour* was produced on Broadway in 1998, and then at the Royal National Theatre, London, in 2003 before a West End revival in 2006. *When the Rain Stops Falling* was produced at Almeida Theatre, London, in 2009 and then at the Lincoln Center Theater in 2010.
2 After *Holding the Man*, Murphy wrote the surreal black comedy *Saturn's Return* for the Sydney Theatre Company, produced in 2008 and then

again in a revised version in 2009. He then wrote the realist dramedy *Gwen in Purgatory*, produced in 2010 in a coproduction between Belvoir, Sydney, and La Boite, Brisbane. His adaptation of J. M. Barrie's *Peter Pan* was produced by Belvoir in 2013, and that production toured to the New Victory Theater, New York, later that same year. Although these plays were undoubtedly successful, given the scale of production, we confine our attention here to Murphy's biographical theater works.

3 *Rupert* was produced by the Melbourne Theatre Company in 2013, before a season at the Kennedy Center's World Stages International Festival in Washington, DC, in 2014. The same production subsequently toured to Sydney's Theatre Royal later that year. The play is a biography of media baron Rupert Murdoch.

4 *Switzerland* premiered at the Sydney Theatre Company (STC) in 2014, before a separate production was performed at the Geffen Playhouse in Los Angeles in 2015. (This arrangement was billed as a co-world premiere.) The STC production was presented by the Melbourne Theatre Company in 2016; a separate production was performed at the Queensland Theatre Company, Brisbane. Two separate productions were performed in 2017: by the State Theatre Company of South Australia in Adelaide and by the Black Swan State Theatre Company in Perth. The play is a biography of the psychological thriller writer Patricia Highsmith.

5 *Letters to Lindy* premiered at the Merrigong Theatre Company, Wollongong, in 2016, in a production that then undertook a major national tour to venues in Canberra, Sydney, and Brisbane, as well as many regional Australian cities. The play is a biography of Lindy Chamberlain-Creighton, whose baby Azaria was snatched by a dingo at Uluṟu in 1980.

6 This is the term colloquially used in Australia for a sheep or cattle station apprenticeship that was sometimes mythologized in twentieth-century life as a masculine rite of passage—a stint in the bush that toughens a wayward young man up and provides discipline, grounding, and direction.

7 One.Tel was an infamous Australian corporate collapse, which became a by-word for the burst of the dot-com bubble—indeed, the company's life between 1995 and 2001 maps almost directly on to the bubble period. One.Tel was founded by Jodee Rich and Brad Keeling, and Lachlan Murdoch and James Packer sat on its board, although it was Rich and Packer who became the avatars of the company's hubris. The company's rise and fall is

charted in Paul Barry's book *Rich Kids* (2003), which carries the subtitle "How the Murdochs and Packers lost $950 million in One.Tel."
8 We might even suggest there is a further haunting here: the actor John Howard, not to be confused with the long-serving Australian prime minister of the same name, also played the titular role in *Mark Colvin's Kidney*, a mere two years earlier in this same theater.
9 Interestingly this moment is not presented in the script, which merely demands "*KERRY turns. The pain is severe. He angles towards the ashtray. He stands. A shot of pain. He hobbles. He gets himself that cigarette*" (Murphy 2019: 11). However, given Murphy was in the rehearsal room throughout the process of bringing *Packer & Sons* to stage, we are confident in attributing the image to both Murphy and Flack.

References

Barry, P. (2003), *Rich Kids*, Milsons Point, NSW: Bantam Books.
Barry, P. (2007), *The Rise and Rise of Kerry Packer Uncut*, Sydney: Bantam Books.
Belvoir (n.d.), "What's On—*Mark Colvin's Kidney*." Available online: https://belvoir.com.au/productions/mark-colvins-kidney/ (accessed February 10, 2021).
Berthold, D. (2006), "A Theatre of Optimism," in *Strangers in between and Holding the Man: Two Plays*, vii–xii, Sydney: Currency Press.
Bovell, A. (2009), *When the Rain Stops Falling*, Sydney: Currency Press.
Canton, U. (2011), *Biographical Theatre: Re-Presenting Real People?*, London: Palgrave Macmillan.
Conigrave, T. ([1995] 2009), *Holding the Man*, Camberwell, Vic.: Penguin.
d'Ancona, M. (2017), *Post-Truth: The New War on Truth and How to Fight Back*, London: Ebury Press.
Farr, M. (2021), "In Less than a Week as Acting PM, Michael McCormack Has Given Conservatives a Licence to Lie," *The Guardian*, January 12. Available online: https://www.theguardian.com/commentisfree/2021/jan/12/in-less-than-a-week-as-acting-pm-michael-mccormack-has-given-conservatives-a-licence-to-lie (accessed February 10, 2021).
Hennessy, K. (2019), "*Packer & Sons* Review—John Howard Is a Brutish Kerry Packer in Generation-Spanning Play," *The Guardian*, November 21.

Available online: https://www.theguardian.com/stage/2019/nov/21/packer-sons-review-john-howard-is-a-brutish-kerry-packer-in-generation-spanning-play (accessed February 10, 2021).

Lyall-Watson, K. (2013), "Biographical Theatre: Flying Separate of Everything," PhD diss., University of Queensland, Australia.

Martin, C. (2013), *Theatre of the Real*, London: Palgrave Macmillan.

Murphy, T. ([1999] 2005), *Troy's House*, Hobart: Australian Script Centre.

Murphy, T. (2006), *Strangers in Between and Holding the Man: Two Plays*, Sydney: Currency Press.

Murphy, T. (2010), "Afterword," in *Holding the Man*, 75–7, London: Nick Hern Books. *E-book.*

Murphy, T. (2017), *Mark Colvin's Kidney*, Sydney: Currency Press.

Murphy, T. (2019), *Packer & Sons*, Sydney: Currency Press.

Murray-Smith, J. (1995), *Honour*, Sydney: Currency Press.

Murray-Smith, J. (2016), *Switzerland*, Sydney: Currency Press.

Rayner, A. (1995), "Improper Conjunctions: Metaphor, Performance and Text," *Essays in Theatre*, 14 (1): 3–14.

Reinelt, J. (2006), "Toward a Poetics of Theatre and Public Events: In the Case of Stephen Lawrence," *TDR: The Drama Review*, 50 (3): 69–87.

Reinelt, J. (2009), "The Promise of Documentary," in A. Forsyth and C. Megson (eds.), *Get Real: Documentary Theatre Past and Present*, 6–23, London: Palgrave Macmillan.

Shand, J. (2019), "*Packer & Sons* Review: The Fathers May Die but Their Sins Live On," *Sydney Morning Herald*, November 21. Available online: https://www.smh.com.au/culture/theatre/packer-and-sons-review-the-fathers-may-die-but-their-sins-live-on-20191121-p53cnz.html (accessed February 10, 2021).

Valentine, A. (2017), *Letters to Lindy*, Sydney: Currency Press.

Williamson, D. (2013), *Rupert*, Sydney: Currency Press.

7

Performing Reality: Tina Satter's Verbatim Staging of an FBI Transcript in *Is This A Room*

Helen Georgas

She was in that tiny house with eleven armed men. It's insane. It's so crazy.

—Tina Satter[1]

Look, I only say I hate America three times a day. I'm no radical.

—Reality Winner[2]

Tina Satter's plays have always been playful distortions of reality. Her source material is personal rather than archival—often informed by a childhood memory and then blown up or spun away (Liska and Copper 2013). Known as a downtown playwright and director, and an avant-garde chronicler of adolescent worlds, she is interested in the strength and intensity of feeling—the way we, at that age, send out flares, looking for connection, for being seen and heard. Experimental in form but set in traditional locales of Americana—the football field, the dance studio—her plays are deep explorations of the strange intimacies that such locales hold (Alker 2018). Satter admits: "I like coded groups, whether it's teen girls or sports plays or four people who happen to be spending an hour in a tap dance class, because of that shared language and shared emotional space that's super specific" (Krane 2020).

With *Is This A Room*, Satter enters, for the first time, the realm of documentary theater, casting light on the shared language of American intelligence and the strange intimacies of an FBI interrogation. On June 3, 2017, a group of armed FBI agents descended upon the home of Reality Winner, a twenty-five-year old Air Force veteran and National Security Agency (NSA) translator, and proceeded to interrogate and then arrest her for leaking classified information to the media. That information confirmed Russia's hacking of the 2016 US election. Winner was tried and convicted under the Espionage Act and was given the longest sentence ever imposed in federal court for the unauthorized release of government information (Phillips 2018). *Is This A Room* is a verbatim performance of the transcript of Winner's interrogation and arrest, giving us the story-behind-the-story of the 2016 presidential election and one of the first theatrical responses to life in Trump's post-truth America.

Critical and audience response took *Is This A Room* from its initial downtown premiere at The Kitchen in January 2019 to an off-Broadway run at the Vineyard Theatre later that year (October 2019–January 2020), followed by touring productions both nationally and internationally. The praise and criticism leveraged at Satter around the play's "truthfulness" were varied. Some said staging a verbatim transcription—not a single word of the performance is invented or altered—was not theater (Hofler 2019). Others said the play was not truthful enough. Eleven FBI agents showed up at Winner's house in Augusta, Georgia, that June afternoon, but only three were portrayed (Teeman 2019). What was real about that?

Even though we are living in a post-truth world in which "facts, the truth, and reality are increasingly undermined" and fiction "has been given a status upgrade," "the relationship between fact and fiction, truth and lie, has become an increasingly tense one" (Wynants 2020: 11). These contestations over the play's "enoughness"—is it true enough? Is it theater enough?—emphasize not only theater's role in post-truth interrogation but also its preferred binary, even within a genre that has always blurred the distinction between reality and fiction.

There is also preference for "the real" to be situated in realism, which "continues to be a strong presence" in documentary theater (Martin

2012: 11). Satter and her theater company, Half Straddle, however, have built a reputation for creating nonlinear and hyper-stylized work. Her plays do not adhere to any traditional (read: patriarchal) notion of plot and are created so that "audiences generate their own meanings from the often-abstract productions in which the performers themselves— their acting styles and embodiment—and the mise en scène—the set, lighting, costume, and sound design—is just as important as the play text" (Del Vecchio 2016: 3). Satter's refusal to lead an audience through the "facts" of plot—to give us agency in meaning-making while still eliciting strong emotions—highlights her ability to take us on a post-truth exploration of r(R)eality.

This exploration is present in every aspect of Satter's production. In bringing *Is This A Room* into the theater, Satter thoughtfully interrogates the authenticity or "truthfulness" of each element of the play's staging: the script, the character of Reality Winner, the play's framing, set design, music, lighting, sound design and costumes, as well as the actors' performances and movements. This production mirrors our post-truth world by grappling with its own questions about what is "truthful," how to replicate or approximate that truthfulness, and when to veer away from replication that feels inauthentic in order to get at larger theatrical, emotional, or cultural truths.

When Satter first encountered the transcript of the interrogation, she was immediately drawn to the document and Winner's story and began to think that "maybe there was something to staging this transcript as a play" ("Playing Reality Winner" 2019). It read like a thriller in the way one knew, within a tight seventy minutes, that things were not going to end well for this woman. Satter was also intrigued by the text of the document—its jargon, shared lexicon, and authentic replication of actual speech:

> From the very first read, at the level of language, it was just so fascinating to me how it was captured on the page, right? Like with the, um, capturing the stutters, noting the coughs, noting sneezes, so you had this amazing, like, I mean what I've been calling like Neo-realism or something. (Satter 2020)

All of the elements that Satter is typically attracted to as a dramatist—the starts and stumbles of human communication, the strange intimacies of specific worlds—but especially her interest in gender, were there in the transcript and in the larger story of Winner and her arrest. Satter's feminism has been described as "post-wave" in that her productions "advocate femininity as consequential, vital, and powerful" (Del Vecchio 2016: 83). She is drawn to characters that have "male energy, but in a really female way" (Williams 2014). Her plays radicalize femininity by normalizing the "likes" of Millennial girl-speak and "say[ing] stupid things when you want to say something really important" (Hammons n.d.). "Putting women's experience at the center" of her work, her plays ask us "how we can invest in the category of 'woman' but still expand and re-imagine it" (Del Vecchio 2018: 310).

In name, intelligence, upspeak, personal style, and in her embodiment of both "feminine" and "masculine" characteristics, Winner could easily be a character created by Satter:

> To me, she's like the women that I've been inspired about and writing into my plays the whole time. If you look on her Instagram, she's this totally girlie girl who also, yeah, owns guns, is totally self-sufficient, speaks Arabic languages, can speak the highest level of security clearance with these dudes in her house because she's done these really intense, typically male things of being in the military and being an NSA analyst/contractor. To me, she's not a leap. That's who I've always been trying to write. (Krane 2020)

Like other Satter characters, Winner feels things intensely and is confused by a world in which those feelings—beamed out—are not reflected back to her. In the predominantly male NSA world in which she worked (as a contractor at Pluribus International), she had trouble fitting in. She was frustrated by all the Fox News at the office and her job translating Farsi documents about Iran's aerospace program was not fulfilling. She wanted to be out in the world—doing good, helping people—and was disappointed that her language skills were not being put to adequate use (Howley 2017):

You know, I—I want—I want to go out with our Special Forces. That's why I got out of the Air Force. I mean, that's why I'm here in Augusta. I wanted my clearance back so I could get a deployment, and it was just at a time when I wasn't applying for deployments. I had, you know, seven, eight months left of a job that didn't mean anything to me because it's Iran, and I'm a Pashto linguist. Like, what am I doing translating Farsi? It just—it just—I felt really hopeless and, uhm, seeing that information that had been contested back and forth back and forth in the public domain for so long, trying to figure out, like, with everything else that keeps getting released and keeps getting leaked why isn't this getting why isn't this out there? Why can't this be public? (United States Department of Justice 2017)

Reality-based theater is "one way that artists are challenging the lies put out by politicians like Trump" (Stephenson 2019). While Satter "regards her work as political," she does "not start from a place of trying to make a political point" (Del Vecchio 2016: 81). Although drawn to the way Winner was "interrogating her own relationship to the United States and its leadership and then taking action on it in a big way" (Krane 2020), Satter and her actors were "really like, old fashioned theater way ... treating that transcript as canonical text ... As if it's Shakespeare, what is in *this*, you know what I mean?" (Satter 2020).

I wasn't at that point, or even now, trying to really tell the larger story of Reality ... Like, to show how those levers of power operated that day, and what Reality went through, it was not, it was just, like, *this* happened [emphasis Satter's]. This is the first word said. This was the last word said. We've put a theatrical imagining of how bodies move in space to hold those exchange of sentences but ... I wanted it to really feel like we're showing and hearing what happened that day and that's the most pure and ultimately interesting and dramatic thing. (Satter 2020)

Even if Satter's motivation was not to reveal the truth-behind-the-truth of Russian interference in America's election, performance "is a place where claims of truth can be tested, ridiculed, transgressed, or reinforced" (Freeman and Jones 2018: 7). Taking a transcript that is in itself a replication of a real event—especially one so closely linked to our current political culture—and treating that text as canonical and therefore worthy of artistic attention speaks to the post-truth possibility of theater as a site of duality and contestation: "a document in a documentary play carries at least two meanings at once ... the meaning it was presumed to have had in its original context and the meaning that the play's creators assign it by repeating it in a new context" (Youker 2012: 20). This possibility is affirmed by Carol Martin: "What makes documentary theater provocative is the way in which it strategically deploys the appearance of truth while inventing its own particular truth through elaborate aesthetic devices" (2010: 19).

With *Is This A Room*, Satter forgoes the usual textual selection and editing together of interviews and other archival sources that is typical of verbatim theater (Hammond and Steward 2008). Unlike documentary plays such as *The Laramie Project* by Moisés Kaufman, there is no textual pointing to the play's "devising process" because there is no textual devising. In presenting, in its entirety, "the real material in its original form," *Is This A Room* is a more complete "fusing of the real and the fictional" (Auerswald 2017: 117).

This "troubling" of reality is made visible only via the play's framing and production design—filtered through Satter's heightened aesthetic sensibility—resulting in a work that is both verbatim *and* imagined, real *and* abstract, performance *and* documentary. The entire experience—our movement between r(R)eality and the theater of r(R)eality—has been thoughtfully negotiated: "that sort of stuff is *very* important to me ... of, like, the second you walk in the door, what are you getting?" (Satter 2020).

Upon entering the physical space of the theater, the focus is on reality and Reality. Flyers ("Stand with Reality") and other materials stress Winner's name, story, and image. At the Vineyard Theatre, an enormous picture of Winner in her Air Force uniform hung from the ceiling. For Satter, this emphasis on "the actualness of Reality" felt important to "that idea of the truth": "the important thing to me was to show the real Reality ... This is a real person, this is what she looked like" (Satter 2020). Projected within the lobby's interior, which I missed (at both The Kitchen and Vineyard Theatre productions) because of crowds and, according to Satter, "the way bodies move through space," was the following, very minimal text: "On May 2017, evidence of Russian interference in the 2016 US election was leaked to the media" (Satter 2020).

In its initial run at The Kitchen in early 2019, Winner's name and the words "verbatim transcription" were included in the play's title—*Is This A Room: Reality Winner Verbatim Transcription*.[3] What I thought was perhaps a signaling by Satter—an indication that this production was an enactment of a real-life event and therefore a departure from Half Straddle's usual, nondocumentary work—was again her commitment to the document itself: "Because that's what's stamped on the front of the actual PDF of the actual transcript. I never could move away from that at first. I'm like this is the title because the first day I looked at that thing I was like this looks like a play" (Satter 2020).

The shift from reality to theater as we enter the main stage is immediate. An almost dangerously thick haze of dry ice filled the entire space as the audience took their seats at The Kitchen. Flo Rida's "My House" blasted through the speakers. The energy was high and very Half Straddle—like we'd just arrived at a really cool downtown party. Music—usually wholly original in composition—is central to Half Straddle's work. Here, Satter and Sanae Yamada (her longtime music director), imagined what a twenty-five-year-old woman, driving back to her house on that summer day in 2017, might have been listening to. They researched what would have been playing that afternoon on a main Augusta, Georgia, radio station:

> And we kind of from, like, our level of ... knowing her from her Instagram, and from the tweets ... we had a little bit more of a sense of her music from some other random ways, but we also liked *imagining* [emphasis Satter's] that she was listening to maybe a pop radio station ... So just situating her emotionally and then a little bit of a nod to that literal time and place. (Satter 2020)

The playlist includes Drake, Kendrick Lamar, Rihanna, Kehlani. Listening closely, the lyrics can be cheeky or haunting, or both, underscoring aspects of Reality's situation and personality: "I'm no man's fantasy / I never plan to be" ("Fantasy," by Kari Faux). The volume of the music is intentional too: "some of the feeling that it's almost too loud, like a girl in her car" (Satter 2020).

Then the music stops, the haze lifts, the party is over. We register immediately the fiction of the staging—a strip of gray carpet with low risers on each side—which does not in any way attempt to replicate Winner's home, or any home at all. Half Straddle's productions are "aesthetically flawless" and "all of the elements are fully-realized and incredibly detailed … The set designs are simple but striking; they often make use of rich color schemes that unify the productions" (Del Vecchio 2016: 80–1). Here, however, the set is highly abstracted—minimalist and colorless—and serves as a strong counterpoint to the mood and energy of its pre-curtain pop-music soundtrack: "I wanted it to be really stark. I wanted people to hear and see this conversation and to have it feel like all the action and emotion and energy came from those humans in space and not from a fake room on a stage" (Schmelzer 2020). Satter's artistic choice to forgo creating some replica of reality—to call out those attempts as "fake"—speaks to how insufficient realism can be in reproducing reality. If the audience recognizes "the fake" in "the real"—is this a room?—the jig is up. Instead, it is through bodies in space—their movements, words, and silences, and the emotions and energy that those bodies collectively generate—that theater can create the conditions under which "the real" might present itself.

It is also striking that Satter does not try to make the set *more* fabulist—none of the colorful accents and glitter that are part of her usual aesthetic—to indicate to the audience a movement further away from reality into the "theater" of a Half Straddle production. For Satter, however, the *suggestion* of a room can be much more evocative than an *actual* room, and presents an interesting ambiguity: "It raises the question of whether this is happening in real life or whether this is happening in a theatre? Like, you set up a theatre as a sort of old-fashioned thing: you go into a room and you make this story happen" (Schmelzer 2020).

Satter's "you" in this case also includes the audience. The abstracted set invites—indeed, necessitates—the audience to become participants in the creative process. We must imagine what Reality's house looked like and pay hypervigilant attention to the words being spoken in order to understand where we are—whether we are outside in her driveway or her yard, or inside, given that the set serves as both exterior and interior space. The single row of audience members behind the stage—who just a few minutes ago seemed to have coveted VIP tickets to the party—now resemble a panel of jurors. Suddenly the set shifts from "empty box" to "courtroom" and the proximity of the panel, along with ours, suggests intimacy, witness, and arbitration of the "realness" before them: "the layout of the theatre space ... implies the act of witnessing an event, which can be greatly intensified through the verbatim form. Because verbatim theatre takes its material from interviews or (court) transcripts, broadly speaking, audiences witness the distilled essence of 'real' public events and 'real' people's opinions" (Auerswald 2017: 113).

Half Straddle's performances "do not emphasize the body" but frequently contain movement and physicality—including dance or dance-like sequences (Del Vecchio 2016: 78). The entire conversation between Winner and the three FBI agents is minutely choreographed by Satter as an elaborate pugilistic dance—a series of micro- and macro-movements as the agents flank Winner, give her space, move practically offstage, only to zero in on her again. This was not done as a replication of the agents' *actual* movement that day but as a moment-by-moment imagining of what was happening—"a heart and brain connection to the language on the transcript" as well as to create "an energetic field of what it would have felt like for Reality" (Satter 2020): "there were all these male presences at work on her, and she was lying to and in conversation with them. I was like, 'I think it's really important that we show this masculine code and energy and physicality up there next to the Reality body'" (Satter 2020).

This choreography of "masculine code and energy" renders all of the funny "ums" and "ahems" of the agents' speech as highly strategic, as if every single cough has been preconceived and carefully deployed. Although one reviewer questioned the truthfulness of the agents' proximity to Winner given their emphasis within the transcript (and the play) on following strict FBI protocol (Hofler 2019), what is "real" is the terrifying intimacy—and performance—of interrogation. Satter's choreography of physical proximity, as it conveys the emotional energy of interrogation, was in fact justified. The agents, for the latter half of their questioning, intentionally took Winner into a small concrete room in the back of her house, one that she hated because it was "creepy":

> When she says I don't really want to go there and they're like "Oh we can go there." That you can see pictures of … in some Democracy Now interview in March 2018. So you can see that room and it was very small … I didn't know that at the time I was making that movement, but then it was like, "Oh we're actually onto something because she was in a very small room." And they took her there on purpose. (Satter 2020)

By following her theater-making instincts, Satter arrived at a truth that "the facts," in fact, bore out. The choreography of "masculine code and energy" is also the choreography of power and can be seen as echoing Winner's movement within the larger patriarchal systems—military, security—that employed her (and that she was up against).

Is This A Room both recreates and complicates gender and its performance, while also "troubling" the r(R)eality of performance. The acting is realistic in that the actors "don't really try to play up any moment in choices of tone" (Roeder 2019) but their performance is not an attempt at *actual* replication either:

> We eventually developed a relationship with Reality's mom where we could have said, "Can you tell us how Reality speaks, do you have any family videos?" … but that was just not the project for us. It was not trying to reproduce exactly who that woman was. It was about an

incredible actor who looks a bit like her taking at face value these words Reality actually said. The truth was created from that. (Satter 2020)

The actors in male roles did not research the real-life FBI agents they portray, nor do they attempt to "play men" (Roeder 2019). But their deferrals and pauses and overlapping dialogue underscore their self-conscious performance of masculinity. Winner's own deployment of "justs" in response to the agents' questioning emphasizes authentic fear but also a strategy of performing femininity—a "girlish solicitousness" (Solomon 2019)—during which she plays her intelligence up or down, depending on what she believes the moment, and the men, require of her.

Satter's theater company has been described as "gloriously queer" and her presentation of "maleness" is further complicated by her casting:

> Half Straddle's drag isn't only girls playing boys and boys playing girls; it's playing on the smart-yet-gleefully-hilarious trespassing between gender, sexuality and age. Girls are women and women are girls, trans and cisgender actors play ambiguously gendered or cisgender characters. Satter creates a very specific cacophony of the gender spectrum, always mediated through adolescence. (Alker 2018)

In this case, two of the three FBI agents are played by trans actors, one of whom also happens to be Black. Although seeing trans actors on stage feels inherently political, and Satter acknowledges what a trans body "portraying a male in an enforcement thing can call up … experientially, impressionistically, and literally," she also "just cast the two best actors for those agents' roles and then the amazing icing is, yeah, they're trans" (Roeder 2019).

Those agents are R. Wallace Taylor (played by T. L. Thompson) and Unknown Male (played by Becca Blackwell), a typically Satter character both in name and in her realization that the character conveys nine different male voices:

> That was fascinating, because there was that non sequitur quality to that text on the page attributed to Unknown Male … For a bunch of reasons, we didn't want to divide this up among nine other

actors—mostly cost and just, like, that's crazy—but then it became this fun thing to play with: "What's the logic with that character?" They actually represented all these male bodies moving around Reality's tiny house and outside it. Those men were photographing everything, moving stuff, cataloguing it, so it allowed us to give all these stupid devices to Becca, like a couple phones [sic] and weird tools, and then find a way that they were saying stuff in the walkies and to some of the other agents to create this logic for that non sequitur quality of the text. (Krane 2020)

As an audience member, unaware of the amalgam (or spectrum) of voices that Unknown Male represented, I found myself wondering: Did someone *actually* say these things? I questioned our continued adherence to the transcription even though I knew that its replication was word for word. The non-sequiturs lend an absurdist quality to the text and trouble our relationship with the play's "truth" and "reality." Notably, it is Unknown Male who provides the strange non sequitur of the title when he asks repeatedly: Is this a room?[4]

This disjointment is also amplified by the play's theatrical embodiment of the transcript's redactions. Early on, the lights flicker and pulse pink with every blackened word. As the redactions build into paragraphs, the entire theater plummets into darkness, bringing the original text, which is itself a replication or facsimile of the event, into our consciousness, suggesting a "calling into question," since we may not know, as audience members, that these descents into darkness, after which bodies on stage have reoriented and we scramble to reorient ourselves in order to keep pace with the hiccupping conversation, represent real omissions of the text. The darkness is accompanied by a low-frequency boom—the sound a microphone might make if used as a gavel. The effect is disorienting—like traveling in a fun-house time-machine that travels just a few seconds or minutes into the future.[5] Or longer. While the transcript-rendered verbatim lasts seventy minutes on stage, it is unclear how long the *actual* interrogation lasted: "What in real life was like, you know, maybe a couple of hours in this young woman's life, we do it in an hour" (Satter 2021). Words (and truths) that have been officially "disappeared" are experienced viscerally as a kind of visual and aural amnesia. For Satter, these blackouts evoke something even more sinister—the threat of knowledge: "When you come to the black box on the page, there's something inherently kind of terrifying about it, like something I can't know or that's dangerous" (Schmelzer 2020).

These redactions occur largely in the play's second "act," which Satter constructed based on her realization of where the "real" interrogation begins within the larger conversation:

> That first third is just all this weird chitchat outside her house. That's when we were like, "the first act is that." The second act is this actual interrogation in this little room, and then once she admits. And then the third act was where, once she's admitted, we were like, "We can really push further on these designs, using tech in it a bit," going further into what it feels like in her head. Voices feel far away. That's where we play more with lights. There's a slowed-down part where the agents talk about her cat. Because we were like, "How surreal would it be for Reality to then hear the agents talking about her cat again?" (Krane 2020)

It is in this third act that the play notably shifts into abstraction. The music—an original nine-synth score by Yamada and Lee Kinney—has, up until now, echoed the darker emotional and psychological realism of the play's first and second acts: tension, expectation, threat, and loss.[6] A low menacing hum is deployed, for example, that culminates in Winner's confession. Here, coupled with the use of slow motion, the music changes mood entirely to become something stranger and out of place: bouncy, dream-like, surreal. This shift from "realism" is still an attempt to replicate something "real": the emotional interiority of Reality. This is the work that theater can do, allowing us access to empathy, which we would not otherwise be able to access because of its absence from the page.

As important as theatrical elements are to Satter, she carefully balanced her artistic impulses with an integrity to the text and its real-life characters: "It was at the level of that design stuff too, that was being, you know, truthful. Let's just keep this direct and clear" (Satter 2020). It is relevant that the "stupid tools"—the old-school walkie-talkies and cellphone—are handled by Unknown Male who, as a composite character of nine male voices, is the most clownish of the three FBI agents. All of the unintelligible sounds documented in the transcript as "[UI]" are attributed to him and rendered by Satter's sound team, via these devices, as "a soundscape of growls, grumbles, zhoozhes, faint gongs, chimey arpeggios, and low drones" (Solomon 2019). Unknown Male also spends a good chunk of the play herding Winner's dog and cat. Even though stuffed animals are a Half Straddle trademark—a baby seal set afloat across a lake in *Seagull (Thinking of You)*, for example, or a swan named Svetlana in the woods of *Ancient Lives*—Satter wanted the stuffed versions to actually replicate Winner's real dog and cat:[7] "We wanted them to look as realistic as possible. We couldn't afford the dogs that looked *so* realistic [emphasis Satter's]. But he does have the colors of the original dogs" (Satter 2020).

Satter's costumes usually register her interest in fashion. Details like the perfect shade of lipstick or the fur that lines a character's pocket are incredibly important to her because such details, being feminine, are "often considered inconsequential and insubstantial" (Del Vecchio 2016: 78). When considering the FBI agents' costumes, however, Satter countered her impulse to substantiate the feminine, citing the ease with which the agents could have been rendered as buffoons:

> Very immediately me and Enver Chakartash, who … just does these beautiful imagined things usually, we felt like it was not that there were these crazy costumes. It wasn't some, like, you know, weird FBI outfit! Then you kind of get excited, the perversity of getting into the normcore of it. So then it was like these have to be sort of plain and real, we're not going to go crazy, there are secret touches for us, and also not totally, totally real, if you look … this is a Half Straddle edge to just everything very, very slightly. (Satter 2020)

While these "secret touches" smuggled in as Half Straddle "truths" might include Unknown Male's mullet, thigh-holster, and the walkie-talkie clipped to the collar of his flak jacket like a pair of aviators, these details still fall within the realm of realism. Emily Davis's costume (the actor who plays Reality Winner) is almost entirely an authentic replication of what Winner was wearing on the day of her June 2017 arrest: "that is like an exact reproduction, overall, of what Reality was wearing that day ... she was wearing low-top yellow Converses in real life and Enver made them high-tops and put a Pikachu on them. So that's a touch to Reality, a little Half Straddle touch" (Satter 2020).

These feminine-masculine, nonbinary attributes—security clearance *and* Pikachu bedspread, part-time yoga instructor *and* CrossFit enthusiast, NSA contractor *and* owner of a Nissan Cube sporting a "Be truthful, gentle and fearless" bumper sticker—which of course drew Satter to Winner and could easily serve as both real-life and Half Straddle "truths," are only minimally included in the play's design. Not even the pink gun Winner owned, I wondered? For Satter, these characteristics are articulated in the text of the interrogation itself, rendering them redundant as visual details:

> Because it's just so perfect when they say is one of them pink? So it lives there, right? ... And I had this whole idea that Reality would change into this really cool dress for her final, and I was just, like, no ... The mention of the pink gun does it. Sanae's songs at the start do it. If you look at her Pikachu sneakers, you know? Like yeah. It couldn't ... it was not right to put that stuff on it. (Satter 2020)

Satter does acknowledge, however, the one place she did "play" with the agents: "when they can't figure out where Reality can go to the bathroom. We don't know if that's actually what was happening, but that's the only way we could read it" (Satter 2020). This "allowance" for "play" was still tempered with a commitment to keeping the agents and the scene "as dry as possible," and is consistent with the characters' use of humor (as tactic, as coping mechanism) throughout the questioning:

> We felt like it could hold that because I think it's present that day in that really creepy nauseous way, you know what I mean? They're trying to joke occasionally with Reality, she's making these dry jokes, she does

the Anderson Cooper thing at the end, and then just the larger cosmic nightmare humor of this whole thing. That like, Paul Manafort's gonna be at his pool and this one person who actually told the truth is gonna go through this and then spend five years in jail, you know? The dark, dark Chekhovian flip of that. (Satter 2020)

Satter's fidelity to the text allows the "dark, dark" surreality of the interrogation to come through. Indeed, this fidelity is such that the whatness of Winner's crime is never stated within the play. If one missed the "actualness" of Reality's story in the lobby, for example, one would eventually come to understand that Winner stuffed a classified document into her pantyhose, exited the building in which she worked, and mailed it to a news outlet, but one would have no idea what the document, or her crime, was about. In this way, *Is This A Room* serves as both theater of the "really real" and theater of the absurd: "Theatre of the Absurd has renounced arguing *about* the absurdity of the human condition; it merely *presents* it in being" (Esslin 2004: 25).

This quality of bothness—where details of the performance can be authentically, heightened Half Straddle *and* still remain truthful to the text and to Winner's story—is one of the mysteries and accomplishments of the play. The kind of deep imagining that Satter does, informed by the documentary record, draws to mind the work of Saidiya Hartman, whose writing, although rooted in the archive, blends history with fiction in imagining the lives of women, especially those women who have been erased from the historical record through omission or misrepresentation. While Winner has not been omitted from the public record, the barrage of headlines and misinformation that constitutes "media" in post-truth America rendered her story—and the truth-behind-the-truth of Russian election interference—as invisible. In lifting this particular document from "the archive," and then reimagining and re-presenting the verbatim experience of this particular woman, Satter acknowledges what theater in a post-truth world can do:

> Reality's story and what went on there, like, theater did give more attention … it nailed down some kind of truth that was being buried

or something ... Like, the act of putting her, that moment, back live, putting it back into the universe over and over again, like, remakes *a* version of *a* truth [emphasis Satter's]. Over and over. Literally, it says look at this. (Satter 2020)

Since putting "that moment ... into the universe over and over again," truths are being remade. In June 2021, after having served four years of her record five-year sentence under the Espionage Act, Reality was released from prison for good behavior. In October 2021, *Is This A Room* premiered on Broadway at the Lyceum Theater, providing another opportunity for citizens to "look" at Winner's story, which, despite her release, remains "not super mainstream" (Satter 2021). In yet another post-truth (in)version of r(R)eality, there was speculation that Winner herself may be able to attend— and therefore witness—the "performance" of her own interrogation and arrest.[8] Given the "Chekhovian flip" of Reality's release, with the person having once been imprisoned now being represented on Broadway, I asked Satter: Does the "truth" of the play get remade in some way?

> I think for a moment in the time she was getting released, I did wonder, I did think does this change it, is there something different around it, and it's because in a way, we've always just tried to be really pure. Here is this transcript we have, now here are the actors we've chosen to do it, here is the set we have decided does it strongest [*sic*], you know what I mean? And that's going to be the same because that's what we have. (Satter 2021)

Though Satter acknowledges that some of the factual information about Winner that appears in the theater-space *before* the performance may change, the play itself will remain "this real deal" whereby "in the back room in a small house on a sunny day in the United States this thing happened" (Satter 2021). Satter, a talented playwright, could easily have written additional material, provided the audience with more context, or made the play more abstract, but she decided (and continues to decide) not to. *Is This A Room* serves as both a troubling of reality and a word-for-word recreation of a troubled "reality." Winner is a young woman who threatened to upset the balance of power at its highest levels by choosing to release a document "that gave us information that we needed to know at a time that we absolutely needed to know it" ("NSA Whistleblower Reality Winner" 2021). Whether or not all of the stylistic particulars of *Is This A Room* are "true," its larger truths—that the world punishes young women, especially smart ones, for *exposing the truth*—are.

Notes

1. Tina Satter (2020), phone conversation with author, December 22. Appears with permission from the author.
2. Howley (2017). Appears with permission from Vox Media.
3. Later, at the Vineyard Theatre, both "verbatim transcription" and Winner's name were dropped from the play's title. By then, with so much discussion about what does the audience need to know beforehand, and how much, Satter said: "It's ok to lose this, you know what I mean? *Is This A Room* can do the work now" (Satter 2020).
4. Satter omits the question mark in the title because—as absurd or obvious as the question already is—she "wanted it to be weirder than that somehow" (Satter 2020).
5. I am evoking here Brenda Shaughnessy's poem, "I Have a Time Machine," published in her collection *So Much Synth* (2016).
6. The original score of *Is This A Room* was released by Vive la Void (Sanae Yamada and Lee Kinney) on Jean Sandwich Records in October 2019.
7. Amanda Villalobos, the prop designer for *Is This A Room*, was nominated for a "Puppetry Design" Drama Desk award for her design of Winner's pets.
8. Even though Winner has been released from prison, she is under home confinement for the remainder of her sentence and was unable to attend a Broadway performance of *Is This A Room*. Without a presidential pardon or clemency, which her family is seeking on her behalf, Winner will forever have certain restrictions placed on her privileges and movements.

References

Alker, G. (2018), "Reclaiming 'Whatever!': Half Straddle as Exemplar of Contemporary Feminist Theatre," *Contemporary Theatre Review*, October. Available online: https://www.contemporarytheatrereview.org/2018/alker-half-straddle-reclaiming-whatever/ (accessed October 23, 2020).

Auerswald, B. (2017), "Promises of the Real? The Precariousness of Verbatim Theatre and Robin Soans's *Talking to Terrorists*," in M. Aragay and M. Middeke (eds.), *Of Precariousness: Vulnerabilities, Responsibilities, Communities in 21st Century British Drama and Theatre*, 109–23, Berlin: DeGruyter. ProQuest Ebook Central. Available online: https://ebookcentral.proquest.com/lib/brooklyn-ebooks/detail.action?docID=5043159 (accessed September 4, 2020).

Del Vecchio, J. (2016), "Straddling Feminisms: Post-Wave Pop Politics and Experimental Performance," PhD diss., Graduate Center of the City University of New York, New York. *CUNY Academic Works*. Available online: https://academicworks.cuny.edu/gc_etds/1348 (accessed September 15, 2020).

Del Vecchio, J. (2018), "'Not 'Just This Girl Theatre': Half Straddle's Feminine Aesthetics Come of Age," *Contemporary Theatre Review*, 28 (3): 310–19. Available online: doi:10.1080/10486801.2018.1475362 (accessed August 5, 2020).

Esslin, M. (2004), *Theatre of the Absurd*, New York: Vintage Books.

Freeman, B., and M. Jones (2018), "Post-Truth?," *Canadian Theatre Review*, 175: 5–7. Available online: muse.jhu.edu/article/699066 (accessed April 13, 2020).

Hammond, W., and D. Steward (2008), *Verbatim, Verbatim: Contemporary Documentary Theatre*, London: Oberon Books.

Hammons, C. (n.d.), Unpublished interview with Tina Satter. Quoted in Jessica Del Vecchio (2016), "Straddling Feminisms: Post-Wave Pop Politics and Experimental Performance," PhD diss., Graduate Center of the City University of New York, New York. *CUNY Academic Works*. Available online: https://academicworks.cuny.edu/gc_etds/1348 (accessed September 15, 2020).

Hofler, R. (2019), "'Is This A Room' Theater Review: A Staged Interrogation of a Whistleblower Named Reality Winner," *The Wrap*, October. Available online: https://www.thewrap.com/is-this-a-room-theater-review-reality-winner-tina-satter-whistleblower/ (accessed March 15, 2020).

Howley, K. (2017), "The World's Biggest Terrorist Has a Pikachu Bedspread," *New York Magazine*, December 25. Available online: https://nymag.com/intelligencer/2017/12/who-is-reality-winner.html (accessed August 20, 2019).

Krane, D. (2020), "Tina Satter Unlocks the Drama of an F.B.I. Transcript," *Extended Play*, February 18. Available online: https://extendedplay.thecivilians.org/tina-satter-talks-is-this-a-room/ (accessed March 15, 2020).

Liska, P., and K. Copper (2013), *OK Radio Podcast*, February 6.

Martin, C. (2010), "Bodies of Evidence," in Carol Martin (ed.), *Dramaturgy of the Real on the World Stage*, 17–26, London: Palgrave Macmillan. Available online: https://doi-org.brooklyn.ezproxy.cuny.edu/10.1057/9780230251311 (accessed October 5, 2020).

Martin, C. (2012), "An Overview," in Carol Martin (ed.), *Theatre of the Real*, 1–21, London: Palgrave Macmillan. Available online: https://doi-org.brooklyn.ezproxy.cuny.edu/10.1057/9781137295729 (accessed August 5, 2020).

"NSA Whistleblower Reality Winner Released from Prison as Family Pushes Biden to Pardon Her" (2021), *Democracy Now*, June 15. Available online: https://www.democracynow.org/2021/6/15/reality_winner_released_from_prison (accessed July 15, 2021).

Phillips, D. (2018), "Reality Winner, Former N.S.A. Translator, Gets More than Five Years in Leak of Russian Hacking Report," *New York Times*, August 23. Available online: https://www.nytimes.com/2018/08/23/us/reality-winner-nsa-sentence.html (accessed January 5, 2021).

"Playing Reality Winner: Turning an F.B.I. Interrogation into Theater" (2019), *NBC News*, January 24. Available online: https://www.nbcnews.com/video/playing-reality-winner-turning-an-F.B.I.-interrogation-into-theater-1431194179574 (accessed March 15, 2020).

Roeder, M. (2019), *No Safety Net Podcast*, December 10.

Satter, T. (2020), Phone Conversation with Author, December 22.

Satter, T. (2021), Phone Conversation with Author, July 19.

Schmelzer, P. (2020), "How Whistleblower Reality Winner's F.B.I. Interrogation Became Powerful Theater," *Fourth Wall*, January 6. Available online: https://walkerart.org/magazine/tina-satter-reality-winner-verbatim-transcription-billie-winner-davis (accessed December 19, 2020).

Solomon, A. (2019), "The F.B.I.'s Interrogation of Reality Winner Was Like a Play—And Has Now Been Turned into One," *The Intercept*, January 2.

Available online: https://theintercept.com/2019/01/02/reality-winner-play-is-this-a-room/ (accessed March 15, 2020).

Stephenson, J. (2019), "In the Post-Truth Era, Documentary Theatre Searches for Common Ground," *The Conversation*, January 3. Available online: https://theconversation.com/in-the-post-truth-era-documentary-theatre-searches-for-common-ground-104445 (accessed March 15, 2020).

Teeman, T. (2019), "The Best Raised Voices Returns from the Past: Harvey Fierstein in 'Bella Bella,' and 'For Colored Girls,'" *Daily Beast*, October 23. Available online: https://www.thedailybeast.com/harvey-fierstein-in-bella-bella-and-for-colored-girls-the-best-raised-voices-return-from-the-past-5 (accessed March 15, 2020).

United States Department of Justice Federal Bureau of Investigation (2017), *United States v Reality Leigh Winner, CR 117–34, Government's Exhibit A: Transcript of Defendant's Interview*, June 3. Available online: https://standwithreality.org/wp-content/uploads/2017/10/092717-100.1-interrogation-transcript.pdf (accessed December 19, 2020).

Williams, B. (2014), "Tina Satter: Interview," *BODY*, January 3. Available online: https://bodyliterature.com/tina-satter-interview/ (accessed September 5, 2020).

Wynants, N. (2020), *When Fact Is Fiction: Documentary Art in the Post-Truth Era*, Amsterdam: Valiz.

Youker, T. (2012), "'The Destiny of Words': Documentary Theatre, the Avant-Garde, and the Politics of Form," PhD diss., Columbia University, New York.

8

Seductive Frames: Digital Aesthetics in Kip Williams's Staging of Bertolt Brecht's *The Resistible Rise of Arturo Ui* (2018)

Susanne Thurow

Across the twentieth century, transformative historical events like the Second World War amplified seismic shifts in Western thought and cultural practices that called into question the very premises on which concepts of reality, society, and identity had been founded. Bertholt Brecht witnessed firsthand the scale of devastation brought about by displacement, persecution, and erasure of entire social groups with endorsement by the majority of society. In this context, the pull of demagogues and their communicative systems proved particularly powerful, bearing eerie parallels to the post-truth effects unfolding in our contemporary digitally saturated cultures. Brecht sought to foster clarity around the cultural and political processes that may lead to such radical abandoning of ethical positions, identifying in particular the role of persuasion when it appeals to emotive intuition at the expense of intellectual reasoning as a key ingredient of antidemocratic fermentation. Drawing inspiration from Marxist ideology to develop a critique of Capitalism as a driver of social alienation, Brecht's enduring legacy remains his rearticulation of theatrical aesthetics as a prompt for critical reflection (Boyle 2016: 18). By continually disrupting immersion through a range of defamiliarization techniques and forcing competing performance styles together without smoothing over the tensions between them, Brechtian theater seeks to position audiences to question performances as engineered mediations on human behavior that always entail a possibility for alternative pathways. In this regard, it already preempted central tenets of postmodern theories, in so far as they conceive the subject as an arbitrary, socially determined, and fluid construction that is established by the historical vagaries of its time as well as sociocultural and geographical place (Zima 2010: xii).

Formulating identity primarily as resulting from performance rather than a preexisting condition, Brecht's work strongly resonates in contemporary times, in which the effective construction of persona has become key to assuming and executing agency both in public as well as private domains (Kalpokas 2019: 70). Yet, Brecht deployed his disruptive aesthetics to lay bare the artifice of cultural performances. He sought to set in motion a "renewal of perception" by inviting a meta-reflection of identificatory processes to encourage the adoption of veracity and truth as pillars of social and political practice (Carney 2005: 19). However, postmodern philosophy dissected such aspirations as forever doomed because the relation between signs/performances and their referents was interrogated as an arbitrary ascription rather than expressing an essential connection (Li 2018: 449). With the dissolution of this stable identification of sign and referent, as argued by thinkers like Jacques Derrida, veracity and discourse have become conceptually divided from each other because signification must be subject to eternal slippage, or *différance* (Li 2018: 449), and truth be deemed ultimately relational rather than absolute. Consequently, adapting Brechtian aesthetics and their political impetus into a contemporary frame requires reckoning with a stark disparity between epistemological horizons and associated aesthetic practices that divide Brecht's historically sited creative agenda from modern-day relational meaning-making processes. As Peter Brooker points out, the ubiquity of disruption as a creative methodology in contemporary times means that it alone does not invariably unfold artistic and political effects (2006: 6). Rather, it requires integration into a broader semantic framework to address the challenges post-truth discourse raises for sociopolitical environments. These are the numbing effects of cognitive dissonance that result from a deliberate and continuous blurring of fact and falsity (McIntyre 2018: chap. 1,

19). In its championing of emotional rather than intellectual reasoning, post-truth discourse establishes a climate of apathy and collusion rather than supporting empowerment and political agency in civil societies (McDermott 2019: 221).

This essay discusses the aesthetic integration of digital and analogue performance in Kip Williams's staging of Bertolt Brecht's *The Resistible Rise of Arturo Ui* (Roslyn Packer Theatre, Sydney, 2018) as an exploration of such adaptation that translates the Brechtian aesthetic program into a contemporary cultural fold while nevertheless retaining and avowing its political agenda. Through analyzing the layered screen and stage performances, it appraises Williams's work as a sophisticated and timely example of artistically thinking through contemporary image-making practices that site the classical text firmly within our age of post-truth and sensory voracity. The key to Williams's approach thereby lies in his conversion of post-truth as a phenomenon of contemporary politics into a structuring principle guiding his theatrical aesthetics. He takes Brechtian aesthetics as a starting point only to funnel them through a postmodern lens that comments on the seductive influence of contemporary image-making practices, which easily bypass the intellectual faculties Brecht was aiming to activate through his aesthetics. The chapter opens with a brief consideration of how both Brecht as well as Williams and playwright Tom Wright evoke political and historical context in their work to achieve a resonance with contemporary zeitgeist. It then reviews those aspects of Brechtian aesthetics that Williams draws on in his reimagination of *Arturo Ui*, segueing into a subsequent analysis of Williams's staging that investigates the configuration of discourses of power, reality, and truth as they intersect across the production's visual and performative design.

As deeply political theater, *The Resistible Rise of Arturo Ui* draws much of its signification and force from resonating with contemporary historical, political, and discursive context. Brecht wrote the play with support from Margarete Steffin in Helsinki, Finland, while waiting to emigrate to the United States. Meditating on the volatility of democratic systems and the ways demagogues may exploit these to usurp power, the play allegorically reflects the rise of Adolf Hitler and his establishment as "Führer" in 1930s Germany. These same events had prompted Brecht to flee his home country to seek safety abroad. The manuscript was completed in 1941, but the play was not produced until 1958—two years after the playwright's death. Brecht had set his play's dramatic action within a city loosely modeled on 1930s Chicago, whose gangster milieu was inspired by dominant tropes he borrowed from then popular movies (e.g., William A. Wellman's *The Public Enemy*, 1931). By choosing a space that represented "übercapitalism" in his time (Wright qtd. in Mumford 2018: 5), Brecht was able to contextualize his arguments about power and greed in direct relation to the economic and political systems whose dynamics he believed to be lying at the heart of social alienation. Contrary to place, the play's dramatic personae and action were more closely modeled on the German context, with many correlating with real-life characters and historical events. As Nozomi Irei points out, each referenced an important persona of Brecht's time: "Ui (Hitler), Dogsborough (Paul von Hindenburg), Giri (Hermann Göring), Givola (Joseph Goebbels), Roma (Ernst Röhm), [and] Dullfeet (Austrian Chancellor Engelbert Dollfuss)" (2016: 153), with some scenes closely resonating with events that took place across the 1930s, such as "Röhm, a Sturmabteilung captain and Hitler's close friend, ... betrayed and killed along with his men on 30 June 1934," which occurs to Ernesto Roma in *Arturo Ui* (Willet qtd. in Irei: 153), and Hitler having taken acting lessons to increase the impact of his public performances (Irei: 153), just as Ui does. In a satirical twist, Brecht made his demagogue Arturo a smalltime criminal who sets his eyes on extorting the local vegetable trade rather than aiming straight for the circles of the rich and powerful. Learning of a popular politician's (Dogsborough) nefarious deals with their lobbyists, Arturo pushes his way to power by violently crushing resistance and using the specter of his reputation to lure or force the support of a growing number of institutions (including the unions, media, and courts) until having usurped the entire city's decision-making systems. True to Brecht's focus on character development through action rather than psychological reasoning, Arturo's rise is presented as a series of decisions that people make to protect or further their individual interests at the expense of collective power, while Arturo's performance centralizes the fabrication of public persona as a conduit to amass power through persuasion by any means. As Jack Teiwes points out, this results in the play capturing not only "one evil man's indomitable will-to-power, but rather the failure, corruptibility, complicity, and capitulation of the system" around him (2018).

The Resistible Rise of Arturo Ui was adapted by Tom Wright for a staging at Sydney Theatre Company's Roslyn Packer Theatre, where it played from March 21 to April 28, 2018. The two-hour, no-interval play was directed by its Artistic Director Kip Williams and featured a multicultural cast, including Hugo Weaving in the title role, as well as Anita Hegh, Ursula Yovic, Peter Carroll, Colin Moody, Mitchell Butel, Tony Cogin, Ivan Donato, Brent Hill, Monica Sayers, and Charles Wu. The production won four prestigious Sydney Theatre Awards and two Helpmann Awards.

Unlike Bruce Norris's 2017 adaptation of the play staged at Donmar Warehouse in London (dir. Simon Evans), Wright and Williams did not "go down the Trump road" (Weaving qtd. in Dow 2018) to allow the play to resonate across time and place (Williams 2021). To nevertheless capture the contemporary zeitgeist and connect with their local audience and their political arena, Wright included subtle verbal and visual references that transposed the action into a recognizably Australian context. These included well-known populist quotes from Australian federal politicians such as "we will decide who comes to this country and the circumstances under which they come" (former prime minister John Howard on the 2001 federal immigration policy), his successor Tony Abbot's "stop the boats" (in reference to the 2013 *Operation Sovereign Borders* policy), or former treasurer Joe Hockey's division of society into "lifters" and "leaners" that he used to justify austerity measures in 2014. Visually, cityscape projections evoked architectural styles dominating Sydney's The Rocks harborside district (formerly a haven for "razor gangs and its fair share of organised crime"

(Felapton 2018)) and cited the interiors of famous establishments in its Chinatown that are frequented by the rich and influential, such as The Golden Century (Wright qtd. in Mumford 2018: 9). Other evocations of place included Arturo reading a copy of *The Daily Telegraph*, a populist newspaper owned by global media mogul Rupert Murdoch, and Arturo setting his eyes on the neighboring town not of Cicero (Brecht's original) but of Millstream, which translates the name of Australia's second largest city Melbourne from Old English (Wright qtd. in Mumford 2018: 9). Woven into a translation and adaptation of Brecht's original manuscript, the 2018 stage adaptation of *Arturo Ui* sketched a realm in which criminals resorted to making rather than breaking the law and instilling a climate of economic crisis, corruption, fearmongering, and violence that uncannily resonated with the dominant politics of contemporary times.

The image of the criminal is physically conjured on stage through activation of Brecht's concept of *Gestus* (comportment) (e.g., Weber 2000). *Gestus* captures the values and identifications that a performer can convey through their physical expression on stage, that is, through a cohesive way of carrying their body, costuming, and gestures. By using an ensemble of recurrent and culturally charged clues, audiences are enabled to decipher performances as quoting a particular social cosmos, recognizing familiar comportment that resonates with their experiences beyond the theater and hence accrues truth value (Weber 2000: 41). Brecht formulated his concept of *Gestus* in direct relation to American gangster films of the 1930s, which had established a pervasive code of how to represent the figure of a criminal simply through a number of nonverbal clues (e.g., swaggering gait, slumping shoulders, intense gaze, etc.) (Weber 2000: 43). For Brecht, this marked representational practice provided an aesthetic blueprint for signaling how audiences may ascribe identity not on the grounds of verbal/dialogical character development but through covertly decoding the assemblage and patterning of collectively shared image associations that are woven into an actor's physical performance (Mumford 2009: 54). For example, Weaving's 2018 Arturo conveys his identity as a petty gangster in Scene Two of Williams's staging through the stark contrast of his unkempt appearance (i.e., greasy hair, bulging pants, and white singlet top) with that of Scene One's elegant business attire of the politician Dogsborough and the lobbyists who entertain him over dinner as well as through his slumping shoulders, swaggering gait, and his aggressive choreographic closing-in on his scene partners when asserting his leadership status amid the gang of dockland criminals. If not for the negative connotations already culturally associated with the *Gestus* of the criminal, the physical and psychological violence that emanates from Weaving's performance predisposed me as an audience member against the character and the type he impersonates, setting the tone for the distribution of sympathies in the play.

However, *Gestus* is leveraged for the project of defamiliarization in *Arturo Ui* by performatively showing the usurping and gradual coalescing of the "Gangster *Gestus*" with that of its initial opposite, namely that of the "Politician," to yield the threatening specter of a demagogue who uses any means available to him to further his thirst for power. The codes that underpin each *Gestus* are rendered transparent and activated as interpretive categories in Scene Seven when Arturo receives lessons in sitting, standing, walking, and orating like a politician by a tutor who verbalizes and mimics the difference between Gangster and Politician *Gesti*. This scene functions as a meta-commentary on the nature of acting (both in life and on stage), emphasizing the artifice both of Weaving's performance as well as that of any identity constructions in our extra-theatrical world (Williams 2021). Thus, this scene has the potential to aesthetically jolt audiences into a critical reflective state by being shown how a public persona is artificially engineered. Williams's directorial approach ostensibly supports this intention, letting stage performance and video stream document the actor from every angle as he converges the tutor's instructions into a faultless and spirited delivery of Marc Anthony's speech taken from Shakespeare's *Julius Cesar*. This form of representation for Williams and his team rendered unnecessary to adjudicate further the obvious parallels to real-world contexts, such as the public communication strategies employed by the 2017–21

Trump administration in the United States (Williams 2021). Instead, the play reached beyond its historical context to capture more universal structures that arise from human behavior and how these articulate as political constellations through time, thereby staying in keeping with Brecht's original political and artistic agenda (Barnett 2015: 75).

Brecht developed this artistic agenda through a dense reflection of dominant creative conventions and past theater traditions, funneling them through a Marxist lens that considered their role in supporting the discursive effects of capitalist evolution. He developed his theories on theater while living through the demise of the Weimar Republic, the rise of fascism in Europe, and its devastating impact across the globe—a time in which emotional persuasion and divisive identity practices dominated politics and dissolved social ties in ways that bear eerie parallels to contemporary developments across the Western world. His artistic legacy lives on in the "epic theatre" style, whose key objective is to prime audiences to adopt and cultivate a critical attitude toward actions and characters presented on stage, with the aim of carrying this style of thinking across into the extra-theatrical realm (Carney 2005: 33). This intended reconfiguration of perception is to be achieved both through selection of adequate subject matter as well as through disruptive aesthetic configuration of representational modes— with each production component assembled to counter any perception of unification and resolution (Barnett 2015: 69–70). Brecht interpreted the latter as hallmarks of a Bourgeois theater tradition that served to affirm and cement its exclusionist cultural prerogative to the detriment of the social majority who did not receive equitable representation in its cultural universe (Brooker 2006: 3). He read the classical canon of works from Shakespeare to Goethe and Wagner through a Marxist lens, arguing that its "grand style" (Irei 2016: 165) entrenches and aestheticizes a classicist cultural narrative of social division, which supports the real-life exploitation of the masses for political and economic gain by the ruling class (Irei 2016). Brecht's opposition to bourgeois culture in particular was grounded in its existential reliance on capitalism, whose systemic telos of perpetual growth had divulged its socially destructive nature in the global economic depression that began in the late 1920s. Brecht aimed to create a new theater that left behind the miring shackles of naturalism (which instated the Bourgeois cultural universe as a worthy object of representation) and the indulgent individualization of expressionism, while circumventing the nihilistic stance of existentialism (Unwin 2005: 35–6). Understanding theatrical aesthetics as key conduits for imparting a new cultural vision, Brecht set out to reformulate the form of theatrical communication to arrive at a theater that could assist in the realization of political subjecthood among the broader public. This political agenda was developed in the face of profound experiences of annihilation and displacement that for Brecht called for an active response from civil society (Mumford 2009: 76). A key question underpinning *The Resistible Rise of Arturo Ui* has therefore been "How did we get here, and how can theatre help us learn to resist such developments in the future?" Williams leverages and transforms this foundational Brechtian aesthetics to reckon with contemporary political ecologies in which capitalist dynamics have absorbed disruptive practices, fermenting a discursive climate in which the Brechtian concept of fostering critical acuity and continual inquiry is increasingly undermined by an interest-driven exploitation of relational notions of truth.

Brecht sought to instill this mode of critical reflection through an aesthetics premised on the principle of "dialectics," namely that insight and advance in knowledge can approximate a higher-level understanding of the world yet would never lead to a complete resolution of the world's contradictions and complexities (Carney 2005: 18). A dialectical structure, hence, keeps in motion a perpetual cycle of action and response that requires a continuous reflective mindset to drive decision making. This aesthetic principle stands in direct opposition to the closed structure of, for example, a Wagnerian *Gesamtkunstwerk* (total work of art), in which every element is integrated to create a harmonious cosmos that in its seamless fusion implies an ideological meta-narrative that can establish absolute meaning and truth (Barnett 2015: 69–70). Brecht rejected the deep immersion that such closed aesthetic systems invite, assuming that the glossing over of disparities would lead to uncritical, passive reception by audiences who would be lulled by the pleasing nature of representation (Mumford 2009: 63). In response, he advocated an aesthetics that maximally emphasizes division to disrupt the theatrical performance and foster awareness of its artifice to get audiences to contemplate alternatives to the arguments presented on stage. To this end, he deployed a range of *Verfremdungseffekte* (defamiliarization tools) that can disturb illusion and reframe action. The arsenal of such tools ranges from, for example, the inclusion of narrator figures who provide meta-commentary on scenes; visual signposts that explain the siting of dramatic action; a mixture of styles that breaks with conventional expectations brought to a performance; a play with intertextuality where origin texts are marked only to be recontextualized and critiqued in their cultural import; to the express valuation of physical and visual performance languages alongside a critical probing of verbal language, which—in Brechtian theater—is refracted as a volatile medium that is easily corrupted and emptied of meaning (Mumford 2009: 66).

Williams overtly quotes these cornerstones of Brechtian aesthetics in his staging, yet he arranges them in ways that gradually undercut their disruptive potential, counteracting the expectation of an emancipatory trajectory with a reflection on contemporary performative image regimes that serve rival objectives of subjugation and domination. The standout aesthetic attribute of Williams's staging of *Arturo Ui* was the use of large-scale projection of livestreamed video that was continually captured of the stage performance by a swirling camera team and spliced onto a towering overhead screen under the direction of cinematographer Justine Kerrigan. Williams adopted this staging approach to deconstruct "the performance of power and the theatre of politics ... to reveal its construction and the ways we are influenced and manipulated by it" (qtd. in Australian Arts Review 2018). As the following analysis shows, this aesthetic choice draws on the full arsenal of defamiliarization techniques to activate a Brechtian interpretive frame, yet—through the beguiling use of cinematographic imagery—continually seduced the audience into a deep immersion that suspended the critical rigor of detached contemplation that Brecht so avidly advocated for, "revealing the ways in which we might fail to [resist the pull of political persuasion today]" (Williams qtd. in Australian Arts Review 2018). Williams's use of defamiliarization effects here did not aim to assist the audience to glean a hidden truth beyond the performance of character. Rather, the seamlessness of capture and reproduction engrained the pervasiveness of performance as the only available reality on stage beyond which no other truth could unfold significant impact. This hermetic closure in its effect mirrors that of post-truth politics that displace the quest for verifiable facts with partisan beliefs that render the concept of truth obsolete (McIntyre 2018: chap. 1, 8). The splicing of physical stage and digital screen performance allowed Williams and team to viscerally probe the very means by which influence and power are accrued and executed in our contemporary visual/digital cultures, using the state as a platform on which to make palpable the pull of emotional over intellectual persuasion that lies at the heart of post-truth politics (Kalpokas 2019: 10).

In our personal interview, Williams stated that a reflection of performance as a mode of being and influencing for him lies at the heart of Brecht's play. While the story traces Arturo Ui's meticulous crafting of an identity as a public leader, Williams read the stage directions as a call for deconstructing this quest to lay bare its interest-driven and nihilistic nature. By presenting Arturo as a figure without a past and solely guided by his will to absolute power—rather than as a means toward a better life—the character emerges as the epitome of a dehumanized politics that threatens to dissolve the connecting fabric of society (Wright qtd. in Mumford 2018: 6). The original Brechtian defamiliarization technique that would foreground the split between flesh-and-blood actors and their theatrical roles (Mumford 2009: 61) aims to point toward the existence of a counterweight to this performed identity, opening a dichotomy of artifice versus an implied natural identity that can function as a touchstone for veracity in the cosmos of the play. A break of character on stage would here hence correspond to indicating that the manipulative universe conjured by the performance would still be tied to another layer of reality in which truthfulness is a significant parameter. Williams used various signposts of Brecht's aesthetic program to activate a Brechtian interpretive frame, for example, via bracketing the play by a narrator, utilizing an open set design that allowed glimpses into the backstage wings, announcing scene changes via text projections, making the act of storytelling transparent through the onstage camera team, and sampling different cinematic and theatrical storytelling genres. These storytelling devices ensured that audiences were continually kept in a perceptual limbo, dividing their attention between stage and screen, as well as diving into the immersion invited by the actors' performances, and again being jolted out of it by the sudden changes in tone, genre, and meta-reflection. This constant flux and its relation to the well-known Brechtian aesthetic paradigm fostered an assumption in me while watching the play that I am witnessing the seduction and coercion of a collective by Arturo from a privileged, detached position.

Yet, by foregoing the Brechtian split between actor and role and instead letting his cast perform seamlessly in character, Williams created a hermetic cosmos in which the artifice of performance was no longer counterpointed by any implied "natural" coordinate. This meant that marked performance in this staging became the only truth available to the audience. The screen commanded attention, placing the actors' livestreamed performance under a magnifying glass and creating anticipation to glimpse a rupture of character. Yet, such ruptures never eventuated, and my expectation of revelation was continually frustrated. Instead, it was countered with a pervasive cinematic performance that served to emotionally captivate and deepen immersion. The effect of this was that the critical distance advocated by Brecht was progressively undermined by the seductive pull of larger-than-life imagery, leading audiences on a path that let them viscerally experience the difficulty of resisting the persuasion of a meticulously crafted performance. By gradually expanding camera angles, the audience was being incorporated into the play's referential horizon, captured in the feed's digital stream, and rendered as the mute mass who Arturo addresses in his final victory speech—a moment that divulged the identification of the audience as entangled and vulnerable matter of performance rather than emancipated subjects partaking in political discourse from a detached, merely intellectually involved position.

Hence, Williams enlisted Brechtian aesthetics as a way of activating a postmodern lens onto identity and performance practice; yet rather than affirming them as capable of supporting agency, he performed a dialectical turn that mapped their limitations vis-à-vis contemporary image regimes. These regimes tend to enlist disruption primarily as a means to capture attention and influence emotional responses via sensual impression, not to foster a critical stance toward the representational device (Kalpokas 2019: 52). They exploit the effectiveness of visual information that through its graphical manifestation and sensory reception implies a measure of truthfulness that evidences more directly than verbal information (Nyhan and Reifler 2019: 224). The onstage camera crew made visible the production processes flowing into the staging to invite a sense of transparency and foster trust in the veracity of imagery through the close coupling of stage performance and its simultaneous screen translation. As François Jardon-Gomez explains, contemporary audiences derive a sense of pleasure from being let into the mechanisms of staging that produce artifice because this leads to experiences of immediacy and realism that other theater traditions, such as Naturalism, have elided by concealing the theatrical apparatus and its mechanical creation of illusion through a unifying aesthetics (2018: 35). The emphasis on artifice unfolds reality effects because it reflects the visual and digital practices that determine much of contemporary reality. This resonance with familiar image practices was able to emotionally connect the audience to the play's aesthetic cosmos by steeping them within a familiar technologically enabled environment that in its contemporary feel created a sense of recognition and expanded entertainment.

However, the politics underpinning Williams's aesthetic framing remained mostly opaque and only gradually emerged. This progressive revelation was achieved through a shift in cinematic languages and strategically timed manipulation of the livestream feed. It expanded the Brechtian critique of capitalism by a dedicated focus on digitally enabled lifeworlds as the locus at which manipulation and execution of power converge in contemporary times and can produce subjected rather than empowered identities. Williams's staging leveraged digital technologies in such a way that they invited audiences to think about their implication in post-truth politics and how it can create a seductive frame that may take us emotionally hostage despite our knowledge of its engineered and interest-driven nature. By utilizing the frames through which we have come to construct reality, the projected live feed provides a larger-than-life looking glass onto the actors and their performance. Most of the early video footage beguiled through long cinematic Steadicam shots inspired by the work of German director Frank Castorf (Williams 2021), making it easy for the audience to match the actors' stage performance with its digital capture on screen. Its correspondence with documentary filmmaking conventions fostered trust in the veracity of the imagery. The multi-angle capture and large-scale projection expanded the audience's viewing angles, affording access to spaces physically closed off from their seated contemplation, creating a sense of privileged access and omniscience. The camera functioned as an allied tool that supports the audience's informational quest by making it easy to clearly ascertain the source and correspondence of projected imagery with action on stage, adding an entertaining and expanded lens onto the actors' performance. It intensified through close-ups and scaled projection, allowing audiences to trace minute shifts in gesture and facial expressions.

As Arturo's circle of influence expands, the style of the filming began to shift, reflecting and supporting the subversion of power and discourse. Cross-cutting of shots occurred more frequently and at intensifying pace. This made it harder for audiences to ascertain at all times which camera was contributing the video feed, beginning to weaken the station of representational veracity and backgrounding the importance of truthfulness in the play's cosmos. Increasingly, audience members had to decide whether to dedicate attention to the act of source-tracing or to be swept along by the frenetic stage action that swayed into slapstick comedic style as Arturo and his men hijack the court proceedings dedicated to investigating allegations of corruption involving Dogsborough and the lobbyists. The lure of their vivacious, over-the-top performance that perverts justice and frames an innocent man for the crimes committed was accompanied by a range of quick video cuts and a dizzying turnover of viewing angles on the towering screen that visually mirrored and amplified the chaos that the characters wreaked on stage. Stage performance and filming here worked together to background the audience's concern for veracity and catered to the hedonistic pleasure of sensory stimulation—luring audiences into a space that calls for emotional rather than intellectual engagement, aesthetically priming them for the descent into Arturo's fascist regime. Yet rather than maintaining the absurdist trajectory, the performance scaled back again, regaining sobriety and preventing a solidifying of style that would have allowed stable orientation in Arturo's emerging universe. While not returning to the calm, cinematic quality of the opening scenes, the Steadicam shots of later scenes were of a more free-flowing, abstract nature—by moving at wider angles that were facilitated at times by mounting a camera on a harness dropped from and lifted back up into the lighting truss. The effect of such capture was that perspectives disconnected from the capabilities of the human body and instead opened compelling angles that imbued the imagery with a surreal quality. These captivating visuals and the integrated stage performance fostered deep immersion, inviting audiences into a realm in which intellectual reflection was no longer coveted but eclipsed by the emotional pull of the visual and physical performance language. This effect was fully exploited for Arturo's nightmare scene, in which his murdered friend Ernesto Roma haunts him with a prophecy of betrayal and doom, resonating with Shakespearean undertones in its intertextual reference to *Richard III*'s pre-battle ghost visitation (V.iii). This is the play's only scene that delves into the inner workings of Arturo's mind. The abstracted camera footage visually translated the ruminations of his feeble conscience, inviting the audience to empathize with his torment. While Weaving's performance revealed this rare human sensitivity in Arturo, the video image mirrored the singularity of this event through an equally singular overt manipulation, in which the live feed was superimposed with prerecorded material to multiply the image of Colin Moody playing Roma, so that the numerous animated renditions of his body consumed the entire projection screen.

Both representational means here divulged a previously hidden capacity to the audience. Yet, neither unfolded effects that would significantly alter the play's trajectory: In the narrative ecology, Arturo's moment of vulnerability only serves to throw into relief his ensuing shedding of all human sensibility as he murderously pushes his way to unchallenged power (Wright qtd. in Mumford 2018: 6), while the splicing of live and recorded visuals alerted the audience to the volatility and easily manipulable nature of the digital image that could propel them to critically reconsider the constitution and role of the video feed in the ecology of the play. However, the occurrence of manipulation within the "dream scene" is sited within a fold that narratively justified and aesthetically glossed over its critical implications. As the manipulation supported the surrealist style of the scene—for which the preceding abstract Steadicam shots had gently prepared the ground—the rupture was able to be experienced as a logical consequence of style and to neatly integrate with previously established receptive regimes rather than as a fundamental call to revise assumptions about the capability of digital images to function as conduits for veracious discourse. This bracketing lulled audiences and made it easy to follow the pull of emotion rather than to engage in critical reflection. Williams here exploits the psychological mechanisms that see us holding on to beliefs until pushed to reconsider under the burden of sustained cognitive dissonance (McIntyre 2018: chap. 3, 15). By keeping the scene brief and stylistically integrated, the disruption is not unfolding a strong enough effect to jolt audiences onto an alternative receptive pathway.

In a subtle way, the staging of Roma's execution had previously reinforced the idea that genre would demand a particular style that may rule out aspiration to veracity in performance: Aiming for a Film Noir feel—in keeping with Brecht's fascination for 1930s Chicago gangster films—Williams concentrated here on delivering the scene predominantly as an imposing screen experience (2021). By letting his cast play to the cameras while introducing overt special effects (such as dry ice for smoke effects), he deliberately turned the stage performance into a subservient set for the film rendition. This simultaneously demonstrated the artifice of acting as well as its compelling effect on screen. It asked the audience to engage in and maintain a "double vision" that would allow them to revel in the witnessing of the creative process as well as to abandon themselves to the illusion conjured on the screen. The argument of style as the motivation and core of performance here replaced the Brechtian aspiration to veracity and made the image and emotional response to it the chief aims of reception. This occupation with representation at the expense of subject matter encapsulates contemporary discursive post-truth mechanisms that enlist this same strategy for the promotion of particularized and vested political interests (Kalpokas 2019: 33).

Following these aesthetic interventions, the audience then witnessed how Arturo embraced his quest for power with unrestrained verve, supported by the videographers who buoyed his ascent with "propagandistic pomposity" (Gallasch 2018). This impression was created by gradually cutting the number of cameras in operation down until only a single one remained. This camera maintained a steady angle, guided by Weaving who—after the "dream scene" in which Ui casts off his last fragments of empathy—had begun to exert increasing control over the camera team, enlisting it as a tool to convey his lines to the audience via unidirectional screen relay. In contrast to the multitude of perspectives and cuts that had attended on his rise to power, this solidifying conveyed the fossilizing of discourse and power relations into a "fascist order" (Gallasch 2018) that centered Arturo as the ruling demagogue over the masses rendered as silent and subjected.

In keeping with the Brechtian code, the fluid aesthetics of Williams's staging kept audiences in a constant limbo in relation to the performance on stage and screen. The multiple, expanded perspectives enabled by the camera team created a dynamism that fostered deep immersion and—as the analysis has shown—encouraged particular interpretive frames for scenes, which colluded in seducing the audience onto a trajectory that would eventually implicate and immure them within Arturo's fascist cosmos. Disruption here was consequently not enlisted to activate and support audiences' critical faculties but to generate impact from the exploration of the gaslighting effects of contemporary visual regimes. These continuously stimulate our senses, priming us for affective resonance (Döveling, Harju, and Sommer 2018: 3), which make them a potent vehicle for post-truth discourse that aims to reconfigure public conversations by leveraging emotional persuasion to derail intellectual arguments (Fridlund 2020: 233). Williams and his team created a visual and performative environment that mirrored many peoples' relationship with politics outside of the theater—watching the theater of politics play out through screens, passively witnessing actions executed in their name with impact on their lives. Inspired by Marxist ideology, Brecht aimed to activate his audiences to engage in a restructuring of the social and political world. Williams's staging addressed the challenges that postmodernism and its deconstruction of grand narratives have heralded for such political objectives, orchestrating the diffraction of critical faculties that can occur when technology is enlisted for the wrong political ends that end up miring collective power in the shackles of violence and terror.

References

Australian Arts Review (2018), "The Resistible Rise of Arturo Ui," *ArtsReview.com.au*, March 26. Available online: https://artsreview.com.au/the-resistible-rise-of-arturo-ui-3/ (accessed April 30, 2021).

Barnett, D. (2015), *Brecht in Practice: Theatre, Theory and Performance*, London: Bloomsbury. ProQuest Ebook Central. Available online: http://ebookcentral.proquest.com/lib/unsw/detail.action?docID=1779015 (accessed December 22, 2021).

Boyle, M. (2016), "Brecht's Gale: Innovation and Postdramatic Theatre," *Performance Research*, 21 (3): 16–26. Available online: https://doi.org/10.1080/13528165.2016.1176733 (accessed December 22, 2021).

Brooker, P. (2006), "Keywords in Brecht's Theory and Practice of Theatre," in P. Thomson and G. Sacks (eds.), *The Cambridge Companion to Brecht*, second edition, 209–24, Cambridge: Cambridge University Press.

Carney, S. (2005), *Brecht and Critical Theory*, London: Routledge. *ProQuest Ebook Central*. Available online: http://ebookcentral.proquest.com/lib/unsw/detail.action?docID=1122974 (accessed December 22, 2021).

Döveling, K., A. A. Harju, and D. Sommer (2018), "From Mediatized Emotion to Digital Affect Cultures: New Technologies and Global Flows of Emotion," *Social Media + Society*, 4 (1): 1–11. Available online: https://journals.sagepub.com/doi/10.1177/2056305117743141 (accessed December 22, 2021).

Dow, S. (2018), "'The Resistible Rise of Arturo Ui': History Is an Infinite Loop," *TheMonthly.com.au*, April 6. Available online: https://www.themonthly.com.au/blog/steve-dow/2018/06/2018/1522973306/resistible-rise-arturo-ui-history-infinite-loop (accessed April 30, 2021).

Felapton, C. (2018), "Review: The Resistible Rise of Arturo Ui—Sydney Theatre Company," Blog, March 25. Available online: https://camestrosfelapton.wordpress.com/2018/03/25/review-the-resistible-rise-of-arturo-ui-sydney-theatre-company/ (accessed May 14, 2021).

Fridlund, P. (2020), "Post-Truth Politics, Performatives and the Force," *Jus Cogens*, 2: 2015–35. Available online: https://doi.org/10.1007/s42439-020-00029-8 (accessed December 22, 2021).

Gallasch, K. (2018), "Kip Williams' Arturo Ui: Democracy's Death Dance," *Realtime.org.au*, May 1. Available online: https://www.realtime.org.au/kip-williams-arturo-ui-democracys-death-dance/ (accessed April 30, 2021).

Irei, N. (2016), "'Abolishing Aesthetics': Gestus in Brecht's Arturo Ui," *Rocky Mountain Review*, 70 (2): 150–74. Available online: https://www.jstor.org/stable/10.2307/rockmounrevi.70.2.150 (accessed December 22, 2021).

Jardon-Gomez, F. (2018), "Violence, Speech, and Reality: The Case of Cinq Visages pour Camille Brunelle," *Canadian Theatre Review*, 175 (Summer): 35–40.

Kalpokas, I. (2019), *A Political Theory of Post-Truth*, Cham: Palgrave Pivot. Available online: https://doi.org/10.1007/978-3-319-97713-3_2 (accessed December 22, 2021).

Li, C. (2018), "Sounding Out Différance: Derrida, Saussure, and Bhartṛhari," *Philosophy East & West*, 68 (2): 447–59.

McDermott, R. (2019), "Psychological Underpinnings of Post-Truth in Political Beliefs," *PS Political Science & Politics*, 52 (2): 218–22.

McIntyre, L. (2018), *Post-Truth*, Cambridge, MA: MIT Press.

Mumford, L. (2018), *On Cue*, Walsh Bay: Sydney Theatre Company Education.

Mumford, M. (2009), *Bertolt Brecht*, London: Routledge.

Nyhan, B., and J. Reifler (2019), "The Roles of Information Deficits and Identity Threat in the Prevalence of Misperceptions," *Journal of Elections, Public Opinion & Parties*, 29 (2): 222–44. Available online: https://doi.org/10.1080/17457289.2018.1465061 (accessed December 22, 2021).

Teiwes, J. (2018), "The Resistible Rise of Arturo Ui | Sydney Theatre Company | Sydney Theatre Company," *AustralianStage*.com.au, April 1. Available online: https://www.australianstage.com.au/201804018685/reviews/sydney/the-resistable-rise-of-arturo-ui-%7C-sydney-theatre-company.html (accessed April 30, 2021).

Unwin, S. (2005), *A Guide to the Plays of Bertolt Brecht*, London: Bloomsbury.

Weber, C. (2000), "Brecht's Concept of Gestus and the American Performance Tradition," in H. Bial and C. Martin (eds.), *Brecht Sourcebook*, 41–6, London: Routledge.

Williams, K. (2021), "Personal Interview," Interview by Susanne Thurow. Zoom, May 24, 45 min.

Zima, P. (2010), *Theorie des Subjekts*, third edition, Tübingen: A. Francke Press.

9

Satanic Panic: Performance in the New Culture War

Lewis Church

According to the 2020 documentary *Out of Shadows*, the visionary live artist and "godmother of performance art" Marina Abramović eats and sexually abuses children as a constituent part of her participation in a global satanic conspiracy. The roots of this accusation originate in highly superficial readings of her performance practice, in a series of leaked emails connected to Hillary Rodham Clinton's 2016 campaign for US president, and in the emergence of a variety of antagonistic right-wing internet subcultures that have intensified the reach and appeal of conspiracy theories.

Within the film these connections play out across a surprisingly slick and well-edited series of talking-head interviews, stock footage, and decontextualized clips from music videos and Hollywood movies. Publicity pictures of Abramović holding skulls or posing with scorpions are provided without qualification to afford her an ominous occult aura, and tiny excerpts of varied documentation from across her nearly fifty years of performance practice are amalgamated together without differentiation to present the worst and most extreme impression of her work. Images now canonically central to the history of performance art, a form (and an area of academic study) that Abramović has "been absolutely central to the development of" (Phelan 2004: 18), such as the artist cutting a five-pointed star into her stomach with a razor in *Thomas Lips* (1975) or scrubbing a pile of cow bones in *Balkan Baroque* (1997) are recast, alongside the artist's association with Lady Gaga and

Tony Podesta, as "evidence" of the pedophilic cabal that supposedly sits at the heart of both the art and entertainment industry and the highest echelons of the national and international elite.

Since its release the film has been viewed over twenty million times on YouTube alone and translated into more than ten different languages, with legal representatives for the film's creator (former Hollywood stuntman Mike Smith) estimating to the *Daily Beast* that its cross-platform viewership is "roughly 100 million" (Hitt 2020). The success of the film reflects the widespread popularity of its outlandish claims among digital communities of conspiracy theorists since 2016 and is troublingly indicative of the wider audience that these ideas can now reach. For although the identification of Abramović as a satanic conspirator is a ridiculous and often tedious exercise in logical leaps, non-sequiturs, and fallacy, the story advanced by the film, its dissemination, and the reactions to it are worthy of close attention for scholars of contemporary performance interested in understanding the strange post-truth cultural context in which such work can rapidly become embroiled. As Abramović herself states in a recent interview, while this "is something I have been deeply bothered by," going on to clarify that "I'm an artist, I'm not a Satanist," she also acknowledges that "they Googled me, and I am perfection to fit a conspiracy theory" (Saner 2020).

The characterization of Abramović in *Out of Shadows* is one that is intrinsically linked to the emergence of the alt-right, alt-light, QAnon, adjacent groups and spin-offs, and the many other strange and hard-to-quantify subcultures that lurk in the darker corners of the internet peddling half-truths, spurious evidence, and disinformation in order to wage a cultural war against the "woke left." It is also a clear example of how and why the alt-right and these related communities might find fertile ground for ridicule and condemnation in live art and performance, and of the consequences that result from such a project. Here I will use the characterization of Abramović in *Out of Shadows* in order to outline the parameters of the "new culture war" that is underway during the first quarter of the twenty-first century, and track some of the historical precedents of post-truth engagements with performance practices by highlighting confluences with the last major period of anglophone culture war in the 1980s and 1990s. For while this new culture war features some particularly egregious examples of sensational nonsense, the strategies pursued by those wishing to denigrate or restrict artistic expression in service to censorious right-wing political ideologies are far from new or unique.

Precedent and Continuation

At root, the new culture war of the 2010s and 2020s repeats and rehearses many of the post-truth strategies from the Western culture wars of the late 1980s and early 1990s, as well as the intense cultural conflict that preceded that period during the social upheavals of the 1960s. During these culture wars, conservative politicians and interest groups (in the United States and the UK in particular) consistently used artists, musicians, theater makers, and writers as supposedly decadent and transgressive examples in their attempts to restrict creative expression they judged to be inappropriate. This is pursued with the goal of limiting state and private funding for the arts and influencing the programming decisions and curation of galleries, theaters, and museums. In turn this is hoped to restrict the parameters of acceptable public discourse and engagement to avoid potentially disruptive or revolutionary concepts and aesthetics shifting social attitudes to bodies, sex, families, and spirituality.

In his history of these late-twentieth-century culture wars in the United States, Andrew Hartman writes that these clashes were

> battles over what constituted art, and over whether the federal government should subsidize art … over transgressive films and television shows, and over whether insensitive cultural programming should be censored. … They involved struggles over the university curriculum, and … were fights over how the nation's history was narrated in museums. (2019: 6–7)

This list of battlegrounds and flashpoints is staggeringly applicable to the current moment of cultural conflict. The same debates—over canon, over values, over the representation of different identities and experiences, over the curriculum in universities, and of the acknowledgment of deficiencies in national and international systems of governance and capital—have again become central to social and political discourses. And so, while the utility of the "culture war" label is sometimes called into question, I argue that there are significant benefits to claiming the current moment as precisely such a continuation of these previous periods of conflict, and the propagation of conspiracy theories like the one attached to Abramović as an operation within it. As Hartman writes in his updated conclusion from 2019, "economic anxiety and class resentment have [today] mapped onto cultural divisions to make the culture wars angrier, more tribal and more fundamental than ever before" (2019: 294). For while it is sometimes said that "the right won the economic war and the left won the culture war," as Angela Nagle puts it in her history of the emergence of the alt-right (2017: 57), it is also true that following the neoliberal domination of the 1980s the economically victorious right wing "were insecure about their power. The national culture—art, music, films and television—seemed to have slipped from their hands" (Hartman 2019: 199).

The emergence of antagonistic, right-wing, and violently repressive discourses and communities online is just the latest and most intense manifestation of this cultural undercurrent of insecurity on the part of the right: an attempt to undo what progressive gains have been made in the last two decades by limiting artistic expression and discrediting artistic practices. Minor improvements in the cultural representation of women, people of color and sexual diversity, for example, are sought to be undermined by a shifting of focus to artworks like Abramović's that might appear shocking or disturbing when removed from their original context. This deflection is designed to suggest that small changes in the breadth of expression and tolerance of different aesthetics, topics, and perspectives will inevitably lead to a cultural decline and the total abandonment of existing moral frameworks. This evocation of the decline of society maps explicitly onto the political ideologies of the extreme right seen in both contemporary manifestations like the alt-right and in influential far-right thinkers of the twentieth century such as Alain de Benoist.

Indeed, this attitude is often formulated as part of the "metapolitical" project of the far-right, a term that originates in the work of Italian Marxist Antonio Gramsci but was later co-opted by European far-right groups such as Nouvelle Droite and their think tank GRECE in the 1970s and 1980s. As the HOPE not hate researchers behind the most comprehensive recent taxonomy of the alt-right write, metapolitics can be described as the idea that activism must "focus on affecting culture before anything else, so as to shift the accepted topics, terms and positions of public discussion to create a social and political environment more open and potentially accepting of an ideology" (Hermansson et al. 2020: 128). Similarly, as cited by Massimiliano Capra Casadio in his interrogation of metapolitical thought in the far-right movements of France and Italy, de Benoist writes in 1983 that "only 'the activity of cultural power'" can affect "civil society," which, through its educative works, is able to determine the diffusion of those "accepted values which are considered 'obvious' by the majority of society" (2014: 52).

As Hermansson and his co-authors write, this metapolitical outlook "sits at the core of the American alt-right's belief that they are in the midst of a cultural war that will precede a political takeover" (2020: 15), and therefore the role of the arts and the place of culture is a key focus for this new wave of populist right-wing movements. While in its twenty-first-century iteration the battlegrounds on which this is played out are perhaps more obviously video games, film and television, and social media, rather than theater and performance, a focus on instances where performance makers are thrust into the fray are nevertheless illuminating in revealing connections to those performance artists and the practices of experimental theater makers that were also positioned on the frontline of the conflict in the 1980s and 1990s. There are remarkable and revealing similarities between the profoundly post-truth defamations of Abramović as a subversive occult mastermind enacted by the contemporary alt-right and examples of artists and their work that were denigrated as corrupting or threatening to public morals during this earlier period.

This includes unmistakable resonances with the "NEA Four" scandal in the United States, where performance artists Karen Finley, Tim Miller, Holly Hughes, and John Fleck were denied their grants from the National Endowment for the Arts following a campaign of smear and disinformation by right-wing lobbyists and politicians that misrepresented or overemphasized the sexual content of their performances. It also echoes the framing of artists such as David Wojnarowicz and Ron Athey by conservative politicians and media figures as representing a corrupting and seditious homosexual anti-family campaign. There are even (and perhaps particularly in the case of Abramović) echoes of the "Satanic Panic" that reached "a fever pitch in the Reagan era" (Janisse 2019: 13), where horror films, tabletop role-playing games, and heavy metal music were characterized by politicians, religious organizations, and tabloid journalists as corrupting occult artifacts that left young people vulnerable to the predations of an international satanic network of child abusers.[1]

In their current form, however, campaigns like the one against Abramović are engineered not by the faith groups, professional lobbyists, and political activists that led them in the 1980s and 1990s, but by the contemporary alt-right and its related communities, loose groupings of internet users circulating memes, abuse, and rumor endlessly online, occasionally breaking through and being amplified by what remains of the broadcast and print media. As before, the veracity of the accusations leveled at artists are incidental to the discrediting of their practices and characterization of artists, performance makers, and their audiences as liberal, subversive, and antithetical to the heterosexist, cisnormative, and archly capitalist attitudes advanced by these groups.

Comparison between these new campaigns and historical strategies of the far-right reveals the confluences, dangers, and potential for worrying outcomes should the contemporary instances of these operations (like the satanic characterization of Abramović) go unchallenged or dismissed as merely absurd and fantastical paranoia by isolated and inconsequential fringe groups. The online communities that propagate damaging and erroneous conspiracy theories like the one leveled at Abramović do so with the metapolitical intention of shifting public discourse, political debate, and wider social attitudes to race, sexuality, gender, and economic inequality, in an attempt to reverse any liberalizing progress made around those issues since the mid-twentieth century.

The new culture war is therefore as significant as earlier iterations in that it has the potential to drastically reshape the way in which contemporary culture is organized, funded, taught, and spoken about, as the culture wars of both the 1960s and the 1980s and 1990s did.[2] Ultimately, as Nagle puts it, "the new online Trumpian trolling right are leading another great push, as important as the culture wars of the 60s and 70s" (2017: 55). To dismiss the significance of this, to refuse to engage with what is a tactical assault on artistic expression and its potential to foster tolerance, diversity, and new models of social interaction, is to surrender to the culturally conservative and repressive attitudes of the extreme right-wing. The warning that the "metapolitical outlook of the alt-right elevates the arts to a crucial battleground in the war for society" (Hermansson et al. 2020) should underscore the scholarly relevance of the at-first ridiculous characterization of Abramović as a baby-eating satanist to broader questions of cultural engagement and reflection, and the importance of directly confronting and debunking misinformation and bad-faith readings of artworks and performance that characterize the post-truth context of a culture war.

Conspiracy Theories, the Alt-Right, and Terminology

The digital does, however, shift the location of these operations. As Stacy Rusnak writes, mass-media "in the 1980s played a pivotal role in disseminating the conservative cultural politics and promoting this cultural war" (2019: 195), with centralized news sources and a public far more restricted in their options for sourcing information allowing a much greater control of cultural narratives by politicians and pressure groups. Rather than through the television and newspapers of the bygone political era of the 1980s though, cultural debates and social imperatives are today won and lost, asserted, interrogated, dismissed and/or adopted, online. Yet despite the shift in the arena of public debate, it is the same strategies of tactical misreading, selective quotation, and decontextualization pursued by reactionary conservative culture warriors in the 1980s that are being reproduced digitally in the 2010s and 2020s.

To begin to fully outline the significance of this through the characterization of Abramović as a cannibal satanist requires an engagement with the disparate groups that foster the post-truth context through which such characterizations emerge. These right-wing internet subcultures are notoriously difficult to quantify and define, existing as overlapping and amorphous social communities played out through memes, trolling activities, message boards, anonymous social media and blog posts, and alternative media (as well the occasional curiously well-funded documentary like *Out of Shadows*). Great efforts have been made in the recent sociological research around these groups to differentiate and delineate the alt-right from QAnon, the alt-light from the manosphere, and other examples, work that is of course valuable and necessary. However, for the purposes of discussing performance's relationship to these groups in the context of the new culture war, I have decided not to engage in an extended and granular definition of the individual parameters of each of these disparate online communities here.

Instead, I have chosen to default to "alt-right" as a broad (if somewhat unspecific) term for the groups and their activity that is relevant to the example of Abramović and the trend it represents. This feels the most appropriate term to deploy as one both firmly established in wider public debate and one that has been used at various points to encompass all of the groups who engage in the activity I discuss, including the nurturing of conspiracy theories around public figures and politicians, the attempted censorship and defunding of art and performance deemed liberal or subversive, and the trolling of artists.

This wider definition of the alt-right is a disparate ecosystem of activity, really only united by what it opposes, pushing the narrative that white Western identity is "under attack from pro-multicultural and liberal elites and so-called 'social justice warriors' (SJWs) who allegedly use 'political correctness' to undermine Western civilisation and the rights of white males" (Hermannsson et al. 2020: 2). This narrative has migrated well beyond the limited online networks in which it once circulated into the political and cultural zeitgeist (perhaps most notably through the election of President Donald J. Trump), largely as a result of the online strategies of the movement. These online efforts "melded with the current fever pitch of anti-elitism" (Wendling 2018: 6) to become a remarkably effective tool in provoking conservative cultural backlash, as the mass media Rusnak describes above was in the 1980s.

While the example of Abramović offers an explicit link between the trolling strategies of the alt-right and the cultural conservatism of those earlier culture warriors, there is an important distinction between the more general action of trolling and the specifically alt-right nature of the activity I discuss, despite the conflation of the two often exhibited in mainstream media and casual conversation. Trolling is an action of baiting and/or attack in a digital space that may be directed at any or no political group or demographic, be entirely random in its targets or simply opportunistic, pursued with an ultimate goal of provoking a response that may then be laughed at ("for the lulz" [sic]). Where trolling as an activity is useful to highlight though is in relation to understanding both the way in which the narrative amplified by *Out of Shadows* operates and the consequences of its success on Abramović and others. In this I draw upon Whitney Phillips's history of trolling, which frames it in part as an act of "cultural digestion," in which trolls "scavenge the landscape for scraps of usable content, make a meal of the most pungent bits, then hurl their waste onto an unsuspecting populace—after which they disappear" (2016: 10). This selective identification of images, words, and concepts that will provoke the most extreme reactions, regardless of the original context or intent, is a process that Phillips refers to as "detournement," by which "the existing meaning of a particular statement or artifact is turned against itself" (2016: 67).

Phillips vividly illustrates this concept when she writes that trolling behaviors can result in a "reverse-snowball form (in that contextualising information is lost over time, not accrued)" (2016: 119). This "reverse-snowball" form is key as a metaphor for the development of post-truth discourses around cultural artifacts, particularly performance, which as an ephemeral event is wildly susceptible to rumor and misrepresentation of what "happened in the room" through the tactical selection of images, video, and documentation. This documentation is then able, and indeed prone, to circulating detached from its original context as one element of a full performance or artwork. This process has been key to the engagement of right-wing culture warriors with performance practices, exploiting the vulnerability that lies in the ontology of its liveness. And so, while Phillips outlines this process of detournement in relation to trolling activity online today, it is a key point of connection between the contemporary strategies of the alt-right and the censorious campaigns against artists of the late-twentieth-century culture wars.

"Abramović Is a Satanist" as a Trolling Operation

The spread of conspiracy theories and targeting of artists like Abramović is trolling of a specifically political type, engineered by the alt-right. As Hermansson et al. write, a more general understanding of the action of trolling outlined above and the alt-right converge "when their antagonism is directed against what they perceive as the left-liberal political and social hegemony" (2020: 123), as is very much the case in the satanic accusation against Abramović and the trend that it represents. Even so, it is still notable that "a *performance artist*, Marina Abramović, found herself tossed into the hollow core of the nation's election news cycle," as Abramović biographer James Wescott writes in his blog post responding to the original framing of the artist as part of Hillary Clinton's satanic network in 2016. As he puts it, after "decades of obscurity in a tiny artworld niche … to now show up on the alt-right's radar is a whole other level of fame" (Wescott 2017). But this was far from accidental, nor is it *incidental* that it was a performance practice deployed in service to this narrative. Rather, as Tony Perucci suggests, it was a "performatively constructed insinuation," designed to connect the then-candidate Clinton to a strange and disturbing artistic practice vulnerable to the operation, an attempt to engineer a "third-hand association with Abramović's 'occult' performance art" (2017: 132).

It was a tenuous connection to Clinton that first brought Abramović to the attention of the alt-right and prompted the first trolling actions against her. During the 2016 US presidential campaign, documents released by Wikileaks pertaining to Clinton's campaign were gleefully leapt upon by alt-right networks devoted to the cause of then-candidate (and at the time of writing, sitting president) Donald J. Trump, a cache that included a 2015 email sent from Abramović to lobbyist, art collector, and long-term friend Tony Podesta inquiring whether his brother John (Clinton's campaign manager) would be attending her forthcoming *Spirit Cooking* dinner.[3] This event was a performative meal hosted by Abramović that derives from what Wescott describes as a "rather throwaway" performance from 1997, which the artist has now turned into a form of "dinner party entertainment" that she lays on for "collectors, donors and friends" (2016).

In the original 1997 *Spirit Cooking* performance Abramović painted abstract instructions onto the white walls of an art gallery in pig's blood, the text commanding the viewer to "lie motionless," "spit inside your navel," and other strange actions. While this bloody text is admittedly a potentially disturbing aesthetic to deploy, it should be said that the original audience were not expected to actually carry out these instructions, particularly as they were often nonsensical and physically impossible to enact (e.g., "drink an earthquake").[4] Even acknowledging the provocation of painting instructions in blood on the walls of a gallery, though, the *Spirit Cooking* dinners discussed in the leaked email bear only a tenuous relationship to the original performance, with Wescott going on to describe them as events where "guests simply made soup" overseen by Abramović in "full-on comedy schoolmarm mode" (2016). No blood, sperm, or breast milk was involved, no children were present or harmed, and no devils were raised. And, as has been comprehensively documented by Abby Olsheiser in *The Washington Post* (2016) and Eric Levitz in *New York* magazine (2016), John Podesta, the "smoking gun" connection to Clinton's campaign, did not even take up Abramović's invitation to attend. It might reasonably be expected that this would render the charge that the event was evidence of an elite occult network that included Clinton and Podesta, with Abramović as high priestess, meaningless.

Nevertheless, following an article from right-wing conspiracy theorist Alex Jones's *Infowars* network, the accusation that John Podesta was into "spooky occult rituals" (Watson: 2016) was taken up, amplified, and disseminated throughout alt-right networks in a prime example of Phillip's detournement. Images from Abramović's original 1997 performance (and not the rather tamer dinner party event she had actually been emailing out invites to) rapidly circulated, as did images from other works, with the conflation of the five-pointed communist star of Abramović's Yugoslavian upbringing in early pieces like *Rhythm 5* (1974) with a satanic pentagram demonstrating exactly the reverse snowball of accelerating decontextualization and divergence from demonstrable fact that Phillips describes.

These images shortly came to form one of the central planks of the "Pizzagate" conspiracy theory, the idea that there is an international network of occult child abusers made up of prominent politicians and celebrities, so called because they use "pizza" as a codeword for the sexual abuse of children (and/or because the fictitious abuse took place in a Washington DC pizza parlor). The narrative of Pizzagate is a constituent part of the QAnon movement now gaining traction across the globe, and is also, in what is far from a coincidence, the central thread of the narrative constructed around Abramović by *Out of Shadows*. But it is important to emphasize once again, as Wendling writes, that Pizzagate is a theory that has been "planted, fed and watered by the alt-right" (2018: 156). The alt-right happily amplified the decontextualized images of Abramović's work because they fit into a metapolitical project of delegitimizing artistic expression they find objectionable and of characterizing those who enjoy it (or even might tolerate it) as immoral—a charge that in this case they were able to level at Hillary Clinton and her political circle.

These narratives can have a profound effect on the public perceptions of performance because, as Perucci writes "performance art is read as being doubly secret: (1) the Clinton campaign concealed its secret performance art, and (2) performance art concealed its secret occult rituals and child sex rings" (2016). The conflation of performance art and sexual deviancy is of course nothing new, reflecting the fact that historically it has been a form that offers artists "access to their own emotional histories and a tool for attacking taboos, whether sexual or social" (Goldberg 2004: 23). Performance art is well known for featuring nudity, violence, and sex (both acts and discussion of), often in the service of directly challenging the heterosexist societal frameworks that the alt-right are devoted to preserving. Just as performance work that featured any of these elements was in the 1980s consistently framed as subversive and/or immoral, an extremely similar operation can be seen throughout alt-right discourses. This is particularly the case when enacted by women, as within the movement any woman seen as "defying their 'natural' subordination by exercising their sexual and political enfranchisement can therefore be portrayed as not only leading to the breakdown of the family unit, but as a threat to the nation" (Hermansson et al. 2020: 185). It is therefore easy to see how Abramović's work, centered around the figure of a powerful woman who is comfortable in asserting both her sexual agency and the materiality of her body, would threaten these groups and require delegitimization, undermining, and dismissal, and provide such a convenient brush to tar their political opponents with.

When positioning this within the framework of a culture war, it is important to recognize these campaigns of conspiracy theory and the discrediting and disruption of artists as a form of attempted censorship and repression, an attempt to subvert any sense of artistic merit and create an attitude of excessive caution in audiences and those being exposed to this work for the first time (the "secrecy" Perucci refers to). As in Peter F. Spooner's writing on censorship, "attitudes precede actions," and therefore a more expansive and broader definition of censorship "might look behind censorial actions to include conditions and attitudes that make it difficult or impossible for people to express themselves or to gain exposure to the expressions of others" (Spooner 1997: 340). The conditions that Spooner describes "result from attitudes like racism, sexism, homophobia, greed, xenophobia" (1997: 341), the motivating attitudes and foundational principles of the alt-right and their efforts to spread "evidence" of the immorality of their perceived opponents.

It is notable that Spooner's work on censorship forms part of his reflection on American painter, performance artist, and writer David Wojnarowicz, who was a major target in the culture wars of the 1980s and 1990s. This again confirms the precedent that this earlier period provides for Abramović's mischaracterization. In 1990, Wojnarowicz was the victim of a deliberate campaign of decontextualization of his art when Reverend Donald Wildmon of the American Family Association clipped and pasted together the explicitly sexual elements of his collages and paintings and mailed the resulting pamphlet to members of the US Congress and selected media networks during the lobbying organization's campaign against the NEA. Wojnarowicz successfully sued the pressure group, ultimately receiving one dollar in compensation. What is notable here is the clipping of sexual elements from an expansive and wide-ranging artistic practice, which were then cropped "to the features that the organisation found most objectionable" (DeLand 2014: 29), in order to misrepresent the artist and to shape the public narrative around their work. This too is the process of detournement that Phillips describes, simply played out through the analogue rather than the digital. It is a stripping back of context and meaning in order to provoke an outraged or disturbed response in those exposed to these practices for the first time.

Conclusion: *Out of Shadows*

While frequently amusing in their absurdity, the reality is that many of these characterizations of artists as degenerate or embroiled in a systematic erosion of public morals can and do have a material impact on the diversity of artistic expression, the ability to experiment, and for artists to access both public and private funding for their work. There have been several real-world consequences from the claims made against Abramović, with actions taken in response to them by trolls, vigilantes, and concerned members of the public as well as major corporations.[5] But to return by way of conclusion to *Out of Shadows*, the 2020 documentary that built on the original scandal of the 2016 email leak to double down and reinforce the imagined connection between Abramović, Clinton, and Satan, reveals the pervasive nature of these narratives, and their damaging potential.

One material result of the resurgence of the narrative and demonstration of the impact of these at-first absurd characterizations of the artist's work is the withdrawal of an advertisement for Microsoft's HoloLens2 headset, which revolved around Abramović and her 2019 augmented reality installation *The Life*. This performance installation, which first took place at London's Serpentine Gallery in 2019, consists of an augmented environment that the viewer accesses through a virtual reality headset, where the artist addresses the audience and interrogates the notion of presence. Following a concerted campaign to "downvote" the ad on YouTube by groups congregating through the r/conspiracy subreddit and other digital venues connected to QAnon and the alt-right, the advertisement was withdrawn, with Microsoft declining to comment on the removal to *ArtNews* or the other publications that then reported on the disappearance of the video.

While much of this reporting suggested that this campaign of downvoting and censorship was prompted by the 2016 *Infowars* article, there is evidence that *Out of Shadows* also played a significant role in prompting the ire of those who took part, and in facilitating the deployment of the old tropes of deviant performance art in service of the alt-right. On the subreddit devoted to the campaign, which is grouped under "r/conspiracy," several users can be seen directing those unfamiliar with the charges against Abramović to the documentary, citing it as supporting evidence of their claims. User "Barrack-HusseinObama" references admiringly "the documentary *Out of Shadows* sweeping the internet," while ModernDayN3rd indicates to those browsing the reddit topic that the artist is "featured in the documentary *Out of Shadows*" before imploring others to "look it up on YouTube."[6]

While the ad featuring Abramović had already been released and the artist already been paid, it is reasonable to assume that the outcry and embarrassing public removal of the ad will nevertheless subsequently influence the likelihood of Microsoft or other major corporations enlisting Abramović as a brand ambassador in the future. But rather more importantly, this removal can be read as a signifier of a more general culture of preemptive paranoia around engagement with artists exploring sensitive issues or aesthetics, such as the one described by Spooner in his work on censorship. The trolling activity of the alt-right, their deployment of selected images of Abramović's work in order to repress engagement with her artistic practice, is clearly demonstrated by the coordinated campaign against this ad. Often, as Spooner writes, an "atmosphere of repression is a more insidious form of censorship within a society because it is invisible as censorship until it is borne out in some covert action" (1997: 341). The removal of this advertisement is just such a covert action, a practical instance that points to and reveals the significance of the metapolitical strategy at the heart of the contemporary alt-right.

Of course, despite her targeting, it should be acknowledged that Abramović's career is, certainly for a performance artist, relatively secure. A forthcoming career retrospective at the Royal Academy of Arts in London, multiple academic studies of her work, biographies, and rather more flattering documentaries than *Out of Shadows* are unlikely to prevent her from being able to create work in the future, or undo her legacy as an artist. But there should be no suggestion that this renders the impact of the characterizations against her meaningless or ineffective operations. The post-truth narratives constructed, performatively distributed, and amplified by the alt-right, now filtering through in documentaries like *Out of Shadows* able to reach larger and less concentrated audiences, can severely impact on contemporary perceptions of performance art. Abramović continues "to be linked with pedophilia on Twitter even after Trump's inauguration" (Perucci 2017: 132), and if such a characterization can be effectively applied to one of the most lauded and successful exemplars of the form, the reality that performance art is highly susceptible to campaigns of detournement is again reinforced.

Out of Shadows purports to reveal the "secret truth" behind Western societies, bringing the light of the filmmaker's analysis to the umbral networks of power that dictate what is seen as acceptable, proper, or realistic. Ultimately, what the narrative put forth by the film actually does is reveal the familiar repressive and regressive ideologies of the culturally conservative right wing, pursued and furthered in what amounts to merely a digital update of their metapolitical strategies. These are the narratives at the heart of the new culture war, the rationale behind the post-truth discourses that swirl through the internet, and it is only by engaging directly and systematically debunking them, by insisting on a recontextualization that undoes the process of detournement, that they can be resisted. Performance, although far from the only art form implicated in this, provides a key opportunity through which to approach the task of fighting back within the new culture war of the twenty-first century.

Notes

1 A guide to the emergence of the "Satanic Panic" and its key flashpoints in the United States, the UK, and international contexts can be found in the collection *Satanic Panic: Pop-Cultural Paranoia in the 1980s*, edited by Kier-La Janisse and Paul Corupe and included in my references.
2 To cite but one example of the material consequences of this kind of culture war for artists, the notorious assault on the National Endowment for the Arts led by Senator Jesse Helms and other right-wing politicians and pressure groups in the 1990s, including the campaign against the "NEA Four," resulted in the removal of individual artist grants for visual art or performance in 1994. These grants have never been reinstated and marked a major victory in the conservative right's systematic pruning back of state subsidy of the arts in the United States.
3 The original email I refer to here can still be accessed through Wikileaks via https://wikileaks.org/podesta-emails/emailid/15893 (accessed January 15, 2021).
4 Documentation of the original 1997 *Spirit Cooking* performance at Zerynthia Associazione per l'Arte Contemporanea in Paliano (Italy) can easily be found on YouTube and is included in my references. Comments below these videos demonstrate the enduring nature of the conspiracy theory and the vehemence with which its adherents pursue it.
5 One of the most serious responses to the Pizzagate conspiracy theory came when Edgar Maddison Welch entered Comet Ping Pong pizza parlor in Washington DC on December 4, 2016, brandishing an assault rifle and demanding access to the basement where the child sex slaves were being held. He then opened fire at the floor, traumatizing customers and staff. The restaurant had no basement.
6 These quotations from reddit are freely viewable via the topic "Microsoft just took down their 'commercial' featuring Satanist, Marina Abramović which had comments turned off, 24k dislikes and now has been fully deleted" posted by u/Barrack-HusseinObama to the r/conspiracy subreddit.

References

Casadio, M. C. (2014), "The New Right and Metapolitics in France and Italy," *Journal for the Study of Radicalism*, 8 (1): 45–86.

DeLand, L. (2014), "Live Fast, Die Young, Leave a Useful Corpse," *Performance Research*, 19 (1): 33–40.

Goldberg, R. (2004), *Performance: Live Art since the 60s*, London: Thames and Hudson.

Hartman, A. (2019), *A War for the Soul of America: A History of the Culture Wars*, second edition, Chicago: University of Chicago Press.

Hermansson, P., D. Lawrence, J. Mulhall, and S. Murdoch (2020), *The International Alt-Right: Fascism for the 21st Century?*, London: Routledge.

Hitt, T. (2020), "Inside *Out of Shadows*: The Bonkers Hollywood-Pedophilia 'Documentary' QAnon Loves," *Daily Beast*, August 6. Available online: https://www.thedailybeast.com/inside-out-of-shadows-the-bonkers-hollywood-pedophilia-documentary-qanon-loves (accessed January 7, 2021).

Janisse, K. L. (2019), "Introduction: Could It Be … Satan?," in K. Janisse and P. Corupe (eds.), *Satanic Panic: Pop-Cultural Paranoia in the 1980s*, 13–16, Godalming: FAB Press.

Levitz, E. (2016), "Report: Clinton Linked to Satanic Rituals Involving Kidnapped Children and Marina Abramovic," *New York Magazine*, November 4. Available online: https://nymag.com/intelligencer/2016/11/spirit-cooking-explained-satanic-ritual-or-fun-dinner.html (accessed January 15, 2021).

Marina Abramović Spirit Cooking (1997). Available online: https://www.youtube.com/watch?v=3EsJLNGVJ7E (accessed January 15, 2021).

Nagle, A. (2017), *Kill All Normies: Online Culture Wars from 4chan and Tumblr to Trump and the Alt-Right*, Winchester: Zero Books.

Ohlheiser, A. (2016), "No, John Podesta Didn't Drink Bodily Fluids at a Secret Satanist Dinner," *Washington Post*, November 4. Available online: https://www.washingtonpost.com/news/the-intersect/wp/2016/11/04/no-john-podesta-didnt-drink-bodily-fluids-at-a-secret-satanist-dinner/ (accessed January 15, 2021).

Out of Shadows (2020) [Film], Dir. Mike Smith, USA: Outofshadows. Available online: https://www.outofshadows.org (accessed January 7, 2021).

Perucci, T. (2017), "The Trump Is Present," *Performance Research*, 22 (3): 127–35.

Phelan, P. (2004), "On Seeing the Invisible: Marina Abramović's *The House with the Ocean View*," in A. Heathfield (ed.), *Live: Art and Performance*, 16–27, London: Tate.

Phillips, W. (2016), *This Is Why We Can't Have Nice Things: Mapping the Relationship between Online Trolling and Mainstream Culture*, Cambridge, MA: MIT Press.

"r/conspiracy: Microsoft Just Took Down Their 'Commercial' Featuring Satanist, Marina Abramović Which Had Comments Turned Off, 24k Dislikes and Now Has Been Fully Deleted" (2020), Reddit Topic. Available online: https://www.reddit.com/r/conspiracy/comments/g0n02q/microsoft_just_took_down_their_commercial/ (accessed January 7, 2021).

Rusnak, S. (2019), "Scapegoat of the Nation: The Demonization of MTV and the Music Video," in K. Janisse and P. Corupe (eds.), *Satanic Panic: Pop-Cultural Paranoia in the 1980s*, 173–99, Godalming: FAB Press.

Saner, E. (2020), "Marina Abramović: I'm an Artist, Not a Satanist!," *The Guardian*, October 7. Available online: https://www.theguardian.com/artanddesign/2020/oct/07/marina-abramovic-im-an-artist-not-a-satanist (accessed January 15, 2021).

Spooner, P. (1997), "David Wojnarowicz: A Portrait of the Artist as X-Ray Technician," in E. Childs (ed.), *Suspended Licence: Censorship and the Visual Arts*, 333–65, Washington: University of Washington Press.

Watson, P. (2016), "'Spirit Cooking': Clinton Campaign Chairman Practices Bizarre Occult Ritual," *Infowars* (article unavailable on January 15, 2021).

Wendling, M. (2018), *Alt-Right: From 4chan to the White House*, London: Pluto Press.

Wescott, J. (2017), "Marina Abramovic's Spirit Cooking," *MIT Press* (blog). Available online: https://mitpress.mit.edu/blog/marina-abramovic's-spirit-cooking (accessed January 7, 2021).

Contributors

William C. Boles holds the Hugh F. and Jeannette G. McKean Chair of English at Rollins College. His previous books are *The Argumentative Theatre of Joe Penhall* and *Understanding David Henry Hwang*. He is the editor of *After In-Yer-Face Theatre: Remnants of a Theatrical Revolution* and co-editor with Anja Hartl of the Methuen Drama Agitations series for Bloomsbury Academic. He currently serves as the director of the Comparative Drama Conference.

Heidi E. Bollinger is an Associate Professor of English at Hostos Community College, CUNY. Her research focuses on contemporary literature, graphic novels, and life writing. Her work has been published in peer-reviewed journals including *Pedagogy, Autobiography Studies, Genre*, and *Studies in the Novel*. Her article "'What If I Don't Wanna Be White?': Black Authenticity and White Privilege in Margaret Seltzer's Fake Memoir" (2016) examines fraudulent autobiographies—another phenomenon endemic to our post-truth culture.

Stephen Carleton is an Associate Professor and Director of the Centre for Critical and Creative Writing at the University of Queensland (UQ). He also teaches the Drama major class at UQ, with research and teaching specializations that include contemporary Australian playwriting, gothic drama, cli-fi, postcolonial drama, spatial inquiry, cultural geography, and Australian theater historiography. His major plays include national award-winning dramas *The Turquoise Elephant* and *Constant Drinkwater and the Final Days of Somerset,* and he has co-authored *Imagined Landscapes: Geovisualizing Australian Spatial Narratives* with Jane Stadler and Peta Mitchell.

Lewis Church is a Lecturer in Theatre and Performance at Birkbeck, University of London. His research is focused on contemporary performance and live art, cultural politics and policy, censorship, subcultures, and interdisciplinarity. This research has been published in *PAJ*, *The First Line*, and *Punk & Post-Punk*, with other writing appearing in *Something Other*, *The Art Story*, *Hackney Citizen*, and *Exeunt*, and for the Live Art Development Agency, SPILL Festival of Performance, Daily Life Ltd., and The Sick of the Fringe. As an artist, dramaturg, and producer he has worked with Ron Athey, Vaginal Davis, Franko B., Stacy Makishi, Sh!t Theatre, and others.

Lynn Deboeck is an Adjunct Assistant Professor of Theatre and Lecturer in Gender Studies at the University of Utah. Her research interests include performance theory, the representation of maternity and motherhood in Western theatrical traditions, pedagogy and directing live performance. Her most recent published work is "Feminist Resistance to the Coded-Male Auteur-Director," in *Frontiers: A Journal of Women's Studies* and her most recent directing work is *Helen* by Euripedes with Salt Lake City's 2021 Classical Greek Theatre Festival.

Helen Georgas is the Literature and Theater librarian and an associate professor at Brooklyn College (of the City University of New York). She is an editor of the digital arts platform *Underwater New York* and served as literary co-editor of the anthology *Silent Beaches, Untold Stories: New York City's Forgotten Waterfront*. Her recent writing about art, performance, and culture has appeared in *The Brooklyn Rail*, *Hyperallergic*, and *Lady Science*.

Chris Hay is an ARC DECRA Senior Research Fellow and Senior Lecturer in Theatre History in the School of Communication and Arts at the University of Queensland, Australia. He is an Australian theater and cultural historian, with a particular interest in how live performance subsidy has shaped the national imaginary and Australian identity. His current funded research examines the development of government arts funding in Australia between 1949 and 1975, and has appeared in the *Australasian Drama Studies* and the *Journal of Australian Studies*. With Stephen Carleton, he is completing a study of Australian theater from 2007 to 2020, to be published as the monograph *Contemporary Australian Playwriting: Re-Visioning the Nation on the Mainstage* (2022).

Victoria Scrimer is doctoral candidate at the University of Maryland where she is completing her dissertation, "Performing Protest in a Postdramatic Age." Her research focuses on dramatic theory and its application in political activism. Victoria is the two-time winner of the Comparative Drama Conference's Anthony Ellis Prize for outstanding paper by a graduate student and her work has appeared in *Critical Stages*, *Etudes*, and *Text & Presentation*. She currently teaches dramatic literature and theater history at the University of Mary Washington.

Mamata Sengupta is Assistant Professor of English at Islampur College, India. Her research interests include postwar British drama, performance studies, postdramatic theater, gender studies, and Indology. She has worked extensively on Arnold Wesker and Caryl Churchill during her MPhil. and doctoral research. Sengupta received the UGC MRP grant in Humanities (2017–19) for a national research project on Sarah Daniels. Her recent articles include "Performing Trauma: Narratives of Rupture in Caryl Churchill's *Seven Jewish Children*" (2021), "Of Women and Witches: Performing the Female Body in Caryl Churchill's *Vinegar Tom*" (2021), and "Female Hysteria and Gender Politics" (2022, forthcoming). Sengupta is currently working on postdramatic theater and alternative performances.

Susanne Thurow is an Australian Research Council laureate post-doctoral fellow and a deputy director at the University of New South Wales' iCinema Centre for Interactive Cinema Research in Sydney, Australia. Her interdisciplinary research encompasses the fields of performance studies and digital media, rethinking contemporary arts practice in light of digital aesthetics. She is a chief investigator on three large-scale research projects, which explore the application of immersive intelligent aesthetics to the creative arts. Her latest book is *Performing Indigenous Identities on the Contemporary Australian Stage* (2020). Her professional background has been further consolidated by work for companies such as Thalia Theater (Germany), the Universities of Melbourne and Sydney, and Goethe Institut.

Index

Abbot, Tony 180
Abramović, Marina 31, 196–7, 206–12
    The Life 210–11
    Spirit Cooking 206–7, 213 n.4
academia 16–20
activism 116, 118, 119, 121, 200
al-Assad, Bashar 109
alt-right 31, 197–8, 199–205, 206–12
alternative facts 29, 72, 77–9, 81, 88–9, 91 n.1
alternative reality 18, 29, 72, 79, 86, 88–9, 98
artifice 42, 143, 177, 182, 185–7, 192
audience 83, 90–1, 100–2, 118–19, 124–6, 162–3
authenticity 41–2, 119–20, 142–3, 157
Axelrod, David 128

Bening, Annette 115, 126–7
Berthold, David 136–7, 140
biographical theater 30, 137–40, 144–7, 150–1
Bok, Sissela 10, 12
Bowling Green Massacre 78–9, 92 n.1
Brecht, Bertolt 31, 176–93
    aesthetics 176–8, 181–8, 192–3
    The Resistible Rise of Arturo Ui 31, 178–93
    livestream filming of 185–93
Brexit 6, 9, 14–15

capitalism 66–7, 176, 183, 189
censorship 204, 209, 211
Charlottesville, VA, *see* Unite the Right rally
Churchill, Caryl 29, 58–73
    Bluebeard's Friends 65–9, 72
    Glass 59–63, 72
    Imp 69–71, 72–3
    Kill 63–5, 72

cigarette companies 1–5
climate change 22–7, 32 n.6
Climactic Research Unit (CRU) (University of East Anglia) 23
Climategate 23–5, 32 n.6
Clinton, Hillary 80, 206–8, 210
    as a character 80–3
Colvin, Mark 140
    as a character 142–4
Comey, James 85
Conigrave, Tim, *see* Tommy Murphy *Holding the Man*
conspiracy theory 28, 40, 71, 196–7, 199, 202–5, 207
Conway, Kellyanne 29, 72, 77–8, 91 n.2, 92 n.3
counterknowledge 31, 58–9, 61
culture war 197–212

de Benoist, Alain 200
deadly theater 116, 119, 127
detournement 205, 207, 210, 212
documentary drama 20–2, 39–43, 54, 114–16, 118–22, 127, 129–30, 137–8, 141–2, 150, 155–60, 163, 170–1

Emmott, Stephen 26–7
    Ten Billion 26–7, 31
experts 22, 26–7, 81–2
    doubting of 2, 4, 5–6, 14–15, 23–4, 44–5

Fairness Doctrine 4
fake news 16, 19, 40, 104, 138, 140–1, 144
false equivalence 6, 44
far right, *see* alt-right
femininity 158, 165

Field, Mary-Ellen 140–1
  as a character 142–4
found theater, *see* documentary theater
fourth wall 29, 97, 99–102

gender politics 129
Graham, Lindsey 107–9

Half Straddle Theater Company 157, 161–3, 165, 168–70
Hill, John 2, 5
Hockey, Joe 180
Howard, John 180
Hwang, David Henry 21–2, 79–84, 90–1
  Soft Power 29, 79–84, 90–1
  Yellow Face 21–2, 91

Intergovernmental Panel of Climate Change (IPCC) 22–3

January 6, 2021 13–14
Johnson, Boris 10, 19
Jones, Phil 24
journalism, *see* news media
journalistic theater, *see* documentary theater

Kavanaugh, Brett 107–9
Kelly, Dennis 21
  Taking Care of Baby 21
King and I, The 79–80
Kirschner, Glen 128
Kline, Kevin 115, 125

Leave campaign 10, 14–15
lies 8–12, 72, 90–1, 96, 98–9, 104
Lithgow, John 115, 124, 126
living history, *see* documentary theater

manipulation 103, 145, 189, 191
Mann, Michael 23

Martin, Trayvon 52
Marxism 176, 183, 193
masculinity 146–7, 165
Matthews, Chris 49
McCarthy, Jenny 5–6, 17
McCormack, Michael 151
media, *see* news media
metapolitics 200–2, 211–12
Microsoft 210–11
misrepresentation 62, 67, 72, 170, 205
Mitchell, Katie 26–7
mockumentary drama 21–2, 102
Moyers, Bill 98–9
Mueller, Robert 30, 115, 125–6, 128–30
  as a character 124–5
  testimony before Congress 117–18
Mueller Report 30, 115, 117–18, 123–6, 130
Murdoch, Lachlan 146
  as a character 148
Murdoch, Rupert 140–4, 146, 150, 152 n.3
Murphy, Tommy 30, 135–51
  Holding the Man 135–8
  Mark Colvin's Kidney 30, 138–45, 150–1
  Packer & Sons 30, 138–40, 145–51
Murray-Smith, Joanna 136, 138
  Switzerland 152 n.4
Murrow, Edward R. 4–5
myth 64–5, 85–7, 89, 145–7, 149–50

NEA Four 201, 213n
news media 4–7, 11–12, 24, 45, 78–9, 103–4, 114, 120, 130 n.1, 141–3, 170
Norton-Taylor, Richard 20–1
Nunes, Devin 117

Obama, Barack 49, 52–3, 77, 89, 104
Office, The 101–2
One.Tel 146, 148–9, 152 n.7
Orwell, George 16, 73
  1984 16

Out of Shadows 31, 196–7, 208, 210–12

Packer, Clyde 146
  as a character 147–8
Packer, Frank 146
  as a character 146
Packer, James 146
  as a character 148–9
Packer, Kerry 146
  as a character 146–9
patriarchy 68–9, 164
pedagogy 17–20
Pelosi, Nancy 106–7
performance art 201, 206–12
Pizzagate 207–8, 213 n.5
Podesta, John 206–7
Podesta, Tony 197, 206
police violence 39, 41, 49–51, 54
political hobbyism 30, 116, 120, 123, 127
post-race 39–55
postmodernism 16–20, 32 n.4, 144, 177–8, 188, 193
press conference 29, 99, 104, 106, 109, 110
public relations 2–3

Q-Anon, *see* alt-right

Rapley, Chris 27
  2071 27
Reagan, Ronald 7–8, 104
redactions 166–7
Richardson, Heather Cox 98–9
Riverside Church 118–19, 121

Satanic Panic 201, 213 n.1
Satter, Tina 30, 155–72
  Is This A Room 30, 155–72
Schenkkan, Robert 30, 118–28
  The Investigation: A Search for Truth in Ten Acts 118–28
Schiff, Adam 117–18, 128

Serling, Rod 84
Smith, Anna Deavere 28–9, 39–57
  Fires in the Mirror 40
  Twilight: Los Angeles, 1992 (film) 46, 47, 48–9, 54–5
  Twilight: Los Angeles, 1992 39–43, 45–53
social media 12, 14, 39, 78–9, 123–4
Spicer, Sean 29, 30, 77, 109–10

Tesich, Steve 7–8
theater of fact, *see* documentary theater
theater of witness, *see* documentary theater
Tobacco and Health 3–4
Tobacco Industry Research Committee (TIRC) 2–5
Todd, Chuck 72, 77
trolling 204–7, 211
Trump, Donald J. 8–14, 29, 30, 79–80, 83–7, 92 n.10, 106–7, 110–11, 115
  as a character 85, 87–90, 124–5
  Covid diagnosis 104–6
  impeachment 104, 106–7, 126–7
  inauguration 77
  lies 9–12, 86–7, 89, 97–9, 104–6
  and Nazis 110–11, 122
  rhetoric 9–11
2016 presidential election 80–1
  Russian interference 30, 58, 115, 117, 123–4, 156
2020 presidential election 10–11, 13, 53
Twilight Zone, The (show) 84

Unite the Right rally 13, 110–1

vaccine controversy 5, 7
Valantine, Alana 138
  Letters to Lindy 152 n.5
verbatim drama, *see* documentary drama
victim 68–9, 106, 108, 141

Washburn, Anne 29, 79, 84–91
  Shipwreck 29, 84–90
  The Twilight Zone 84, 91
Waters, Steve 25
  The Contingency Plan 25
Weiss, Peter 121–2
  The Investigation: Oratorio in 11 Cantos 121–2
Wildmon, Donald 209

Williams, Kip 31, 178, 180, 182–93
Winner, Reality 156, 158–9, 169–72, 172 n.8
witness testimony 42
Wojnarowicz, David 209
Wright, Tom 178, 180

Yamada, Sanae 161, 167

www.ingramcontent.com/pod-product-compliance
Lightning Source LLC
Chambersburg PA
CBHW062217300426
44115CB00012BA/2108